UNDERSTANDING ENTERPRISE, ENTREPRENEURSHIP AND SMALL BUSINESS

UNDERSTANDING ENTERPRISE, ENTREPRENEURSHIP AND SMALL BUSINESS

Simon Bridge
Ken O'Neill
and
Stan Cromie

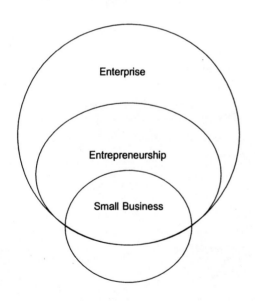

palgrave

Published by
PALGRAVE
Houndmills, Basingstoke, Hampshire RG21 6XS and
175 Fifth Avenue, New York, N. Y. 10010
Companies and representatives throughout the world

PALGRAVE is the new global academic imprint of
St. Martin's Press LLC Scholarly and Reference Division and
Palgrave Publishers Ltd (formerly Macmillan Press Ltd).

ISBN 0–333–68347–1 hardcover
ISBN 0–333–68348–X paperback

This book is printed on paper suitable for recycling and
made from fully managed and sustained forest sources.

A catalogue record for this book is available
from the British Library.

10   9   8   7
06   05   04   03   02

Typeset in Great Britain by
Aarontype Limited, Easton, Bristol

Printed and bound in Great Britain by
Antony Rowe Ltd, Eastbourne

Transferred to digital printing 2001

■ Contents

■ List of Tables

■ List of Figures

■ List of Boxes

■ Acknowledgements

The author and publisher gratefully acknowledge the following for permission to reproduce copyright material in this book.

Chapter 1: the bare facts for the UK, from C. Handy, *The Future of Work* (Oxford: Basil Blackwell, 1984) pp. 16–17; and an excerpt from T. Peters, 'Travel the Independent Road', *Independent on Sunday* ©, 2 January 1994.

Chapter 2: excerpts from the University of Ulster's material on *Enterprise in Higher Education*; J. B. Cunningham and J. Lischeron, 'Defining Entrepreneurship', *Journal of Small Business Management* (January 1991) p. 47; entrepreneurial or enterprising attributes, from A. A. Gibb, 'Enterprise Culture – Its Meaning and Implications for Education and Training', *Journal of European Industrial Training* (1987) p. 6; influences on the development of entrepreneurial ideas and ambitions at different stages of life from Gibb (1987) ibid., p. 13; the components of enterprise culture from Gibb (1987) ibid., p. 14; the focus of learning from Gibb (1987) ibid., p. 17; entrepreneurial v. corporatist management – some contrasts, from Gibb (1987) ibid., pp. 21–2; 'Hunting the Heffalump in the World of the Enterprise Industry' by F. Coffield, from *The Independent* © 29 August 1990.

Chapter 3: promotional material used by the Department of Trade and Industry; three types of small business owner, from R. W. Hornaday, 'Dropping the E-Words from Small Business Research', *Journal of Small Business Management*, vol. 28, pp. 22–33; framework for identifying enterprise competency, from S. Caird, 'Problems with the Identification of Enterprise Competencies', *Management Education and Development* vol. 13, (1992) p. 16, © Sage Publications; change management competencies, from D. Buchanan and D. Boddy, *The Expertise of the Change Agent* (Hemel Hempstead: Prentice Hall, 1992) pp. 92–3; intentions model of entrepreneurial potential, from N. F. Krueger, *Prescriptions for Opportunity: Communities Can Create Potential for Entrepreneurs* (Washington, DC: Small Business Foundation of America, Working Paper 93–03, 1995).

Chapter 4: various short excerpts from pp. 10, 63, 74, 111, 117 and 159 and selections from tables on p. 67 and p. 73, from G Hofstede, *Cultures and Organisations* (London: HarperCollins Publishers 1994), © G. Hofstede; G. Redding, 'Three Styles of Asian Capitalism'; in *Mastering Enterprise*, no. 7, *Financial Times* ©, 13 January 1997, p. 10; the triangle of enterprise, from O. R. Spelling, 'Enterprise in a Cultural Perspective', *Entrepreneurship and Regional Development*, vol. 3 (1991) p. 39, © Taylor & Francis Publishers.

Chapter 5: network capitalism, from G. Redding, 'Three Styles of Asian Capitalism', in Mastering Enterprise, no. 7, *Financial Times* ©, 13 January 1997,

p. 11; autonomous and community entrepreneurs, adapted from B. Johannisson and A. Nilsson, 'Community Entrepreneurs: Networking for Local Development', *Entrepreneurship and Regional Development*, vol. 1, no. 1 (1989) p. 5; W. Hutton, 'Ethics Man Finds No Place in the Enterprise Era', from *Guardian* ©, 21 March 1994; K. Gold, 'Must We Buy Schooling from Marks and Spencer?', *The Observer* ©, 21 January 1990.

Chapter 6: the five stages of business growth, from N. C. Churchill and V. L. Lewis, 'Growing Concerns: The Five Stages of Small Firm Growth', *Harvard Business Review*, May–June 1983, pp. 31, 32, 33 and 34; growth process as reflected in possible growth paths, from E. Garnsey, *A New Theory of the Growth of the Firm*, 41st World Conference of ICSB, Stockholm (June 1996) p. 4; diverse trajectories of a cohort of businesses, from E. Garnsey (1996) ibid., p. 18; influences on the entrepreneurial decision, from A. C. Cooper, 'Technical Entrepreneurship; What Do We Know?', *R & D Management*, vol. 3 (1973) pp. 59–64; Vickery's model from B. Garnier and Y. Gasse, *An Experience in Training in the Area of Entrepreneurship and Starting a Business in Quebec: The Project 'Becoming an Entrepreneur'*, October 1986; entrepreneurial success from R. Peterson and R. Rondstadt, 'A Silent Strength: Entrepreneurial Know Who', *The 16th ESBS, efmd IMD Report*, (86/4) p. 11; the self employment spectrum from R. Lessem, 'Getting Into Self-Employment', *Management Education and Development* (Spring, 1984) p. 31, © Sage Publications; an analysis of a business start-up, from M. Scott and R. Bruce, 'Five Stages of Growth in Small Business', *Long Range Planning* (1987) vol. 20, p. 48, © 1987 Elsevier Science Ltd; business survival rates: percentage of enterprises surviving after 1, 2 and 5 years, from *The 3rd Annual Report of the European Observatory for SMEs* (Netherlands: EIM Small Business Research and Consultancy, 1995) p. 87.

Chapter 7: the layers of the small business support network from A. A. Gibb, 'Towards the Building of Entrepreneurial Models of Support for Small Business', paper presented at the *National Small Firms Policy and Research Conference* (Cambridge, 1988); six phases of reaction to unemployment, from J. Hayes and P. Nutman, *Understanding the Unemployed* (London: Tavistock, 1981); debt structure by country, from P. Burns and O. Whitehouse; *Financing Enterprise in Europe 2* (Milton Keynes: 3i Enterprise Centre, 1995).

Chapter 8: previous academic approaches to understanding small business growth from A. A. Gibb and L. Davies 'In Pursuit of Frameworks for the Development of Growth Models for the Small Business', *International Small Business Journal*, vol. 9, 1990 pp. 16–17; managing factors and stages from N. Churchill, 'The Six Key Phases of Company Growth', in Mastering Enterprise; © *Financial Times*, 20 February 1997, p. 3; management weaknesses as a constraint on growth: internal barriers to growth (percentage of respondents citing factor as important) from Binder Hamlyn and the London Business School 'The Quest for Growth', reprinted from *Managing to Grow* (London: CBI, 1995) p. 11; constraints for small business growth, from ESRC Centre for Business Research, *The State of the British Enterprise* (Cambridge Small Business Research Centre, 1992).

Chapter 9: who is the entrepreneur?, adapted with permission from G. Pinchot III, *Intrapreneuring* (New York: Harper & Row, 1985) pp. 54–6, by Gifford Pinchot III; manager mindset and behaviour for innovation, from © The Foresight Group Diagram, S Hamngatan 37, 41106 Goteborg, Sweden.

Chapter 10: objectives of small firm policy, from D. J. Storey, *Understanding the Small Business Sector* (London: ITBP, 1994) p. 260.

Chapter 12: UK government SME policies, from D. J. Storey, *Understanding the Small Business Sector* (London: ITBP, 1994), p. 269; SME policy areas, from European Network for SME Research, *The European Observatory for SMEs 2nd Annual Report* (European Network for Zoetermeer; EIM Small Business Research and Consultancy, 1994); policy fields and instruments, from K. de Lind Van Wijngaarden and R. Van der Horst, 'A Comparison of SME Policy in the EU Member States', *Business Growth and Profitability*, vol. 2, no. 1 (March 1996) p. 40; overview of SME start-up support policy in the EU, from K. de Lind Van Wijngaarden and R. Van der Horst (1996) ibid., p. 43.

Chapter 13: monitoring and evaluation, from the work of the late R. Scott based on his work at Northern Ireland's Department of Economic Development.

Note: the Ten Commandments of Innovation (pp. 190–1) is based on material presented at a Department of Trade and Industry presentation on innovations but we have been unable to trace the owner of the copyright. Every effort has been made to contact all the copyright-holders, but if any have been inadvertently omitted the publishers will be pleased to make the necessary arrangements at the earliest opportunity.

■ Preface

Over the last two decades in many countries a new industry has developed. It is that of enterprise promotion and support. The world has been changing, and the role of the individual has become increasingly more important, with individual initiative becoming increasingly necessary for economic success. This process has been referred to as the development of an enterprise culture, and its benefits have been widely sought. Enterprise and its associated concepts of entrepreneurship and small business are all widely promoted and their development supported. This has been done by government departments, by local economic and enterprise agencies, by community initiatives, by private ventures and by academic organisations. This process is also being repeated in countries, such as many of those in Eastern Europe, with less well-developed market economies and where enterprise development seems therefore to be an attractive route to economic growth.

For those working in this field, however, especially when they are new to it, there can be considerable confusion about what is involved. The new industry has developed policies, practices and a language of its own, but often without a clear objective or strategy. For those unfamiliar with it, and even for many who have some familiarity, it is hard to grasp what is being done and why. Nevertheless, employment in the industry is already substantial and is still growing, and those working in it or close to it need to try to make sense of it.

Comprehensive overviews of the subject have not been available, however. There has been considerable research done, but it has of necessity been rather specialised, often not very widely published and of a piecemeal nature. Guides in the form of books and pamphlets that are available for enterprise and small business often turn out to be about how to start a small business: a useful subject for those who are doing just that, but not for those who seek a wider insight into enterprise and its associated concepts in order better to promote or support it. This book therefore attempts, for the first time, to address their needs. It is targeted at policy makers, staff of business support organisations, researchers, staff and students of further and higher education establishments and the informed public. Its content is relevant in countries with developed or developing economies: where people, for whatever reason, wish to know more about enterprise and its context. It seeks to present them with a sound introduction to the key concepts and issues as a grounding for understanding and work in this area and as starting point for further explorations of more specialised aspects.

In our work of writing it we have been conscious of many people who have helped and encouraged us. We owe them considerable thanks. We would however like especially to highlight the patience and support shown by our wives, who have had to put up with many evenings and weekends of work and many late phone calls and interruptions. We are very grateful to them. We would also like particularly to thank Ella Bennett for her superhuman patience in dealing with phone calls, faxes, urgent typing requests, meetings to be arranged, messages to be passed and many, many other small (and not so small) tasks which made our work much easier.

Belfast

SIMON BRIDGE
KEN O'NEILL
STAN CROMIE

■ Introduction

This book seeks to introduce the concepts of enterprise, entrepreneurship and small business and their interrelationships. It is not intended to be a comprehensive theoretical study, but instead it tries to provide a practical guide to the subject for those working in this field, be they promotion and support agency staff, civil servants, advisers, counsellors, trainers or academics. It aims to provide a beginner's guide to the key facts, ideas, theories and thinking about enterprise and entrepreneurship, to look at their relationship to small businesses, and to consider the methods that are taken to promote them.

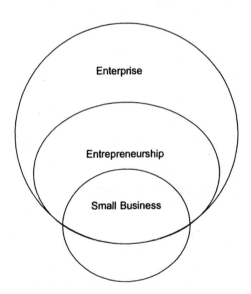

The word 'enterprise' is, at present, much used in a variety of contexts and with a wide range of meanings. Within this range there are narrow meanings of the word specifically related to business and there are wider meanings indicating a way of behaving that can apply in a variety of contexts, including business. The narrower meanings are closely linked to entrepreneurship, and, in turn, the concepts of enterprise and entrepreneurship embrace much that would be considered to be expressions of small business activity. Indeed, the words enterprise, entrepreneurship and small business often appear to be used interchangeably, but it is also argued that there are many small businesses that do not demonstrate much enterprise.

The variety of uses made of the word 'enterprise' and the variety of contexts in which it is applied are indicative of the appeal of the concept and its various applications. Evidently, the main reason for this appeal of enterprise is jobs. Small businesses are frequently net creators of jobs, more so than big businesses. Those, therefore, who wish to encourage and promote more jobs are interested in small businesses and often in what can be done to develop more of them. It is this interest, and these aspects of it, that this book seeks to inform.

The book consists of three parts. Part I starts with an examination of why the concept of enterprise has been presented by many people as something desirable and worth pursuing in practice. It explores the variety of ways in which the word is used and the spectrum of meanings it can have. In particular it refers to the narrow and broad definitions. It presents a number of theories about enterprising behaviour in individuals and it looks at the external environment in which individuals and groups operate and at the influences that cultural, economic and political conditions can have on enterprise.

In Part II small businesses are explored. They are often the reason why people are interested in enterprise. There are many varieties of small business, which differ from each other as much as they differ from larger businesses. Small businesses are not, however, smaller versions of large businesses. They have many distinctive features, and those who wish to understand and influence the development of small businesses need to be aware of these distinctions. A popular category of small business is the 'growth' business, because this is frequently seen as offering the best job-creation prospects. Therefore small business growth is considered, as is the issue of 'intrapreneurship' or the application of enterprise inside larger businesses.

If enterprise and small business are beneficial then there will be a desire to have more small businesses. In the third part the issues of how, and why, to promote enterprise are explored. Small business is important for a variety of reasons, including diversity, social stability, and to support the competitiveness of other businesses. Particular attention has however been focused on them because of the indicated links between small business and job creation. Governments, especially in times of high unemployment, want more jobs. They are therefore prepared to intervene to secure the development of more enterprise.

Intervention is the subject of Part III of the book. We start by considering the reasons for intervention and the benefits sought from it. We then consider a number of theories and assumptions about the nature of the enterprise process in order to see how intervention might work and what intervention might be successful. The possible areas for intervention and the forms it might take are then examined, and this is followed by a look at the issues of evaluating interventions and the results indicated by some of the relevant research.

The Concept of Enterprise

■ Introduction

Part I of this book looks at the concept of enterprise to see why it is being examined so universally, by whom, and what they interpret it to mean.

It starts in Chapter 1 by examining why enterprise has been presented by many people as something desirable and worth pursuing and why, therefore, it is the subject of considerable interest in government, academic, business and other circles.

Chapter 2 explores the concept of enterprise and the variety of ways in which the word is used and looks at the spectrum of meanings it can have. In particular it refers to two definitions: a 'narrow' definition, in which enterprise means the

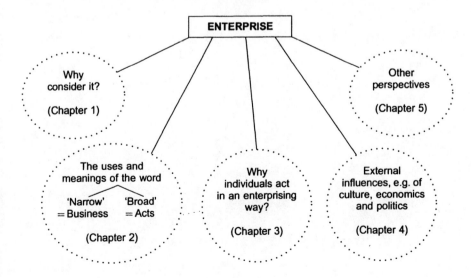

same as entrepreneurship and is specifically concerned with the start up and development of business, and a 'broad' definition, which considers enterprise as the behaviour resulting from the exercise of a set of attributes that can be demonstrated in a variety of different contexts.

These attributes are considered further in Chapter 3, which looks at a number of theories about enterprising behaviour and what it is in individuals that influences them to engage in enterprising acts. Chapter 4 in contrast looks at the external environment in which individuals and groups operate and at the influences that cultural, economic and political conditions can have on enterprise.

Finally, in Chapter 5 some other perspectives on enterprise are presented and its future relevance to many economic and social objectives considered.

CHAPTER 1

Why Talk About Enterprise?

We must have an enterprise culture, not a dependency culture.

Lord Young

There are a number of generally recognised human rights, but the one that probably commands the greatest recognition, if not the greatest observance, is the right to freedom. But can a government ensure freedom for its subjects? Good laws, it has been said, can promote freedom, whereas bad laws can prevent it. Despite its recognition as a right laws cannot therefore, of themselves, ensure freedom; they can only help to set the conditions in which it can exist.

Another human benefit sometimes recognised as a right is an education. Education, however, differs from freedom in that, whether it is seen as a right or not, a government can take steps to provide at least a basic education for its citizens. An education, it is generally recognised, is within a government's gift.

1.1 The right to a job

The other day one of the authors was having a Saturday morning coffee in his favourite café. He happened to know the two people at the adjacent table. He had said hello to them when they came in before resuming his attempts to solve the crossword in the daily paper. Suddenly something one of them said impinged on his consciousness. 'Everyone' she said, 'has the right to a job.' What are the implications of that, he wondered, how can such a right be ensured and how does it fit into an enterprise culture?

But can the same be said of work, and is the right to work the same as the right to a job? That 'everyone has the right to work' is enshrined in the Universal Declaration of Human Rights signed by the members of the United Nations. The desirability of full employment as a political objective is often debated, however, not so much because people don't want full employment, but because

3

questions are raised about the practicality of achieving it and the implications it might have. Is employment like health or education, where a government can provide a basic level of service or provision for everyone? Or is it more like freedom, in respect of which a government's powers are more negative than positive, where it has the power to deny freedom but cannot itself directly provide freedom for everyone? Can a government provide a basic job for everyone who wants one? Governments do directly create some jobs but, at least in Western societies, they are not the main sources of direct employment, and they cannot themselves create enough jobs for everyone who might want one.

It is businesses that create most jobs. Governments can encourage businesses to create jobs, they can try to provide a supportive environment for the creation of jobs and they can legislate for people to have an equal opportunity to get the jobs that do exist, but that is not the same as offering the right to a job. That would mean that everyone who wanted a job could have one, but how can a government maintain that when it can't actually create enough jobs itself? If a government cannot create enough jobs then is it practical to talk about the 'right to a job'?

For many people a key feature of the communist-inspired systems of government was that they guaranteed a job for everyone. Actually, it would seem that that was not really the case and that it might be more accurate to say that they provided everyone with an employment contract and a wage whether or not they really had a full job to do at their official place of employment. However, to do even that required the centrally controlled economies, which are now largely deemed to have failed. A job for everyone who wants one nevertheless remains a very desirable aspiration.

Earlier this century, after the upheavals of the Industrial Revolution and the First World War, there did seem to be some prospects that a job for everyone might become the norm. Then, in the Western world at least, there were the traumas of the 1930s. Following the Wall Street crash in 1929 it appeared that there were indeed fundamental problems with the structure of capitalist economies in maintaining full, or nearly full, employment. However, by the end of that decade major job creation initiatives had produced significant reductions in unemployment and John Maynard Keynes had in theory suggested how unemployment might continue to be controlled. In addition, by 1940 there was again a war, which increased the demand for armaments and other requirements for the military struggle and brought an end to the remaining unemployment.

After the war, economic prospects seemed to be much better. Keynesian economic theory seemed to be working, the experiences in the 1930s of practical employment creation seemed still to be valid and in Britain unemployment seemed to be relatively steady at about a quarter of a million. This was a manageable figure, which offered support to the view that full employment was realistically achievable. Alarm bells did not ring loudly when by the end of the 1960s this figure had doubled to about half a million. Although history is lived forwards it is viewed backwards, and it is only in retrospect therefore that it

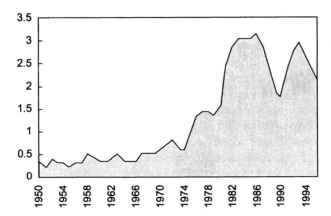

Source: CSO, *Labour Market Statistics.*

Figure 1.1 UK unemployment (millions)

would now seem that this was a turning point. Half a million now looks like a relatively small figure, and it was during the 1970s, when the figure grew to one and a half million, and the 1980s, when it rose again, to three million, that notions about the practicality of achieving full employment were finally shattered (Figure 1.1).

1.2 The bare facts for the UK, as set down by Charles Handy in 1984*

- There are fewer jobs than there were, but not that many fewer
- But jobs have been continuously squeezed out of business
- Jobs were picked up by the public sector, however – but no longer
- In general, jobs had continuously moved from manufacturing to service
- Meanwhile the labour force had been expanding...and was going to go on expanding for the next twenty years
- Demand for jobs had consistently exceeded supply and looked like continuing to do so.[1]

* In 1997 they are still relevant!

What was going on? One person who has studied this matter is Charles Handy. He, and others saw that what was happening in the 1970s and 1980s was a fundamental restructuring of work. For millennia of human history the major source of jobs was agriculture. Then, with increases in industrial production and increases in agricultural efficiency, work for many became based in industry through the process which came to be known as the Industrial Revolution. Was that revolution itself, however, now being superseded?

In his introduction to *The Future of Work*[2] Handy points out that it was during the 1970s that visible changes began to appear in what had until then been the normal working life. Large organisations began to decline and concepts such as redundancy and long-term unemployment became more familiar. Britain was no longer primarily an industrial nation. Since the early 1970s the gross profits from the service sector had exceeded those from manufacturing. Internationally it was the same. Similar changes had taken place throughout the industrialised world. The problem for many, however, was not the change to new jobs but that the generation of the new jobs did not seem to be keeping pace with the reduction in the old ones.

In this situation there was a natural tendency to look back to the 1930s when job creation measures had worked, and to try to repeat that prescription. A number of solutions were proposed. Expanding the business sector was one solution considered, although to an extent business output was already expanding, but through increases in productivity not in jobs. Some businesses were simultaneously increasing output and shedding jobs – a phenomenon referred to as 'jobless growth'. Other suggestions included expanding government employment to take up the slack in jobs – a Keynesian type of solution that suggested increased government spending on infrastructure, health and education. That however looked problematic, because of the numbers who would have to be employed, the cost and the potential impact on inflation. Governments struggled to find something that might work and certainly still hoped that business would make a major contribution.

It was in this situation in 1979 that David Birch published the results of his research into employment in the USA. He concluded that it was small firms, defined as those with 100 employees or fewer, which had in the early 1970s created over 80 per cent of net new jobs. Net new jobs is the difference between the total of new jobs created and the total of jobs lost during the same period, and is sometimes used as a reasonable indicator of economic growth. The implication therefore was that it was small firms which were responsible for much of the economic growth, and were the prime source of employment creation in the USA. Many people discounted Birch's work when it was first published, as this conclusion was contrary to the perceived wisdom of the time. Nevertheless, the issue was important enough to stimulate others to try to replicate his work. (For more on this see Chapter 7.)

While the statistical debate still continues, it can be seen that it was the work of Birch, followed by that of others, that challenged the previously common belief that economic benefits of business such as jobs and growth came always from big business, and that small business was almost incidental to this. This work led to a recognition that the bulk of the new jobs being created to maintain, or to grow, employment levels was actually coming from small businesses. Those looking for an expansion of business employment, or even for

Table 1.1   Self-employed and
employers in the UK

Year	Total (million)
1951	1.65
1961	1.72
1971	1.79
1981	2.06
1991	3.30

Source: Labour Force Survey.

a maintenance of existing employment levels, looked increasingly to small businesses to do this. Small businesses therefore became a focus of interest for policy-makers, and they wanted to know more about them. They were seen as a fundamental component of any effort to increase employment. There was a desire to promote more of them and therefore to understand and promote the concept of 'enterprise' that is thought to underlie them. Enterprise was becoming a vogue word, and the number of businesses and the extent of self-employment were increasing, as shown for the UK by Table 1.1.

Essentially what Birch had done was to challenge a particular assumption that the future was a continuation of the past, and had shown it to be wrong. He looked at what was already happening and demonstrated that it was not what many experts had assumed. Others have also highlighted aspects of the present and used them to suggest that there are changes that many have not perceived. At the same time as Birch was releasing his work, Alvin Toffler was writing *The Third Wave*[3] in which he described large-scale industrial mass production as 'second wave' industry and forecast that both the office and the factory would be revolutionised over the future decades in a way which would affect the structure of industry, the size of work units and even the location of work. In effect, Toffler analysed reasons for the change that gave rise to the developments Birch had recorded.

Charles Handy also talked about the 'shamrock organisation'.[4] It had been the assumption, he suggested, that an organisation should do as much as possible in-house with its own permanent workforce. Indeed, vertical and horizontal integration was seen as the norm for business development. However organisations in future would most likely have three distinct categories of people working for them, like the three leaves of a shamrock. The first category was the professional core, the second was the contractual fringe and the third was the, mostly part-time, flexible labour force. The result he suggested was that in the UK, by the end of the 1980s, already about one third of the paid workforce were part-timers or self-employed, and it could be 50 per cent by the end of the century. Subsequent experience has show the truth of this. The proportion of part-time workers in organisations and self-employed workers contracted to them has increased, with consequent changes in employee loyalty and in length of service expectations.

1.3   Contracting out

'Contract out everything except your soul!', exhorted management expert Tom Peters.

The airline is going to examine every part of its operation and decide which services it can buy more cheaply elsewhere...Over the past four years...it has contracted out its security arrangements, heavy engineering and much of its catering. It has recruited small external 'franchise' airlines to fly several routes on its behalf.... 'There is no part of the operation that we are not going to look at', said one source.

Rolls-Royce last year signed a deal with EDS to provide all its IT needs for 10 years.

J P Morgan is paying a consortium of suppliers $7bn over seven years.

Source: Excerpts from business articles in the *Observer* © on one Sunday in 1996.

A generation ago Handy said,[6] we used to work for 47 hours a week, for 47 weeks a year and for 47 years, or about 100 000 hours in a lifetime. Now he suggested this may be down to 50 000 hours for someone just starting work. This may be $37 \times 37 \times 37$, or it could still be 47 hours a week for 47 weeks a year but only for 25 years in an intense professional job, or possibly 22 hours a week for 47 weeks a year for 50 years of part-time work extending well into one's sixties as it is a continuing part, but not the whole, of life.

The 50 000 hour job is just one of the unanticipated outcomes of the shamrock organisation, and there are going to be many more. It was already clear, however, that the employee society had changed fundamentally and would not readily change back. Half as many people in the core of the business, paid twice as much and producing three times as much may make economic sense for a business, but what did it mean for the assumption of permanent jobs for life? Other attitudes to employment will be needed. Those not in the core will not have a job but may be offered work for which fees are paid. They will have to find such work, to contract to do it, and to manage its delivery. Such behaviour has been described as enterprising.

Tom Peters also looked at trends in business organisation. He foresaw the time when the organisation as we know it would not exist. Instead there would be smaller, flat and flexible network organisations. To get beyond your own brain-dead management, he said you must subcontract everything. The future, he went on to suggest, even for larger organisations, is to deconstruct the organisation and to organise work by small teams. Otherwise the responsiveness needed for true competitiveness would be impossible to achieve.

Changes in the organisation of many businesses are already clear. The hands-on management style, flexible structures and consequent fast response times of small firms can be very beneficial in the rapidly changing modern world and bigger businesses have sought to benefit from them. In effect they have been diminishing the disadvantages of bigness by contracting out many production and service functions. As Mintzberg notes,

> This is what NASA did in the 1960s, when its attention was focused on the Apollo project, whose singular goal was to put an American on the moon before 1970. NASA conducted much of its own development work but contracted production out to independent manufacturing firms.[7]

It is also possible to contract in. Self-employed people can take on specific responsibilities 'within' large businesses, working in effect for a price not for a wage. This form of organisation is not new. Clawson[8] shows that it was an important aspect of industrial organisation in textiles, transport and iron and steel in the transition from craft organisations to the fully fledged factory in eighteenth-century Britain.

There is another discernible trend among large organisations: the creation of federal structures. As large organisations divest themselves of their divisions in pursuit of the benefits of smallness, the task of managing all divisions from the centre – and a much reduced centre, at that – becomes increasingly problematic. The solution, Handy argues, is to create a federation, or network, of connected units in which the core organisation acts on behalf of its constituent parts. This only works when the centre

> genuinely is at the middle of things and is not a polite word for the top... the centre must cling to its key functions of new people and new money, but its decisions have to be made in consultation with, and on behalf of, the chiefs of the parts.[9]

While such arrangements do provide large organisations with greater flexibility they do have potential drawbacks. They do mean a lessening of commitment on both sides, with employees and subcontractors having to look out themselves for the best deals and for new opportunities. A lessening of paternalism has been accompanied by a lessening of employee loyalty. It is increasingly a case of everyone for himself or herself.

These developments have major implications for individuals. If a job for life is no longer either the norm or a realistic aspiration, if even a succession of different jobs may not always be easy, if businesses will contract out work rather than employing people to do it, and if those who do have jobs will be working in smaller more independent business teams, then people themselves will have to be more proactive in arranging and managing their own economic activity. If there will no longer always be an employer to find work to arrange materials and facilities and to pay wages, then people will have to do it themselves. There will be an increase in the number of people, either from want or necessity, who will be thinking and acting to establish their own smaller work units. That process has also been called 'enterprise', and the changes outlined above stimulated a desire for more of it and an exploration of what it involved.

> *People do realise that job security is gone, but many don't realise what it has been replaced by. The driving force of a career must come from the individual, not the organisation.*
>
> **(Professor Homa Babrami**[10]**)**

As well as individuals perceiving the advantage of being able to fend more for themselves, there has also been an interest in reversing the apparent tendency of many people to look to government, or at least to someone else, for the provision of whatever seems to be missing in society. Some saw this change as the essence of what in the UK was called Thatcherism, and in the USA Reaganism, but, whatever its label there has been, in many developed countries, a reduction in the perception of government as the universal provider. There have therefore been corresponding moves to make the individual more aware of his or her own ability to do things, to accept responsibility and to foster more communal and social development. This has been labelled an 'enterprise culture', and associated with it are views that there are general economic and social benefits to be gained from having a more enterprising culture, society, family or person. 'Enterprise' has therefore been on many agendas.

The changes mentioned above were not apparent initially, they were not instantaneous, and they did not proceed smoothly. Nevertheless they were, and are still, being felt, and the responses that were perceived as necessary to accommodate them were described as 'enterprise'. Whether it was a move at government level to promote more small business, or an individual response to changed employment market conditions, or something in between, the word 'enterprise' came to be attached to it. 'Enterprise' became seen as an important part of the way forward to a stronger economy, to a less dependent society or to a more prosperous future.

For all these reasons 'enterprise' became the thing to explore, to understand, and to promote. This resulted in a growth of research about 'enterprise' topics, a proliferation of courses or programmes with 'enterprise' in their title, and an increased readiness to apply the label 'enterprise' to anything remotely connected to small business or to the attitudes or behaviour associated with it. It began to be seen almost as some sort of universal cure-all for economic ills.

What enterprise consisted of was not always clear, however. For some it would appear to have meant simply small business and the activity of starting and running a small business. For others it was a set of personal qualities that made their holders more ready than others to seek their own solutions to economic or other problems. In this wider sense, an enterprising person was one who saw opportunities not problems, who looked to the future and not to the past and who was more creative than analytical. There was, however, a spectrum of ways in which the word was used, rather than one narrow definition.

To address only one definition of enterprise would not be relevant to other uses of the word. The first part of this book therefore addresses the question 'What is enterprise?' by looking at the range of contexts in which the word has been used and the spectrum of different meanings that these usages imply. It explores some of the components associated with these concepts and examines the ideas associated with enterprise from a number of different perspectives. It concludes by considering the implication of some current and potential future developments in society on our need for enterprise or for aspects of it.

Those wishing to study enterprise are often interested in one or other of two key aspects. As noted the word 'enterprise' is often used to refer to small business, and for many policy-makers, especially, this aspect of enterprise would appear to be of prime importance. In Part II of this book, therefore, small business is explored from the point of view not of the small business practitioner or the person thinking of starting a business, which is the approach taken by many writers on small business, but from the question of what constitutes a small business and what particular insights are helpful in understanding them for those who might desire to encourage more of them. The issues of small business growth and other associated concepts such as entrepreneurship and innovation are also linked in to this.

The second aspect, covered in Part III, is the issue of how to promote the growth of enterprise and within that the growth of small businesses in general and in particular. The possible reasons for such external interventions are considered, together with some of the more common or useful theories and assumptions about intervention in enterprise or small business development. Specific intervention categories and methods are then explored, where possible together with some indication of their apparent results. Evaluating the effectiveness of such measures is crucial to determining the efficiency and effectiveness of intervention, and this part therefore concludes by considering the possibilities, limitations and pitfalls of measuring and evaluating results.

Key points

- The last twenty years have been a time when a number of parallel developments have become clear.
- Following the relatively successful attempts to address unemployment in the 1930s, and the apparent ease of maintaining virtually full employment after the war, a belief had arisen that permanent full employment was possible and that it was the duty of the government to maintain that position.

- In the 1970s and 1980s, however, unemployment rose considerably, without apparently being susceptible to government attempts to reverse it. Actually employment was not falling, but the number looking for employment was rising.
- Another development was that industry, the traditional main source of employment, was itself changing. It was actually increasing its output, but through increased productivity, not through increased numbers of employees. Expanding output no longer automatically increased employment.

    Birch, however, showed that the bigger businesses were actually losing jobs, and that the source of the increased number of jobs to maintain employment levels was small businesses. Governments therefore wanted to promote more small business development, in order to maintain economies and to promote more employment.
- Other commentators showed that the structure of employment was itself changing. The mass, long-term employment resulting from the Industrial Revolution was being replaced by a much more flexible employment structure.
- The implication of this was that business would be increasingly likely to be offering people, not jobs, but work to undertake. People would therefore need skills and aptitudes for utilising opportunities to be paid a fee for an amount of work done, instead of finding jobs in which they would then be paid for an amount of time spent. They would have to be more flexible themselves, and more prepared and able to find their own sources of such work. In other words, they would have to be more enterprising.
- In addition to the benefits to individuals of being more enterprising, there are also perceived benefits to society of a more enterprising culture in general that would result in less dependence on government to address all society's ills.

CHAPTER 2

What Does Enterprise Mean?

Enterprise – Undertaking, esp. bold or difficult one; readiness to engage in such undertakings; enterprising, showing courage or imaginativeness.

(The Oxford Handy Dictionary)

Mastering Enterprise: all you need to know about starting and developing a successful business.[1]

Many things have been described as 'enterprise'. It has been a popular label for a variety of initiatives.

2.1   Enterprise

The British sense of enterprise
DTI: The Department of Enterprise
The Enterprise Initiative for Industry
Enterprise Allowance
The Business Enterprise Scheme
Training and Enterprise Councils
Local Enterprise Agencies
Enerprise in Higher Education
Young Enterprise
and even
The Starship Enterprise

However, like many fashionable labels, it appears sometimes to have been applied more for the cachet it brings with it than for the appropriateness of its application. Dictionary definitions of 'enterprise' are some help, but language evolves and the meaning of words can change as their usage develops. This book is concerned *inter alia* with understanding what people actually mean when they use the word 'enterprise', and its implications, rather than trying to isolate an abstract concept of 'enterprise' or trying to impose a single uniform meaning for it. In this chapter, therefore, some of the key usages are considered and the meaning, or meanings of their authors extracted or deduced.

■ Examples of 'Enterprise' Usage
■ UK Government Initiatives

> *Lord Young, when he was the UK Secretary of State for Employment, said that: 'We must have an enterprise culture, not a dependency culture.' When he was asked what he meant by 'enterprise' he described it as: 'Get up and go – not sitting back and accepting it. Think positive and things can happen; if you are passive and think negative then nothing happens. It's a mental attitude.*[2]

> *This budget puts Britain on course to be the enterprise centre of Europe.*
>
> (Kenneth Clarke, Chancellor of the Exchequer, Budget speech, 28 November 1995)

The DTI (Department of Trade and Industry) launched its Enterprise Initiative in 1988, which brought together many of the schemes of support provided by the DTI for industry and commerce. At its launch the DTI considered whether its plans were an industrial policy, but concluded that

> the phrase itself is unfortunate, because it appears to concentrate on industry rather than consider all the factors which affect the ability of industry and commerce to create wealth; it also carries the flavour of the DTI taking responsibility for the fortunes of individual industries and companies. It will be obvious that neither is consistent with the philosophy of this paper... But the government have a coherent set of policies towards industry and commerce. That set of policies is better described as an enterprise strategy than an industrial policy.[3]

The DTI described its objectives as follows:

> The needs and demands of society can only be met by increasing prosperity. The prime objective of the Department is to assist this process throughout the

economy and then to champion all the people who make it happen, rather than just individual sectors, industries or companies... We seek to:

- produce a more competitive market by encouraging competition and tackling restrictive practices, cartels and monopolies;
- secure a more efficient market by improving the provision of information to business about new methods and opportunities;
- create a larger market by privatisation and deregulation;
- increase confidence in the working of markets by achieving a fair level of protection for the individual consumer and investor.

We will encourage the transfer of technologies and cooperative research, the spread of management education and the growth of links between schools and the world of work. Our objective will be to produce a climate which promotes enterprise and prosperity.[4]

In the 1988 White Paper describing the role of DTI, encouraging enterprise was described as 'one of the major economic goals of the Government'. 'Enterprise', the DTI said,

is fundamental to a dynamic and growing economy. Lack of enterprise played a major part in the relative decline of the British economy; its return has played a major role in the recent economic revival. The key to continued economic success lies in the further encouragement of the enterprise of our people... The change of approach is reflected throughout DTI's activities. DTI will be the department for Enterprise.[5]

2.2 Pathfinder initiatives – 1

In Northern Ireland the Department of Economic Development (DED) launched an interim report on their 'Pathfinder' initiative in 1987. Its aim was 'to find new and better ways of building a stronger economy in Northern Ireland... to find new ways to build on our strengths and to correct our weaknesses'. Among those weaknesses were the 'lack of an enterprising tradition: Northern Ireland is proud of its "work ethic", but this is essentially an employee ethic. As a result there are few role models or mentors for those who wish to enter business and the option of self-employment is novel in many areas.' 'Enterprise', the report defined as: 'the propensity of people to create jobs for themselves and for others by engaging in and creating a legitimate activity which will earn them a living or by developing their existing jobs.'[6]

The Local Enterprise Development Unit in Northern Ireland (now known as LEDU: The Small Business Agency) is sponsored by the

Department of Economic Development and was tasked to implement many of the Pathfinder recommendations. Its aim is to strengthen the Northern Ireland economy by encouraging enterprise and stimulating improvements in the competitiveness of both new and existing businesses.

These examples are all taken from UK government initiatives and publications. The major thrust of government industrial policy in the UK under the Conservatives in the 1980s and 1990s was the creation of a climate that stimulated enterprise and thereby sought to increase prosperity. In this context, as the above examples show either explicitly or by implication, the concept of enterprise is concerned with business, with the creation of new businesses or with the development of existing ones. Some reference is made in the DTI literature to the need for links between business and education, and the DED's Pathfinder plans included producing a more positive attitude to enterprise. These aspects, however, are in support of the overall aim of economic improvement. This was expected to come from business development, which in turn was to come from more enterprise.

▌ Training and Enterprise Councils and Local Enterprise Agencies (TECs and LEAs)

The Training and Enterprise Councils (TECs) in England and Wales, and the Local Enterprise Companies (LECs) in Scotland, were formed as the result of central government initiative. According to the government's strategic guidance paper, 'Improving the competitiveness of business and people is one of the central purposes of TECs.'[7]

The central interest of most TEC directors is enterprise.

**(Charles Mitchell, Chairman,
TEC National Council Manufacturing Task Group[8])**

Birmingham TEC was set up to stimulate Birmingham's economy by investment in both training and career development, and business support.

(Information leaflet issued by Birmingham TEC[9])

[To] *serve and support the business growth, performance improvements and management development needs of all industry and commerce within the Greater Nottingham area.*

(Aims of Greater Nottingham TEC[10])

> *The Leicestershire Training and Enterprise Council is one of a number of similar organisations recently set up in the UK to help stimulate the local economy. In short, the Leicestershire TEC is here to help you build* better *jobs,* better *businesses and a* better *future.*
>
> **(*Guide to Services*, Leicestershire TEC[11])**
>
> *To improve the economic prosperity and quality of life for all in Sheffield, through a training and enterprise partnership and investment in people.*
>
> **(Long-term goal of Sheffield TEC[12])**

An Enterprise Workshop was held in May 1991, organised by the Employment Department. It was the first major opportunity for TECs, LECs (Local Enterprise Companies) and government to meet together to discuss how to develop and take forward their small firms and enterprise remit. There were five main conference themes:

- helping people to set up in business
- providing advice and support to established small businesses
- financing business growth and development
- developing and supporting the owner-manager
- developing a business through its people.

Among the conclusions of the workshop were that:

TECs/LECs need to have a clear vision for enterprise and to firmly establish the area of their role in small business support:

- Is the TEC primarily in the business of alleviating the effects of unemployment, offering services to small firms or designing programmes which impact on local economic regeneration?
- Should resources and effort be primarily concentrated on business start ups or on growth businesses?
- Should the TEC directly deliver training and support services or play a facilitating role in coordinating existing provision?[13]

Local Enterprise Agencies have been around for longer than TECs. Their formation was due not primarily to a central government initiative but to a series of local initiatives. Their aims are therefore more diverse that those of the TECs. One example is the London Enterprise Agency (LEntA), which

> exists to enable a group of the UK's leading companies to work together to tackle some of the economic and employment issues facing inner-London . . . the LEntA member companies aim to foster job and wealth creation, and to improve the economic prospects of the least advantaged among inner-London's residents.[14]

Local Enterprise Agencies vary greatly in size and in the range of services offered. But they all have one thing in common, one core activity: counselling of clients looking for advice in starting up or expanding small businesses.

(Business in the Community booklet[15])

The remit of the TECs, and the way it is put into practice, clearly indicates that in this context enterprise is taken primarily to mean business growth and competitiveness. The LEAs may, between them, encompass broader remits, but again their primary focus tends to be business start-up and development and its contribution to local economies. Little recognition is given to a wider meaning of 'enterprise'.

■ Enterprise in Higher Education

The Enterprise in Higher Education initiative was introduced by the Secretary of State for Employment in December 1987. According to the Training Agency,

> the main aim of EHE is to assist institutions of higher education develop enterprising graduates in partnership with employers. There are as many definitions of 'enterprise' as there are people defining the word! However, there is a great deal of common ground, and most people would agree that the enterprising person is resourceful, adaptable, creative, innovative and dynamic. He or she may also be entrepreneurial. However, the qualities of enterprise are as useful in the employee as the employer, and equally important in the public, private and voluntary sectors . . . The broad aims of the initiative are that:
>
> ■ Every person seeking a higher education qualification should be able to develop competencies and aptitudes relevant to enterprise.
> ■ These competencies and aptitudes should be acquired at least through project based work, designed to be undertaken in a real economic setting, which should be jointly assessed by employers and the student's higher education institution.[16]

The aim of the Enterprise in Higher Education programme in one university is described as

> to provide the opportunity for all full-time undergraduate students to acquire enterprise competencies, without compromising academic and intellectual standards. Students will be afforded the chance to develop both personal skills, such as leadership, creativity, problem analysis and solving, self awareness and flexibility; and interpersonal skills such as team building, negotiation and persuasion, conflict resolution and all forms of communication including IT.

This is also expanded as

> giving all full-time undergraduate students the opportunity to develop their enterprise competencies as an integral part of their academic programme. The university has chosen to adopt a broad definition of enterprise, based on personal transferable skills. These include:

- Communication skills: written reports, oral presentations, media awareness
- Group-work skills   leadership, teamwork, group dynamics
- Personal skills   self-awareness and self-appraisal
- Organisational skills   time-management, task management, objective setting
- Interpersonal skills   listening, negotiation and persuasion, mutual confidence and respect
- Problem-solving   problem analysis, creative thinking and decision making
- Social and community awareness   sensitivity to others, moral and ethical bases of decision making
- Resource management skills   economic awareness, costing and budgeting.[17]

While the Enterprise in Higher Education initiative was launched by government, it interprets the 'enterprise' it is promoting as a range of skills. These are not just business and business-related skills, but a range of personal skills that are useful, both in the environment of work and also in a wide range of other contexts. Indeed the Training Agency makes a distinction between enterprise and entrepreneurship, the latter being a possible subset of the former.

■ Young Enterprise

The Young Enterprise initiative has its origins in the Junior Achievement programme in the USA. In the UK it is a national educational charity, founded in 1963, with the mission of providing young people (mainly in the 15 to 19 age group) with an exciting and imaginative practical business experience, enabling them to develop their personal and interpersonal skills, knowledge and understanding of business objectives and the wealth creation process. It does this primarily by giving young people the chance to learn from setting up and running their own companies during one academic year. By 1994 more than 33 000 students from 1700 schools and colleges were participating each year in the UK, supported by 2000 businesses and 6500 volunteers. The benefits it delivers to its participating 'Achievers' include improving their business knowledge, influencing their career and study preferences, improving their attitudes and skills such as the ability to work in a team and self-confidence, and supporting qualifications in business core skills.

Young Enterprise therefore sees 'enterprise' in the context of business, but within that context it is concerned with the acquisition of attitudes and skills that involve discovery, confidence and achievement, as well as the specific business skills of marketing, finance, communication and organisation.

■ Other Examples

An enterprise culture is one in which every individual understands that the world does not owe him or her a living, and so we act together accord-ingly, all working for the success of UK plc. The gross national product is earned by companies. Successful companies which regularly make profits and grow are the flagships of the enterprise culture. Directors who lead those successful companies are heroes of the enterprise culture. Any of our products or services which lead the world are the pride of the enterprise culture.

In an enterprise culture we expect that some of the wealth will be used for public goods and services, but we believe that wealth creation comes first.

(Peter Morgan[18])

How is the 'enterprise culture' to be regarded? Just like some handy little slogan? A simple shorthand way for describing developing small business activity? Some proverbial wisdom about such? Small businesses' new guiding spirit? Or just some well-promoted party political trademark? Maybe the latest populist catchphrase? A carefully sanitized euphemism which glosses over something else?

(John Ritchie[19])

2.3 Enterprise in action

- *The Enterprise Allowance Scheme* was introduced to direct financial support to unemployed people wishing to become self-employed. Its aim was stated as to encourage unemployed people to create thriving new businesses.
- *Graduate Enterprise* provision is a scheme to raise the awareness and preparedness for self-employment among undergraduates.
- *Scottish Enterprise* is the successor to the Scottish Development Agency. Its remit is to help to generate jobs and prosperity for the people of Scotland.
- *British Coal Enterprise* is a wholly owned subsidiary of British Coal set up in 1984 to help to create alternative job opportunities in areas associated with coalmining,
- *Enterprising Nottinghamshire* is an initiative designed to promote an awareness and understanding of the creative potential of people. Its aim was 'to develop and encourage an enterprising culture in Nottinghamshire' and a presentation on its achievements indicated that 'an Enterprising Person was someone who displays initiative, makes decisions, manages resources, shows drive and determination, influences others and monitors progress'.[20]
- *Enterprise culture* is a complex set of economic, social and political attitudes.

*One can be **enterprising** both by making a million before one's fortieth birthday and by shepherding passengers out of a burning aeroplane.*[21]

Enterprise is having ideas and imagination and using them.[22]

*The mission of the **Starship Enterprise** is 'to boldly go where no man has gone before'.*

These other examples of the word 'enterprise' demonstrate that the word has, in normal usage, a wide variety of meanings. In some cases its meaning is limited to the business context, but in others, for instance when applied to the Starship *Enterprise*, it is an attitude to life, an attitude of exploring, of developing, of leading and of taking initiatives, which, while it may help in the business context, has much wider applications.

Narrow and Broad Meanings of Enterprise

Endeavour to be firm (10 letters)

(Crossword clue[23])

In many of the examples examined above the implication is that 'enterprise' is seen, at least primarily, as connected with the promotion of business, small business and/or business starts. The later examples however suggest that, for some people at least, it can have a wider meaning. Writing on 'enterprise culture' the author of an OECD monograph indicated that

> there are, in effect, two definitions of, or approaches to, the word 'enterprise' and the practice of it. One, which can be termed a 'narrow' one, regards enterprise as business entrepreneurialism, and sees its promotion and development within education and training systems as an issue of curriculum development which enables young people to learn, usually on an experimental basis, about business start-up and management. The second approach, which can be termed the 'broad' one, regards enterprise as a group of qualities and competencies that enable individuals, organisations, communities, societies and cultures to be flexible, creative, and adaptable in the face of, and as contributors to, rapid social and economic change.[24]

In answer to the question, 'What do we mean by enterprise?', another commentator replied:

> Two schools of theory and practice are evident, each based on different although not contradictory answers to the question. They can be called the 'economy school' and the 'education school'. The 'economy school' says that enterprise is what entrepreneurs do and entrepreneurs create business and jobs and wealth and those things all contribute to, indeed they comprise, the economy... The 'education school' says that enterprise has a broader meaning and application than that... It says that many types of initiative which need to be taken, many types of responsibility which need to be discharged and many types of problems which need to be resolved require the individual to act in an 'enterprising' manner. Thus this school sees business-type entrepreneurialism as just one context in which people act in 'enterprising' ways. It says that enterprise involves using the imagination, being creative, taking responsibilities, organising, identifying ideas, making decisions, dealing with others in a wide range of contexts. It says that as society becomes more complex and as it changes towards greater complexity, people

need to be more and more enterprising. At the heart of this approach is, therefore, personal development and, in particular, the development of self-confidence.[25]

Enterprise is about attitudes and skills in whatever sphere of life.

The Narrower View of Enterprise: Entrepreneurship – Business Creation and Development

The 'narrow' or 'economy' school view is the one behind many of the examples quoted in the introduction to this chapter. In that context it is not possible to explore enterprise without also examining 'entrepreneurism' and 'entrepreneurship', because frequently the words are used interchangeably, and do indeed have a common root.

The evolution of the concept of the entrepreneur can be traced back to an Irish economist living in France called Richard Cantillon, who introduced the word into economic literature in his *'Essai sur la nature de commerce en général'*, said to have been written in 1734 but not published until 1755, twenty-one years after his death. The word is derived from the French *entreprendre* meaning 'to undertake'. Cantillon's implicit concept of the entrepreneur is a broad one, but it is based on the entrepreneur as a person with the foresight and confidence to operate in conditions when costs may be known but rewards are uncertain. Jean-Baptiste Say (1767–1832), the first professor of economics in Europe, produced a narrower definition of the entrepreneur that involved the combination and coordination of the factors of production to accommodate the unexpected and overcome problems. It was however earlier, in 1776, that the capitalist concept had been first described as a relatively complete theory by Adam Smith in his book *The Wealth of Nations*.[26] This work was the foundation of the classical capitalist economic theory, and it identified the capitalist as the owner or manager who, from basic resources of land, labour and capital, constructed successful industrial enterprise. By the middle of the next century the word 'entrepreneur' was being used to indicate the owner-manager of an industrial enterprise.

By the start of the twentieth century a further refinement in theory of the capitalist economy had been developed, by the neo-classical school, in particular Leon Walras and Alfred Marshall. Its key component is that of market equilibrium, when supply equals demand in a perfectly competitive market. This theory does not, however, have a place for the 'entrepreneur' as a cause of economic activity. Suppliers should instead respond to market pressures: if prices rise they should supply more, and if they fall, less. They should not upset this equilibrium by introducing innovative products or services. Classical economists, however, and in particular a group in Austria, objected to this absence of entrepreneurialism. One of their students was Joseph Schumpeter, who went to the USA early in his career. He believed that the concept of innovation, described as the use of an invention to create a new commercial product or service, was the key force in creating new demand and thus new wealth. Entrepreneurs were the owner-managers who, in this way, started new businesses to exploit invention. If successful they thus created wealth for themselves and employment for others from their ability and ambition, rather than only from ownership of land or capital.

Leibenstein, whose first theoretical observations on entrepreneurship were published in 1968, distinguished between two processes: the process of the entrepreneur who introduces innovation in product or process, and the process of the manager who establishes or runs a business in traditional ways. Schumpeter argued in 1934, in *The Theory of Economic Development*, that entrepreneurs were different from those who solely managed businesses without innovating, and it was these entrepreneurs who were the key to wealth creation and distribution in capitalism. Innovations create new demand and entrepreneurs bring the innovations to the market. This destroys existing markets and creates new ones, which will in turn be destroyed by even newer products or services. Schumpeter called this process 'creative destruction'. This is a dynamic process, which contrasts sharply with the static, equilibrium theory of the neo-classicists. Nevertheless it was the almost scientific appeal of the latter that remained as the dominant theory for much of the twentieth century.[27]

Whyte in his book *The Organizational Man* (1956) suggests that the American experience of the Depression followed by the military training of the Second World War created a belief in or at least an obedience to bureaucracies.[28] America had thus become conditioned to believe in the large corporation as the major, and as the preferred, source of employment. In 1967 John Kenneth Galbraith published *The New Industrial State*, in which he highlighted the benefit of economies of scale in production, as evidenced by Henry Ford's assembly lines.[29] As production organisations become larger, the theory went, greater specialisation of labour and machines was possible, which in turn reduced the unit cost of production. Large firms therefore have lower costs of production than small ones and, as there are no theoretical limits to their size, they will dominate society. Galbraith thus believed that large corporations would work with government and large unions and, based on a shared view of organisation life, they could in effect run the state.

The idea of economies of scale fitted in well with neo-classical economic theory and evidence for their existence appeared to be provided by management information and by plant engineers' calculations. The fact that researchers had difficulty in documenting real examples did not impinge on mainstream economic thought. Big business ruled, and the dominant perception of entrepreneurs was summed up in the saying that 'Entrepreneurs are people who start their own business to avoid getting a job'.[30] It was the results of Birch's economic analysis that changed this perception. He concluded that in the USA, in the period between 1969 and 1976, small firms created the majority of the net new jobs, a result that was initially discounted by most economists.[31] While Birch's conclusions have been challenged by some subsequent work, the importance of the entrepreneur and the relevance of Schumpeter's theory were at last established and became accepted by mainstream economists.

Although this central role of the entrepreneur, and therefore of entrepreneurship, in business and economics is now accepted, this does not now mean that there is a single accepted definition of what an entrepreneur is. On the contrary, there are a range of possible meanings, derived from different ways of looking at the entrepreneur and how he or she operates. Table 2.1 summarises the main approaches (some of which are also explored in more detail in Chapter 3).

It is this contribution of entrepreneurship to economic development that is one of the areas of meaning assigned to 'enterprise'. In this context the words enterprise and entrepreneurship can be synonymous. The word 'enterprise' is also used to mean a unit of business, the processes of business start-up, and the process of being in business and of business growth and development. In other words, it is used to refer to the various elements that contribute directly to economic development and to job creation. These are the 'narrow' meanings of enterprise: it is a form of behaviour devoted to the successful development of business.

■ The Broader View of Enterprise: Attributes and Resources

2.4 The enterprising individual

An enterprising individual has a positive, flexible and adaptable disposition towards change, seeing it as normal, and as an opportunity rather than a problem. To see change in this way, an enterprising individual has a security, born of self-confidence, and is at ease when dealing with insecurity, risks, difficulty and the unknown. An enterprising individual has the capacity to initiate creative ideas..., develop them, and see them through into action in a determined manner. An enterprising individual is able, even anxious, to take responsibility and is an effective communicator, negotiator, influencer, planner and organiser. An enterprising individual is active, confident, purposeful, not passive, uncertain and dependent...

Source: OECD/CERI.[32]

The makeup of the entrepreneur has been explored by a number of people. McClelland looked at motives, and identified three underlying ones: the need for achievement, the need for affiliation and the need for power (see also Chapter 3). According to him, the person motivated for high achievement has optimism, wants responsibility, enjoys challenges and novelty and is a moderate risk-taker.[33] Others have looked at the need for autonomy and the desire for influence. What however is generally being described is a set of attributes that

Table 2.1   Summary of approaches for describing entrepreneurship

Entrepreneurial model	Central focus or purpose	Assumption	Behaviour and skills	Situation
'Great Person' School	The entrepreneur has an intuitive ability – a sixth sense – and traits and instincts with which he or she is born	Without this 'inborn' intuition, the individual would be like the rest of us mortals, who 'lack what it takes'	Intuition, vigour, energy, persistence, and self-esteem	Start-up
Psychological Characteristics School	Entrepreneurs have unique values, attitudes, and needs that drive them	People behave in accordance with their values; behaviour results from attempts to satisfy needs	Personal values, risk-taking, need for achievement, and others	Start-up
Classical School	The central characteristic of entrepreneurial behaviour is innovation	The critical aspect of entrepreneurship is in the process of doing rather than owning	Innovation, creativity, and discovery	Start-up and early growth
Management School	Entrepreneurs are organisers of an economic venture; they are people who organise, own, manage and assume the risk	Entrepreneurs can be developed or trained in the technical functions of management	Production planning, people organising, capitalisation, and budgeting	Early growth and maturity
Leadership School	Entrepreneurs are leaders of people; they have the ability to adapt their style to the needs of people	An entrepreneur cannot accomplish his or her goals alone, but depends on others	Motivating, directing, and leading	Early growth and maturity
Intrapreneurship School	Entrepreneurial skills can be useful in complex organisations; intrapreneurship is the development of independent units to create, market, and expand services	Organisations need to adapt to survive; entrepreneurial activity leads to organisational building and entrepreneurs becoming managers	Alertness to opportunities, maximising decisions.	Maturity and change

Source: J. B. Cunningham and J. Lischeron, 'Defining Entrepreneurship', *Journal of Small Business Management*, 29, January 1991, p. 47.

Table 2.2   Entrepreneurial or enterprising attributes

- Initiative
- Strong persuasive powers
- Moderate rather than high risk-taking
- Flexibility
- Creativity
- Independence/autonomy
- Problem-solving ability
- Need for achievement
- Imagination
- High belief in control of one's own destiny
- Leadership
- Hard work

Source: A. A. Gibb, 'Enterprise Culture – Its Meaning and Implications for Education and Training', *Journal of European Industrial Training* (1987) p. 6.

can be used in a number of situations. Often, however, the starting point for identifying these attributes has been the entrepreneur.

The list of attributes in Table 2.2 was prepared by Gibb, who describes enterprise as the exercise of this set of attributes and the entrepreneur, he suggests, is someone who demonstrates a marked use of these attributes in a particular task or context, usually in business or commerce. However, if

> entrepreneurship is defined solely in terms of a set of attributes, used in a certain task context, it follows that there are entrepreneurs in all kinds of organisations, for these attributes are displayed and developed by a wide variety of people working in many different circumstances – these are 'enterprising' people. There is for example, much scope for entrepreneurial behaviour within bureaucracies, although when this behaviour is frustrated or cannot be contained within the organisation and is regarded as deviant, then job change, or indeed self-employment, may be pursued as a means of exercising these attributes. This is in line with the idea of the entrepreneur as a 'marginal man': put simply, this is someone who does not fit easily into the conventional organisation. Within the conventional employee role, there may be more or less scope for exercise of entrepreneurial attributes, depending on the structure and purpose of the organisation (or parts of it) and the amount of individual freedom. Motivation to develop and exercise entrepreneurial attributes, whatever the nature of the work or location, is important. It is clear that, in some organisations, the exercise of such attributes will be seen as 'desirable'; in others it will be labelled as 'deviant'. The issue of 'desirability' of entrepreneurial behaviour is an important one not confined only to the culture of the work place, but also clearly of importance in terms of society as a whole.[34]

If enterprise, or entrepreneurship, is the exercise of a set of attributes or behaviours then those attributes can also be illustrated by the process by which they might, or might not, be developed. Gibb has analysed and described the relevant attributes, ideas, ambitions and culture and their development through a number of diagrams.

At almost all stages of life there are factors that can influence the development of enterprising/entrepreneurial ideas, these are summarised in Table 2.3.

An enterprise culture is generally one in which several influences combine to reinforce the development of enterprise (Figure 2.1).

Table 2.3   Influences on the development of entrepreneurial ideas and ambitions at different stages of life

Childhood	Adolescence	Early adulthood	Middle adulthood	Late adulthood
Parental and wider family class and class mobility	Parental/wider family influence on educational choice	Choice of further education/ training	Occupational and class mobility	Class attained and income/ wealth achieved
		Own class ranking	Nature of work	
Parental and wider family work situation	Parental and wider family influence on vocational preference	Friendship and community attachment	Own family and friendship	Family situation Communal attachments
Parental and wider family educational choice	Choices of vocational education available	Residual family influence	Working relationships Reward systems and job satisfaction	Extra work opportunities
Parental and wider family values and 'life goals'	Education as provider of values and goals	Possible own family Nature of work	Job satisfaction Interactions with environment socially and at work	Job satisfaction Pensions and early retirement facilities
	Friendship and community attachments		Business training and development	

Source: A. A. Gibb, 'Enterprise Culture – Its Meaning and Implications for Education and Training', *Journal of European Industrial Training* (1987) p. 13.

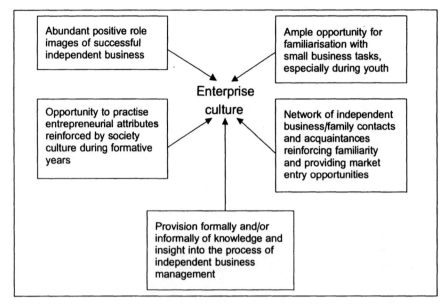

Source: A. A. Gibb, 'Enterprise Culture – Its Meaning and Implications for Education and Training', *Journal of European Industrial Training* (1987) p. 14.

Figure 2.1 The components of enterprise culture

Our youth is the stage of life when we are most susceptible to the influences of an enterprise culture. Often, however, the focus of our formal education is different from that of enterprise, as Table 2.4 shows.

Later in life also we are subject to influences that are not enterprising ones. Gibb, for instance, also contrasts the values and systems embodied by a

Table 2.4 The focus of learning

Education focus on	Entrepreneurial focus on
The past	The future
Critical analysis	Creativity
Knowledge	Insight
Passive understanding	Active learning
Absolute detachment	Emotional involvement
Manipulation of symbols	Manipulation of events
Written communication and neutrality	Personal communication and influence
Concept	Problem or opportunity

Source: A. A. Gibb, 'Enterprise Culture – Its Meaning and Implications for Education and Training', *Journal of European Industrial Training* (1987) p. 17.

Table 2.5   Entrepreneurial v. corporatist management – some contrasts

Entrepreneurial management	Corporatist management
Values, beliefs and goals	
Growth by green field management	Growth by acquisition
Short time horizons	Long time horizons
Informal strategic project planning (policy and practice interlinked and changing and emerging)	Formalised planning systems (policy laid before practice)
Failure means missed opportunity	Failure means resource-centred misdemeanor (variance from standard)
Seeks incremental development as a means to reduce risk	Seeks large-scale development with risk reduction by analysis/information
Pursues action strategies with negotiation as and where necessary	Pursues pre-negotiation strategies for decision making (personal risk reduction)
Management evaluation on task completion	Management evaluation as routine aspect of organisation
Status equals success in the market	Status equals control over resources
Avoidance of overhead and risk of obsolescence by high subcontracting	Seeks ownership of all resources with objective of power and control
Pursues effectiveness in the marketplace	Pursues efficiency information to justify control
Organisational contrasts	
Flat organisational structure	Hierarchical organisation structure
Challenge to owner legitimacy	Clear authority
Need to trust others for reward	Clear reward system defined
Organic relationship emerging.	Rational/legal structures.

Source: A. A. Gibb, 'Enterprise Culture – Its Meaning and Implications for Education and Training', *Journal of European Industrial Training* (1987) pp. 21–2.

corporate and/or bureaucratic approach to those of an entrepreneurial management system (Table 2.5).

The issue of enterprise within business relates both to business founding owners, who might be expected to have some enterprise, and business managers, who might be more inclined to take the corporist approach. In the 1950s and 1960s, when markets seemed more stable, many managers saw the efficient utilisation of resources and the perfecting of performance in marketing and production as their primary tasks. They implemented plans, coordinated disparate activities and controlled behaviour.

In the relatively more turbulent world of the 1980s this behaviour no longer brought continued success. Rapid changes in knowledge, in markets and in education meant that organisations needed to strive for both efficiency and the customisation of goods or services. Several writers have highlighted the role of managers in energising adaptable employees to use all their skills and knowledge in a flexible manner to provide customers with satisfaction. High-quality customised products provide benefits, but they can only be produced by committed flexible employees, not alienated ones maintaining rigid demarcations.[35] Thus, for Salaman the essence of management is the ability to enhance the performance of subordinates by 'doing the right things, doing things right and then better, or learning to do new things'.[36] While new small businesses may play an increasing role in net job creation, increasing enterprise in established businesses is also critical to at least the continuance of existing jobs.

This focus on excellence and continuous improvement was recognised in the Management Charter Initiative in the UK.[37] It was claimed in the mid 1980s that managers in Britain did not possess the education, knowledge and skills required for international competitiveness, and the MCI set about articulating the competencies required for effective management performance, and developing several dimensions of personal competence, one of which highlighted the competence of 'showing concern for excellence'. For effectiveness in this domain managers are required to be adept at setting and expressing high performance goals, doing things better, identifying and overcoming constraints on excellence and being opportunity-oriented in a changing situation. These behaviours are commonly exhibited by all enterprising people, and further confirmation of this link is provided by the then British Institute of Management (now the Institute of Management). It reviewed the literature on key managerial competencies as depicted by a variety of influential writers and concluded that a number of attributes and behaviours underpinned a concern for excellence. These include achievement orientation, efficiency orientation, proactivity, entrepreneurial drive and entrepreneurial skill. Thus enterprising managers are concerned constantly to improve what they and their people do. This is in contrast to bureaucratic managers, who tend to protect the *status quo*.

This contrast between an entrepreneurial, or enterprise, approach and the one to which we might have been accustomed, particularly in the workplace, has been recognised in other situations also. The attributes and resources required for enterprise in a business context are applicable to enterprise in whatever situations it is manifest. This has been summarised as

the change of social policies and practices towards the development of policies that, as in the work place, make the best use of all available human resources. They are called 'enterprising' policies and practices, in which a new balance of power is being achieved between the institution and the individual... Because of these changes all organisations and wider society need to be enterprising. The desired results are systems and structures which encourage and enable the individuals who work in them and are served by them to be enterprising. When and where this happens, we have an enterprising culture... While the changes that are going on in modern societies are complex and manifold, there is a common thread passing through all of them. What they amount to is a change in the balance of power, and a parallel change in roles, between what individuals do for themselves and what others (especially society's institutions) do for them. As the balance changes, we move towards the creation of an enterprising culture.[38]

2.5 Possible models of the distribution of entrepreneurial attributes

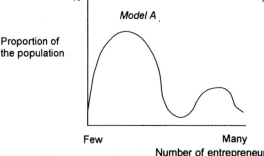
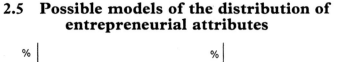
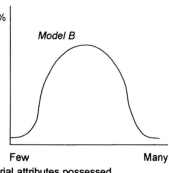

Number of entrepreneurial attributes possessed

There is a tendency to think that the distribution of entrepreneurial attributes among people is like that illustrated in Model A with two distinct groups: those with few attributes and those with many. Actually it is probably more like the Model B. A key difference is that, if the first model is correct, it will imply that making incremental changes in the distribution will not have much effect: there will still be few people with many attributes. In the second model, though, an incremental change will have the effect of increasing the number with many attributes.

Within the debate on enterprising attributes and culture it has been pointed out that the characteristics that are required for the wider application of enterprise are also those needed for the narrower one. It is not possible to develop attributes only in, or for application in, a business context. If someone has these attributes then he or she is liable to use them wherever they appear to be appropriate, whether it be for an economic, a social, a political, an environmental or other purpose. Further, if these attributes are, at least in part, acquired during upbringing and through education then that happens often before career choices are made. To get more enterprise in business it would therefore be necessary to try to develop more enterprise for all contexts.

2.6 Enterprise and happiness

There appears to be an assumption, in the way in which the desirability of enterprise is sometimes promoted, that being enterprising can somehow be equated with being happier That association is however rarely overtly stated, and can therefore be very difficult to pin down.

It can be argued that the results of enterprise can lead to greater happiness. As a result of enterprise a person may have a more rewarding occupation, in terms of financial reward or other benefits such as variety and interest. It can lead to a person achieving more, which is particularly appropriate for those with a high need for achievement (see Chapter 3). It can lead to a person avoiding an otherwise less favourable scenario. However, being enterprising *per se* does not necessarily directly produce happiness.

■ Other Aspects of Enterprise

A further development of this debate has taken place more specifically in the context of enterprise as applied to business start-up. The more traditional view of enterprise has been largely that it is an attribute that exists and can be measured and encouraged, but which is not evenly distributed among the population. Some have more of it than others, and it is those with more of it who tend to display enterprising activity such as starting businesses. The implication has been that if more of those individual levels of enterprise could be raised above some sort of implicit enterprise threshold then more enterprise activity and more business start-ups would be the result. This view of enterprise does not however fit with some of its observable aspects. For instance it is not static, but the threshold theory makes no provision for the dynamic effects that can be observed when enterprise behaviour snowballs and people are influenced by the example of others. Enterprise is not one-way: people can move out of it as well as into it. Enterprise is complex and there are many influences on whether an individual shows enterprise activity and therefore raising levels of enterprise attributes, if that is possible, may be swamped in its effects by other influences.

An alternative view of enterprise, and of enterprising behaviour, is based on the attributes and resources that an individual may possess at any point in time. It is suggested that it is the interaction between these factors produces a rational response, on the basis of available information, when the opportunity occurs for a business start-up. This theory acknowledges however that there is inertia in individual behaviour and that it may take a discontinuity in work, or in life, to trigger a review of an individual's situation. Whether this review will lead to an individual trying their own enterprise will then depend on the attributes and resources they have accumulated and on their perception of environmental factors such as the availability of grants and training. (This concept is developed further in Chapter 3.)

Gibb and Ritchie[39] have summarised the necessary condition for enterprise as the possession of

M otivation
A bility
I dea
R esources

A close examination of what is taught under the name of enterprise reveals, however, that instead of the consensus claimed by leading practitioners, the organisations that are teaching this new culture are all working with different lists of the core skills.

Part of the confusion stems from the fact that the word 'enterprise' is used in different ways, sometimes referring to an individual ability considered amenable to improvement and at other times to a form of economic activity, usually in small business.

We are not dealing with a tightly defined, agreed and unitary concept but with a farrago of hurrah words such as creativity, initiative, and leadership.
(Professor Frank Coffield[40])

■ Conclusions

As indicated earlier there are many different usages, and therefore definitions, of the word 'enterprise'. These different meanings are related to each other, however. There are not just two or three distinct discrete meanings but instead a spectrum: a range of meanings, each one merging with those close to it but perceptibly different from those far from it. It is not possible to indicate that one particular meaning is the correct one. The word is in practice used in these different ways, and those trying to understand it need to be aware of what it means to whoever is using it.

The UK government, however, has almost always used it in the context of economic growth through (small) business start-up and growth. That is what their 'enterprise' schemes are aimed at. Training and Enterprise Councils, Enterprise Agencies and similar organisations have had the same usage. Other initiatives, however, such as Enterprise in Higher Education, have treated enterprise more as a set of attitudes and competencies that may have a wider application than just the world of business. Possibly its most famous application, the Starship *Enterprise*, the spacecraft in the Star Trek series, has nothing to do with business and everything to do with a readiness to explore the new.

One end of the spectrum of meaning could be considered to be the 'narrow' definition of enterprise, which could be summarised as:

Enterprise = Entrepreneurship = Starting up a business,
Being in business, *and*
Growing and developing a business.
(or = a business)

The other end of the spectrum could be enterprise as a positive, flexible, and adaptable attitude to change. It is the exercise of enterprising attributes. It is a new balance in power between the institution and the individual. In this context it has a far wider application than just business, as such attributes can be applied in all walks of life. It could be summarised as:

Enterprise = Innovative attributes and behaviour.

The spectrum analogy is not perfect, however, because a broad meaning can include a narrow one. To get the enterprise that is sought in business, some believe, it is necessary to promote a culture of enterprise that is much broader than business. For them it is all or nothing: you can't only have enterprise in business and not in other fields – you must have both or neither.

The application of enterprise in practice, however, takes more than just an aspiration to be enterprising. For someone to behave in an enterprising way, he or she may need at least some of the right attributes combined with some of the relevant resources with which to apply the attributes, and then it may take a specific trigger to start it off.

'Enterprise' in the way people apply the word is, however, very varied. Some further aspects of that variety are now explored in the rest of Part I of this book.

Key points

- In recent years 'enterprise' has been a popular word to attach to a variety of initiatives. However, it has often seemed that it has been used more for the cachet of a supposedly desirable label than because it is the most appropriate word in the particular circumstances.
- The way it is used nevertheless indicates that it has a wide continuum of meanings. In some case its use implies a meaning that is limited to a business context, and it can even be used as a synonym for business. Other uses, however, imply a wider meaning: it is often associated with an attitude to life: of exploring, of developing, of leading and of taking the initiative. Such an attitude can be very helpful in the business context, but it also has much wider applications.
- These different uses have been described as the narrow and broad meanings of 'enterprise'. The narrow meaning regards enterprise as business entrepreneurialism, and in that context the words 'entrepreneurship' and 'enterprise' are usually interchangeable. The broad one, on the other hand, regards it as a set of qualities and competencies that

enable individuals and groups that possess them to be flexible, creative and adaptable in the face of change. These two approaches have also been labeled the 'economy school' and the 'education school': at the heart of the latter is the concept of personal development and the development of self-confidence.

- In a business context, the word 'entrepreneurship' is often used in a the same way as the word 'enterprise'. Its use can be traced to eighteenth-century France and, with the development of the concept of capitalism, the entrepreneur came to be seen as essential to the process of wealth creation. When very big businesses developed, the entrepreneur seemed to have been supplanted by the manager in business relevance, but the recent demonstrations of the potential and achievements of small businesses has once again highlighted his or her importance.

- Those who have looked at the makeup of the entrepreneur have identified entrepreneurship, or enterprise, as the exercise of a set of attributes. The possession of at least some of these attributes has been particularly helpful in times of change, but their exercise need not only be limited to a business context. There is however no clear agreement on precisely what these attributes, skills, or attitudes are.

- Further, the possession of such attributes, skills and attitudes is not necessarily sufficient for a person to act in an enterprising manner, especially when that implies taking the initiative in business formation and development. What is also needed may be the resource with which to act and a trigger to start it off.

- 'Enterprise' therefore is a varied concept, both in its application and in its explanation. It is however the subject of considerable interest.

CHAPTER 3

Enterprise in Individuals

■ Introduction

Chapter 2 showed that the word 'enterprise', in the way it is actually being used, has a range of meanings. Some of these overlap, some embrace others and some appear to be very different. Within this range there are two main areas of meaning: those reflecting the 'broad' or 'education' approach, in which enterprise is a type of behaviour that can be exhibited in many contexts, and those representing the 'narrow' or 'economy' application, in which 'enterprise' is sometimes used as a synonym for small business or the process of starting one. The latter use is sufficiently common and important to be explored further in Part II. However there are many aspects of the 'broad' definition to be considered first.

The 'broad' or 'education' approach is largely based on the concept of enterprise as something demonstrated in the actions individual people take: actions that can be enterprising in a variety of situations, not just in business. These actions are in turn due to a considerable extent to the makeup of the individuals concerned: to their attributes, competencies, attitudes, skills, ideas and resources. The context the individuals operate in is also of relevance, because enterprise in some aspects and in some contexts seems more due to group dynamics, than to individual ones. This chapter, however, explores enterprise from the perspective of the individual; the group aspect is considered in Chapter 4.

In looking at the personal aspects of the broad definition of enterprise, it is. worth considering how far they apply also to the narrow definition and therefore, by implication, whether the two are inconsistent with each other. One definition regards enterprise as synonymous with business founding, while the other sees it as the application of an array of adaptable skills to new, unique or complex tasks. Enterprising individuals often initiate and develop projects; they do not sit around and wait for things to happen but take control and see issues through to their conclusion. Although there is an apparent difference between the two aspects of enterprise, the distinction may be more apparent than real. In reality, founding a business can be just as much an enterprising act as any other, and that aspect of enterprise can be seen as one component of a larger domain. The 'narrow' definition is therefore just an example of the 'broad'.

Consider the act of initiating and developing a business venture. In developing a business idea, many potential proprietors will have a futuristic and opportunistic orientation and think creatively about different ways of satisfying human needs. In locating and marshalling necessary resources and suppliers of funds, they will be imaginative and persistent. In recognising and overcoming unique problems they will display proactivity and flexibility. And in keeping going in the face of innumerable setbacks they will draw on all their self-confidence, perseverance and dynamism. However, numerous acts in other environments can be considered as enterprising, such as those of the university dean who successfully introduces a radical way of teaching graduate students, the nurse who revolutionises postoperative care, the community leader who convinces his council to care for the homeless or the missionary who improves the conditions of the underprivileged. It might be considered that such actions are specific to their different situations, but they do appear to have many common features. However, before they can all be described as enterprising, it will be helpful to have some idea of what constitutes an enterprising act.

■ Enterprising Acts

Entrepreneurship has been described as 'the creative extraction of value from environments',[1] which emphasises the outcome as well as the process and is a starting point in considering enterprising acts as enterprising outcomes. In the context of business, few doubt the often enterprising nature of business formation and development. One possible indicator of the degree of enterprise to be found in individuals in a community or in an economy is therefore the number of small firms in existence there. It is relevant to note, however, that business formation rates fluctuate widely, and that many self-employed people and small firms fail each year. How, then, should business failure be regarded? If the act of starting a small business is enterprising, what is a subsequent failure? Does it negate the enterprise of the original act? There are no obvious answers to these questions but they do highlight the complexity of coming to terms with the notion of enterprise.

If it is difficult to say unequivocally whether an action is enterprising in a business context, what are the prospects in other contexts? Consider a welfare officer faced with a serious teenage drugs problem. The officer has ideas about what might be done. She mobilises parents, community groups, medics, police and others connected with the problem to take action. She communicates with the teenagers and elicits their views on the issue. She lobbies, politiks and hassles to obtain the physical and monetary resources to create a day centre manned by advisers with access to medical personnel. One year after her intervention the drug problem has not gone away, but teenage suicides have decreased in the area, fewer teenage pregnancies are reported and large numbers attend group therapy sessions. Was this an enterprising process? The individual concerned displayed many of the qualities usually associated with the business formation process and the outcome of this project would be regarded by many as reasonably successful, even if the original aim was not achieved. Many would therefore describe the individual concerned as enterprising.

There are innumerable undertakings of this nature in business, family and private life that can be described as enterprising and, though it is a relative and not an absolute term, it can be considered appropriate to enumerate the key characteristics of such undertakings. In doing so it can be helpful to distinguish between the nature of the task and the manner in which it is tackled. Broadly, however, the label 'enterprise' might be applied when:

- the task is non-routine
- the task is somewhat complex
- the task is goal-directed
- the goal(s) are demanding but attainable

also when:

- the task is tackled in an adventurous manner
- the task is approached in a determined and dynamic manner
- the task accomplishes the set goals (or comes near to so doing).

A project has been defined as 'a task requiring considerable or concerted effort'[2] and, in short, it might therefore be considered that an enterprising act is one in which a project is undertaken in an energetic, bold and adaptable manner.

Defining enterprise in this way can accommodate both the narrow and broad approaches to the subject outlined in Chapter 2, and underpins the importance of newness, change and flexibility for enterprise. This definition also emphasises the relevance of success. Bold, dynamic acts that fail to meet predetermined goals may not always be considered to be enterprising. Those goals, however, need not be economic, and success in enterprise is not just limited to commercial success. In addition, actions that appear to be or indeed are, initially successful and would be regarded as enterprising, but which then subsequently fail, would usually still be regarded as having been enterprising. Enterprising acts take place within a time-frame, and outside it conditions can change radically.

■ Enterprise and Entrepreneurship

As indicated in Chapter 2, the term 'entrepreneurship' is frequently used in conjunction with issues of business formation and development. Further, the ways in which entrepreneurs are said to act when seeking business opportunities, and in coordinating resources to cope with business problems, are very similar to what has been described as enterprise in looking to the future, initiating projects and managing them in a creative and adaptable manner. Entrepreneurship is in effect, the same thing as enterprise in its narrower sense and therefore, in this chapter, analysis of entrepreneurship has also been included in the discussion of the makeup of enterprise.[3]

■ Invention and Innovation

The concepts of invention, creativity and innovation are also closely associated with enterprising outcomes. Invention, it is generally agreed, is the origination of a new concept or idea as the result of a process of creativity. However, there is less agreement on what innovation is. For some it is the development or adoption of new concepts or ideas, while for others it is the new or adopted ideas themselves. These approaches are linked, however, and there is general agreement that invention precedes innovation and that the latter can be viewed as the successful exploitation of new ideas, but not the origination of the ideas.[4] Creativity is having the idea, and innovation is its application. Creativity is not itself enterprising, because it does not generate change; that does not happen until the innovator takes the idea and does something with it.

The place of innovation in commercial success has been illustrated in Figure 3.1, and this can be extended to the successful exploitation of new ideas that leads to any form of increased organisational or social benefit.

What skills are needed by successful innovators? Forehand[5] suggests that innovative behaviour 'includes the development and consideration of novel

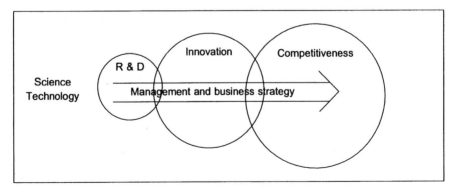

Source: DTI promotional material.

Figure 3.1   The role of innovation

solutions to...problems, and evaluation of them in terms of criteria broader than conformity to pre-existing practice...', and argues that self-reliant, inquiring, flexible, original and independent people are most likely to engage in innovative behaviour. It will be seen that there is considerable similarity between these attributes and those linked with enterprising behaviour. However, the inclusion of originality and enquiry underline the importance of uncovering new ways of doing things. Moss Kanter[6] considers that innovators must develop a vision of something new, must generate a power base to progress the idea, and must build commitment and systems to sustain the new endeavour. For Moss Kanter, visions emerge from kaleidoscopic thinking. Some people have the capacity to view existing structures and behaviours from a variety of perspectives and, unrestrained by existing assumptions, are able to see useful new combinations of resources. Once envisioned, this new possibility must be enthusiastically and articulately communicated to others.

This is very similar to the language used to describe successful enterprise, and it would appear therefore that there are many similarities between innovation and enterprise. Both involve extended and concerted effort; enterprise requires boldness because its steps are often new, while innovation employs novel solutions that may take boldness to implement; implementation of both takes place in uncertain conditions and may require consideration of technical, economic, social and political dimensions; and both are likely to draw on change management skills, including networking, for success. However, enterprise is concerned with initiating and managing tasks and projects, and may not involve many new or unique approaches. On the other hand, innovation is vitally concerned with novel approaches, new ideas, enquiry and originality, and is the means by which ideas are exploited for competitive advantage.

■ Enterprising Individuals

Enterprising acts, whether in business or in a wider context, and whether incorporating original ideas or not, are generally acts initiated, or led, by individuals. Those individuals are said to display enterprise. To a considerable extent it can therefore be considered that there is something within those individuals that makes them disposed to and prepared for, such acts. Enterprising acts are defined as such because they have particular characteristics and certain individuals may be predisposed to perform such activities well. Many have therefore seen the individual as important for enterprise, indeed as key to its success. Lord Young had suggested that 'the basis for the enterprise culture lies with the restoration of the age of the individual.'[7] This is not necessarily so, however. The completion of an enterprising project often requires the involvement and cooperation of numerous people, but individuals and small groups are the building blocks for community and society, and it therefore seems unlikely that an enterprise culture will develop in the absence of a critical mass of enterprise in individuals.

▉ Why are some Individuals More Enterprising than Others?

Identifying what it is that makes some individuals more enterprising than others has been a challenge to a number of researchers. Among the theories explored in the study of this question are the following:

- Personality theories
- Behavioural theories
- Economic approaches
- Sociological approaches
- Other approaches, including values, beliefs and goals.
- And a number of integrated approaches.

These theories are described in more detail below.

■ Personality Theories

Personality theories of enterprise consider that it is the personality of individuals that explains their actions. The simplest theory suggests that it is the possession by individuals of a trait, or traits, that predisposes them towards enterprising behaviour; the traits most often proposed are achievement motivation, risk-taking propensity or the desire for control. Other personality theories consider combinations of traits. The psychodynamic approach views the enterprising individual as someone who is 'deviant' in society, and the social psychological approach also views the context in which the individual operates. Then, in the context specifically of enterprise as exemplified by business formation, there are attempts to produce owner/founder typologies to provide a theoretical framework for dealing with different types of business founders/owners.

■ Personal Qualities – Traits and Attributes

There is a considerable literature on those factors or traits that purport to predispose individuals to behave in an enterprising, or entrepreneurial, fashion. McKenna points out that traits can relate to motives, temperament, style and ability.[8] Many commentators consider that entrepreneurs have a strong need to achieve and to control their own destiny, and we can readily see why people with these dispositions might be interested in tackling enterprising tasks.[9] The successful accomplishment of an enterprising task would provide individuals with a strong sense of achievement and confirm their capacity to control their lives. Others consider that risk-taking tendencies are characteristic of entrepreneurs, although there is a debate about whether they take high, moderate or calculated risks. Stevenson and Gumpert do not define the degree of risk taken, but note that entrepreneurs continuously seek business opportunities without being concerned about the necessary resources.[10] They take a chance on resources, and consider that suitable quantities will be forthcoming. Timmons considers that people with persevering, problem-solving and reliable temperaments will have entrepreneurial tendencies, but his list of traits is long and it is unlikely that many entrepreneurs will exhibit all the traits he mentions.[11]

In addition to these traits there are a plethora of qualities that are purported to predispose people to being enterprising. Such personal qualities include being purposeful, proactive, dynamic, active, positive and able to take the initiative; being able to regard change as an opportunity; being able to identify ideas; being innovative, imaginative, creative, flexible and able to tolerate ambiguity; being adaptable, trusting, moderate risk-takers, at ease with risk; being determined, persistent, capable of seeing ideas through to fruition; and being responsible and self-confident. These qualities may emerge from traits, life's experiences or the structure of organisations and society, but their antecedents are less important than their link with enterprise. There are numerous variables, but we can see that these attributes are clustered, and research by Durham University Business School[12] on enterprising tendencies reveals that enterprising people tend to have a strong need for achievement and autonomy, an internal locus of control, are strongly proactive and independent, have a creative tendency, and are moderate risk-takers. Others add self-confidence, persistence, an ability to deal with failure, and trust.[13]

Some of the main traits or qualities identified are described below.

□ *Achievement Motivation*

Enterprising people have a strong need for achievement (sometimes referred to as NAch), which stimulates them into action. When they accomplish something they consider to be worthwhile, their self-esteem is enhanced and they are encouraged to seek other demanding assignments. Thus enterprising people are constantly on the lookout for challenges.

Content theories of motivation suggest that individuals have basic needs, and from time to time these needs are not fulfilled. When this happens the person experiences unease and attempts to satisfy this need. He or she does this by attaining goals that have the capacity to meet the need. Once these are satisfied, the unease or tension diminishes and will not motivate an individual until, once again, the need is not realised. Note that achievement is not an innate need like the need for food; it is learned, most probably during childhood. It has been suggested that strong-willed children, with parents who make their expectations known and who provide feedback, become high achievers, although McCelland also argues that NAch can also be developed in adults.[14]

The importance of NAch for enterprise is not generally in dispute, but how can an individual with a high NAch be recognised? McClelland argues that such a person

> is more self confident, enjoys taking carefully calculated risks, researches his environment actively, and is very much interested in concrete measures of how well he is doing. Somewhat surprisingly . . . he does not seem to be galvanized into activity by the prospect of profit; . . . [he] . . . works hard anyway, provided there is an opportunity of achieving something.[15]

High achievers often regard money as a measure of achievement, not an end in itself, but they do need feedback of evidence of their achievement, and money can provide such feedback.

3.1   An achiever

A business founder, when asked why she created her firm replied: 'the major attraction is self esteem . . . the ah . . . carrying a job through from beginning to end . . . ah . . . I suppose putting my standard on things. I had four children and so all I felt I was good for was being a mum and you don't always get a lot of appreciation for this.'[16]

☐ *Risk-taking Propensity*

Proactive achievers break new ground, but there are considerable risks in this behaviour. There are many failures that can spell disaster for an organisation or a career. The outcomes of enterprising events are less certain than for conservative ones, and therefore enterprising individuals will need to have the capacity to tolerate risks: to have the psychological makeup and resources to cope with any failure.

While they must be able to countenance risk, that is not to say that enterprising people are high risk-takers. Entrepreneurial research suggests that effective entrepreneurs are moderate risk-takers, while Durham Business School believe that enterprising people are calculated risk-takers. They assess situations thoroughly and do not pursue options which they consider to have a small probability of success. In this vein Drucker argues that successful entrepreneurs 'try to define the risks they have to take and to minimise them as much as possible'.[17] They search for opportunities, give them serious consideration and if promising, capitalise on them. Drucker goes so far as to say that successful entrepreneurs tend to be cautious and are opportunity-focused, as opposed to risk-focused. For him, 'defending yesterday' rather than 'making tomorrow' is really risky.

□ *Locus of Control*

'Locus of control' refers to being in control of events. Enterprising people believe that they personally make things happen in a given situation, and underplay the importance of luck and fate. They make things happen; things do not happen to them. In essence they feel that they exercise considerable control over events in their everyday world. Rotter was instrumental in assessing this aspect of personality, and he designated those who feel in control as 'internals' and those not in control as 'externals'. 'Internal' declarations emphasise the importance of ability, hard work, determination and planning in achieving outcomes, and their outlook is epitomised by the statement 'What happens to me is my own doing.'[18]

There is some evidence that 'internals' become leaders in organisations, more often than 'externals', when they can then exercise control over events[19] but there are those who argue that 'organisations are structures of control'.[20] Individual behaviour can be severely curtailed by rules, norms, and ever-present bosses, and this is something 'internals' dislike. Enterprising people in organisations may well become frustrated, and as a consequence many frustrated, individuals leave organisations and set up their own ventures. It is interesting to note that these entrepreneurs consistently outscore managers on Rotter's 'internal' scale. Business founders are more likely to be able to claim that 'What happens to me is my own doing'.[21]

□ *Need for Autonomy*

'Autonomy' refers to the independence from other people, of being in control of one's own destiny. This can accompany 'locus of control', which involves control of events beyond the individual, but it is not the same thing. Enterprising people have a strong desire to go it alone. In interviews with enterprising people they constantly refer to a need to control their own lives. Phrases such as 'I want to be in control,' and 'What I do with my life is my own doing,' are used regularly.[22] Individuals in many groups, organisations and societies are expected to adhere to the norms, rules and regulations of collective social organisms. Conformity is the price for membership. However, independent people often resent these constraints and regard them as counter-productive in developing innovative proposals. Enterprising people want to reduce barriers to progress, and though they may see some merit in the stabilising impact of rules and behavioural norms, they see more merit in independent thought and action. They can be regarded as headstrong and disruptive in social settings.[23]

There is however a possibility that apparently independently minded people may not be negating the forces for conformity in social entities, but merely 'having problems dealing with authority and working for others'.[24] People who do their own thing regardless of others or who disregard with impunity rules that constrain them could be considered as disruptive dissenters. Independence may produce negativity, but enterprising people tend to be freethinkers who need to break away from the shackles imposed by collective social institutions. When asked why they wanted to start their own firm, aspiring entrepreneurs in one study most frequently cited autonomy, and the need to achieve, as the most important factors in their decisions.[25]

☐ *Determination*

Enterprising people also possess determination. They normally complete projects and a degree of persistence is necessary for success. If individuals wish to exercise their individuality in meeting 'standards of excellence' then they will need to explore alternatives, overcome difficulties and make their plans work. Being in control is important, as is the freedom to exercise ingenuity, but a determination to see a difficult project through is also vital.

☐ *Initiative*

In addition to those qualities discussed above, the enterprising individual will need to be proactive. A person may have a strong need to achieve, may possess determination, may welcome the chance to do his or her own thing and to exercise control over his or her environment in pursuit of an assigned project, and may, when presented with an opening, exhibit many enterprising qualities. If, however, he or she does not actively take the initiative and seek openings and opportunities, then their enterprise is limited.

Enterprising people take bold steps and have a propensity to seek new opportunities. The search for newness can often lead to uncharted waters, and proactive people generally seize the openings that present themselves and outdo others. In so doing they may become abrasive and competitive, but for them this is the best way to advance knowledge and create wealth. More conservative people may feel that if problems do not present themselves then it is best to leave well alone; not so the assertive opportunists. They consider that by actively seeking opportunities they are much more likely to come across potentially rewarding projects and keep ahead of the competition. In general they take the initiative and 'act on rather than react to their environments'.[26]

☐ *Creativity*

The enterprising person is often concerned with developing new products, processes or markets, but the ability to 'bring something new into being' is not evenly distributed within the population. Such people tend to have more originality than others and are able to produce solutions that fly in the face of established knowledge. They are also inclined to be more adaptable, and are prepared to consider a range of alternative approaches. They challenge the *status quo*, which can sometimes bring them into conflict with their colleagues. They dismiss their detractors and are sometimes regarded as aloof.[27] Creative outcomes seldom emerge in an instant: a recognised process is involved, even if it appears to be rather chaotic. It begins with recognition of a problem or anticipation of an opportunity, and then, through understanding the situation and reflection in the issues, new linkages are contemplated and possible new combinations of components are aired. From this viable solutions or possibilities emerge that are subjected to evaluations, which may be continuous with judgement being suspended while the search process is prolonged in pursuit of genuine newness.

Enterprising individuals take bold creative steps but situations encourage creativity. Thompson summarises the situational requirements for creativity succinctly. He feels that creativity is enhanced when people have 'some freedom, but not too much; high internal commitment to the task, but not too high a commitment; a high proportion of intrinsic rewards, but some extrinsic rewards as well; some competition but not winner-take-all competition'.[28] It is, however, important to recognise, as indicated earlier, that an enterprising outcome depends on the process of innovation following creativity, not on the creativity alone.

☐ Self-confidence and Trust

It has been argued that enterprising individuals seek out demanding tasks that produce the intrinsic rewards of achievement, that they act on their environments in uncovering these opportunities rather than responding to changes, that they impose their independent authority to explore creative risky options for problems or opportunities. It is most unlikely that people who lack self-confidence could undertake these tasks. Proactivity, creativity and achievement are not accomplished without major change and, as Gibb has argued, enterprising persons have 'a security borne of self-confidence' in uncertain situations. Self-confidence seems therefore to be indispensable for enterprise.

If, as a result of their endeavours, projects are successfully completed, self-confidence will be reinforced. Success generates more success and may encourage individuals to take on ever more enterprising projects. But what of failure? In such an uncertain environment failure is common and may be viewed as a learning experience, but if failure is repeated then it can dent the confidence of the most self-assured. Continuing enterprise would seem to rely on regular or intermittent success.

Along with self-confidence generally goes trust. Some people consider enterprising individuals, especially in a business context, to be selfish, exploitative and uncaring, with a short-term, get-rich-quick approach to business. In reality, however, successful enterprise requires the coordination of disparate inputs, and a degree of faith, trust and cooperation between contributors is essential. 'Studies of entrepreneurs indicate that many are highly ethical and socially responsible compared to the general population.'[29] Good entrepreneurs have faith in the intentions of those who assist them in their endeavours and do not exploit them.

☐ Comments

The traits and qualities described do impact on behaviour, but this approach to explaining enterprising behaviour has its critics.[30] It is pointed out that personality theories depict general tendencies and are rarely situation-specific, that the methods used to measure entrepreneurial traits are diverse and that the results are conflicting. Some studies find that entrepreneurs do conform to a general psychological profile, while others do not. In addition, several studies also show that other groups, managers for example, exhibit an entrepreneurial profile. It is accepted that most entrepreneurs do not possess all the enterprise traits identified, and many of the traits are also possessed by those who would not be described as entrepreneurs.

■ Psychodynamic Approaches

Psychodynamic approaches are the product of Freud's psychoanalytic theory of personality. Freud considered that individuals have instinctive drives, and that a part of the personality seeks instant gratification for these desires. However, the pursuit of instant gratification can get the person into trouble and as people develop their *ego* emerges to constrain instinctive behaviour. This controlling mechanism protects the individual from the unpleasant consequences of pursuing innate desires. With further development the individual realises that behaviour can meet with the approval or disapproval of significant others and a *superego* develops to limit behaviour to that which is in keeping with the moral code of parents and society. Freud argues that there are many conflicts between these forces, and that the resolution of these conflicts is instrumental in creating the personality. If instinctive behaviour is severely constrained then it can lead to frustration, and psychodynamic approaches to entrepreneurship consider that this frustration is the source of much entrepreneurial motivation.

Psychodynamic approaches are based on three basic premises: that most behaviour is goal-directed and is caused by a force within the person, that much behaviour originates from the unconscious mind, and that early childhood experiences are crucial in the development of the personality. One of the leading advocates of this approach in the entrepreneurial field is Kets de Vries, who suggests that early frustrations are the product of unhappy family backgrounds.[31] Fathers, in particular, are seen as controllers and manipulators who are remote. In addition they are often seen as deserters who place an unwarranted burden on heroic mothers. These negative images of fathers may have little basis in reality, but perception is all-important. As a result of these experiences or perceptions, these individuals develop an intense dislike of authority figures and develop suppressed aggressive tendencies towards persons in control.

These unconscious motives impact adversely on careers. Rejection of controlling others in organisations leads these individuals to be classified as 'deviant' or 'marginal' men, with the result that they change jobs on a regular basis. While they cannot tolerate direction and control in organisations, the variety of job experiences provides them with a range of skills that are indispensable for running a business. As a consequence of their behaviour these individuals make a determined effort to start their own business. In this milieu they are in control, are answerable to no one and are 'at the centre of action'.

☐ *Comments*

Psychodynamic theories have, in general, been criticised because of their subjective nature and the lack of empirical evidence. Their ability to explain enterprise, especially in the context of entrepreneurship, have been found wanting because they do not cover all situations, such as a business start prompted through unemployment; because not all deviants start businesses and many characteristics associated with deviancy are not typical of successful entrepreneurs; and because, in addition, entrepreneurs tend to create their ventures in their thirties or later when many of life's experiences, not merely childhood ones, will influence their behaviour.[32]

■ Social–Psychological Approaches

Social psychological approaches take into account the context in which the individual is operating as well as his or her personal characteristics. Enterprising or entrepreneurial behaviour is more likely in some contexts than others. Chell and her associates constructed a categorisation using this approach that attempted to distinguish entrepreneurs from other business owners and to identify those characteristics which typify the entrepreneur. They presented their business owner subjects with certain critical incidents and asked them to describe their likely behaviour in these situations. The researchers noted how often and how consistently behaviours were exhibited before classifying them as prototypically entrepreneurial. They also took into account the growth orientation and stage of development of the subjects' businesses and considered that, compared with other types of business owner, entrepreneurs are more likely to own growth-oriented businesses. These researches classified the prototypical entrepreneur as 'being alert to business opportunities, proactive, innovative, a utiliser of a variety of sources of finance, a high profile image maker, restless, adventurous, an ideas person and an agent of change'. Some business owners had all of these characteristics, some had none and others were in between. A hierarchical model was therefore conceived with four categories of owner: the entrepreneur, the quasi-entrepreneur, the administrator and the caretaker.

☐ *Comments*

This theory is based on quite a narrow sample and does not yet appear to have been validated by other researchers. It is, however, useful in pointing to the influence of context on behaviour.[33]

■ Owner Typologies

Owner typologies look specifically at the small business context of enterprise and have been built on the presumption that small business owners are not all the

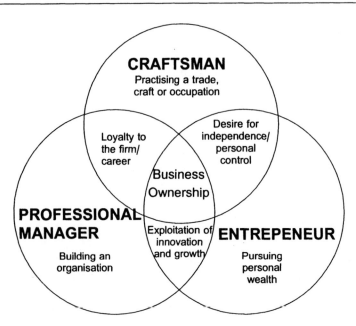

Source: R. W. Hornaday, 'Dropping the E-words from Small Business Research', *Journal of Small Business Management*, vol. 28 (1990) pp. 22–33.

Figure 3.2   Three types of small business owner

same. They present a theoretical framework to deal with the differences. Most studies identified three main types of owner, typically labelled 'craftsman', 'entrepreneur' and 'professional manager' (see Figure 3.2).

☐ *Comments*

There are a number of drawbacks to this approach. There is for instance a problem in maintaining consistent labelling between different studies. In addition, the typologies apply only to businesses, which means that they cannot be applied to other examples of enterprise, and the question of whether small business owners can change from one typology to another has not been given much attention.[34]

■ Behavioural Theories

The behavioural approach to studying enterprise views an enterprising act in the context in which it happens, a context that is often complex. The study of the enterprise of individuals should therefore focus on the behaviours they display in this context, rather than on what they themselves are. Two approaches with particular relevance to this theory are the examination of individual 'competencies' relevant to a specific event and the study of the change of behaviour over time, in particular at different 'stages' of business development.

■ Competencies

Competence has been described as the modern terminology for ability. Nevertheless, there is now considerable interest in enumerating the key competencies of successful entrepreneurs, which is due in particular to the work of Boyatzis in America, and a competence-based approach has become a popular method for development and training. However, there is still considerable confusion around the concept, in particular with regard to what the term 'competency' means.

There are two broad approaches to the question. Boyatzis considers that competency relates to the 'personal characteristics' of individuals, while the Management Charter Initiative in the UK adopts a work-functions approach. The former focuses on the person and on the characteristics that make people competent, while the latter looks at the job and details those job functions that competent people can perform effectively.[35]

In both approaches, attention has been paid primarily to managerial competency, rather than to enterprise competency. Some work has, however, been carried out in the area of enterprise by Caird.[36] She reviews some of the ways in which competency is assessed and considers their applicability to enterprise competency. She concludes that there are four aspects of competency: knowledge, performance, skill and psychological variables, which specifically relate to a field of expertise.[37] Her model is presented in Figure 3.3.

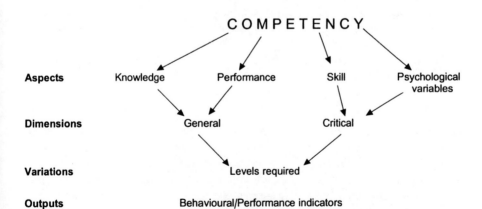

Source: Reprinted by permission of Sage Publications from S. Caird, 'Problems With the Identification of Enterprise Competencies and the Implications for Assessment and Development', *Management Education and Development*, vol. 23 (1992) p. 16. © Sage Publications

Figure 3.3 Framework for identifying enterprise competency

Caird feels that, while the requisite knowledge and skill is contextual, the underlying psychological variables may be more generic. She points out also that it is important to distinguish between the everyday aspects of competency and those aspects that are critical in separating very enterprising people from the only adequately enterprising. The former can cope with complex and variable situations, while the latter may not. In addition, different levels of competency are required in different jobs and business ventures. Caird's work is useful in clarifying concepts, but she notes that there still 'is no clear understanding of what enterprise competency means', with the result that the concept 'runs the risk of meaning everything and nothing'.[38]

There are a number of lists of possible enterprise competencies that overlap but do not coincide, and the lists of enterprise competencies also overlap with lists of enterprise traits or attributes. The following are some of the enterprise competencies frequently cited:

Dedication	Creativity	Technical competencies
Decision-making	Confidence	Sensitivity to changes
Goal-setting	Innovation	Networking and contacts
Planning	Risk-taking	Developing relationships
Responsibility	Insight	Project management

It can be seen that these competencies include personal qualities set alongside skills and individual orientations. It would also seem that they have much in common with the competencies identified by Boddy and Buchanan in relation to the 'perceived effectiveness of change implementation'.[39] This is not surprising, because enterprise thrives in a changing environment and therefore requires change management ability. Boddy and Buchanan have, from their empirical work, identified fifteen change management competencies, which they have grouped in five clusters (see Table 3.1).

□ *Comments*

A major problem with the competency approach, as with some other approaches, is that it is not definitive. There appears to be no competency that is possessed by all entrepreneurs, and many examples exist of non-entrepreneurs who appear to possess more entrepreneurial competencies than some people who clearly are entrepreneurs.

■ Stage Model Approach

Those who take a longitudinal view of the development of business have identified a number of stages in this process (which are considered further in

Table 3.1 Change management competencies

Goals
1. Sensitivity to changes in key personnel, top management perceptions, and market conditions, and to the way in which these impact [on] the goals of the project in hand.
2. Clarity in specifying goals, in defining the achievable.
3. Flexibility in responding to changes [outside] the control of the project manager, perhaps requiring major shifts in project goals and management style, and risk-taking.

Roles
4. Team building abilities, to bring together key stakeholders and establish effective working groups, and clearly to define and delegate respective responsibilities.
5. Networking skills in establishing and maintaining appropriate contacts within and outside the organisation.
6. Tolerance of ambiguity, to be able to function comfortably, patiently, and effectively in an uncertain environment.

Communication
7. Communication skills to transmit effectively to colleagues and subordinates the need for changes in project goals and in individual tasks and responsibilities.
8. Interpersonal skills, across the range, including selection, listening, collecting appropriate information, identifying the concerns of others, and managing meetings.
9. Personal enthusiasm, in expressing plans and ideas.
10. Stimulating motivation and commitment in others involved.

Negotiation
11. Selling plans and ideas to others, by creating a desirable and challenging vision of the future.
12. Negotiating with key players for resources, or for changes in procedures, and to resolve conflict.

Managing Up
13. Political awareness, in identifying potential coalitions, and in balancing conflicting goals and perceptions.
14. Influencing skills, to gain commitment to project plans and ideas from potential sceptics and resisters.
15. Helicopter perspective, to stand back from the immediate project and take a broader view of priorities.

Source: D. Buchanan and D. Boddy, *The Expertise of the Change Agent* (Hemel Hempstead: Prentice-Hall, 1992) pp. 92–3.

Chapter 6). The stage model approach has two important aspects: it considers the types of problem encountered at each stage and the abilities required to deal with them, and it indicates therefore the changes required in the behaviour and practices of managers if they are to progress successfully from one stage to another.

■ Economic Approaches

The economic theories of enterprise are also specifically concerned with entrepreneurship and the function that an entrepreneur serves in an economy. They see the entrepreneur as the seeker of opportunities and the innovative coordinator of resources in the pursuit of profit. Equilibrium theories of economics consider that these profits will be short-lived as competition increases, but Casson considers that their foresight and effective judgement about sources and combinations of resources allows entrepreneurs to reap economic rewards.[40] Economic motivation is important, but the successful initiation of a venture could well afford a sense of achievement to individuals. Of all the theories of entrepreneurship, economic theories have the longest standing, because they go back at least to the time of Cantillon (see Chapter 2).

However they do not indicate why some people emerge as entrepreneurs and others do not. To some extent therefore they describe but do not explain.

■ Sociological Approaches

Psychological and economic approaches to entrepreneurship emphasise the degree of choice exhibited by individual potential entrepreneurs, but some sociologists consider that individuals are seriously constrained in making career choices. They argue that choices are limited by the experience and expectations that individuals face in the social world. Indeed, Roberts goes so far as to say that careers follow patterns that are 'dictated by the opportunity structure to which individuals are exposed first in education, and subsequently in employment'.[41] He contends that ambition is moulded by 'the structures through which' people pass. Others, who would not deny that individual choice plays a part in career decisions, still emphasise contextual awareness. Opportunity structures vary from person to person, and different structures will lead similar individuals towards the development of differing levels of knowledge, skill and drive.

Different opportunity structures expose people not only to different possibilities but also to different expectations from other people. Individuals are socialised to behave in ways that meet with the approval of their role set. To take an example, a young person with a business owning parent may well be expected to join the family business, and not to do so would create a vacuum in the business. The son of an unemployed labourer will be socialised quite differently. The dominant values of close associates will translate into expectations which strongly influence individual behaviour.

Some sociologists emphasise the importance of entrepreneurial opportunity in the entrepreneurial process. For example, Reynolds argues that the decision to seize opportunities are made when the opportunities present themselves. It has been argued however, that enterprising individuals do not just sit around and wait for opportunities to emerge but, if a society does present numerous opportunities, this will quite clearly act as a catalyst for entrepreneurship.

If we accept that entrepreneurs require ideas, opportunities, resources, skills and motivation for success then the social structures and situations to which they are exposed will impact on the choice process. It could well be for example, that socio-economic factors such as social class, family composition and background and parental occupation will strongly influence entrepreneurial decision making. In the UK at least, it appears, for instance, that individuals whose parents, or other close relations, have had their own business appear generally much more likely to have businesses themselves, and certain social groupings, such as ethnic minorities, produce proportionately more entrepreneurs than others.

Furthermore, actual and perceived entrepreneurial skills are acquired over time and consequently age has an impact on entrepreneurship. For example, it has been suggested that many people aged thirty or less may not have acquired sufficient organisational experience while those aged forty-five or more may no longer possess the required energy.[42] Length of experience is important, but so is the relevance of that experience. If people can acquire technical skills that are in demand and that do not require commensurate capital investment for realisation then, they will emerge as likely entrepreneurs.

Localities that allow individuals to develop problem-solving and marketing skills, which contain institutions geared to the support of small businesses and that are favourably disposed to the notion of entrepreneurship, are likely to encourage and sustain more entrepreneurship than other regions.[43] These and other related matters are important aspects of the cultural dimension of entrepreneurship and will be examined in more detail in the next chapter.

In general, sociological approaches recognise the importance of social structures on individual decision-making and are a counter to those who might extol the virtues of rugged individualism as the sole determinant of entrepreneurship. However, while they do tell us quite a lot about the kind of people who become entrepreneurs, they do not tell us much about the process by which social factors actually influence decision-making.

■ Other Approaches

■ Values, Beliefs and Goals

Gibb has suggested that an enterprise culture is 'a set of values, attitudes and beliefs supporting the exercise in the community of independent entrepreneurial behaviour in a business context'.[44] He has illustrated (see Table 2.5) the difference between 'entrepreneurial management' and the more traditional corporate or bureaucratic management by looking at their respective values, beliefs and goals. The implication of this approach is that enterprising individuals differ from others in at least some of their values and beliefs and in their goals and ambitions, although these are not necessarily directly observable characteristics.

■ Integrated approaches

Each of the theories so far considered has drawbacks, in particular because no single theory seems to cover all aspects of enterprise. Therefore attempts have been made to amalgamate parts of two or more theories to produce an integrated approach with more general application. Two of these attempts are Krueger's model and the attributes-and-resources approach, now discussed.

■ Krueger's Model

Krueger[45] produced a model of entrepreneurial potential (see Figure 3.4), which, in view of the similarity of enterprise and entrepreneurship, would seen to apply also to enterprise in its wider meaning. Krueger argues that intentions to act entrepreneurially are underpinned by the development of potential, which is in turn built upon credibility.

Krueger argues that to be credible to oneself and to others, entrepreneurs/ enterprising persons must both perceive the probable outcome of their endeavours in a favourable light and believe that they have the wherewithal to succeed. Perception is all-important in this process; indeed it may be more important than reality. This favourable light is a product of personal preference and social approval for enterprise/entrepreneurship and the wherewithal comes from experience, from innate and learned attributes that might enhance enterprising propensity, and from skills, knowledge and resources that increase self-efficacy. That light and that wherewithal alone, however, are not necessarily

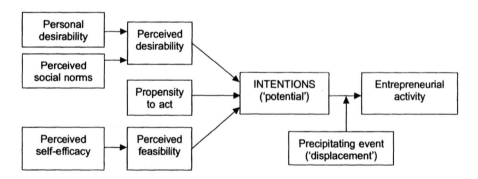

Source: N. F. Krueger, *Prescription for Opportunity: How Communities Can Create Potential for Entrepeneurs* (Washington, DC: Small Business Foundation of America, Working Paper 93-03, 1995) p. 10.

Figure 3.4   Intentions model of entrepeneurial potential (simplified)

sufficient. A trigger or key event may be necessary to start the individual on an enterprising course of action.

■ Attributes and Resources

Perceived self-efficacy is an important aspect of Krueger's model, and it corresponds with a view of enterprise, and of enterprising behaviour, that is based on the attributes and resources an individual may possess at any point in time. Attributes may include self-confidence, diligence, perseverance, interpersonal skills and innovative behaviour. Resources may include finance, experience, knowledge, skills, a network and a track record. It is suggested that it is the interaction between these factors that produces a rational response, on the basis of available information, when the opportunity occurs for a business start-up.

This view, however, also acknowledges that there is inertia in individual behaviour and that it may take a discontinuity in work, or in life, to trigger a review of an individual's situation. Whether this review will lead to an individual trying his or her own enterprise will then depend on the attributes and resources he or she has accumulated, together with his or her perception of environmental factors such as the availability of encouragement, and support such as advice, grants and training. This is illustrated in Figure 3.5.

The implications of this view are that the start-up decision will be affected by the attributes and resources acquired *prior* to the trigger for taking the decision, and that there is scope for initiatives to enhance the acquisition of those attributes and resources. (For a list of possible attributes and resources, and how they are acquired, see Table 3.2.) It does not deny that, at the time of the decision, the availability of support such as grants and training is influential on that decision. It does, however, indicate that, whether or not grants and training are available, more people are likely to decide to try a business start-up, and with more chance of success, if they are in possession of the relevant attributes and resources. There should therefore be economic benefits to be gained from enhancing relevant individual attributes and resources.

Figure 3.5   Attributes-and-resources model

Table 3.2   Attributes and resources, and how they are acquired

Attributes	Resources
Attitude	Ideas
Inter-personal skills	Technical Skills
Self-confidence	Interpersonal and communication
Enthusiasm	skills
Diligence and perseverance	Information, and access to it
Initiative	Network
Independence	Finance
Persuasiveness	Experience, e.g. of small business,
Positive outlook	of marketing, of planning
Perception	Track record
Attitude to risk	Direction

How acquired	
Attributes can be acquired from both nature and nurture. The nurture influences can include family, education, culture, work experience, role models, peers, economic structure, lifestyle and stages of life.	Resources are acquired through many of the processes of working and living. They will, however, be more readily acquired if this acquisition is planned and targeted.

Entrepreneurial Profiling and Enterprise Prediction

One particular application to which the different theories of enterprising behaviour has been put has been to try to construct a profile of an enterprising person. This has been done primarily in the field of entrepreneurship with the objective of predicting who is most likely to succeed as an entrepreneur. However, with a lack of consensus on the definition of 'enterprise' and of an 'entrepreneur', and in the absence of a single accepted model of enterprise/ entrepreneurship, this approach has so far had little success.

■ Postscript

This brief review of some of the forces that impel individuals to act in an enterprising fashion has indicated that there are a broad range of variables in any model of entrepreneurial choice and behaviour. Not all variables will impact on all enterprise, but many of these factors will be considered, implicitly or explicitly, by those taking enterprising actions, and will help to determine whether an individual does or does not become an entrepreneur. It is important, however, to note that enterprising individuals are not homogeneous and that therefore different approaches looking at different groups at different stages of organisational development will result in a complex picture. In general there are many variables that can impact on enterprise but, in spite of calls to develop multidimensional models, few have taken up the challenge to do so. The complexity of such modules, and the enormous difficulty in using multivariate analysis with so many variables that are difficult to measure, have daunted researchers.

Key points

- Enterprise is generally recognised in the outcomes of acts by enterprising individuals. They can be called enterprising outcomes. They can be seen in the narrower definition of enterprise synonymous with entrepreneurship, or small business formation, and in the wider approach of enterprise, which applies to any task that is non-routine and goal-directed and is accom-plished in a determined and adventurous manner.
- Enterprise activity is dependent on enterprising individuals. There have been many studies and approaches to analysing what makes some individuals more enterprising than others. They include:

  - Personality theories considering traits in individuals that predispose them to enterprise, psychodynamic approaches that look at the enterprising personality, social psychological approaches that take into account the context in which an individual operates, and owner typologies that look at different types of small business owner.

  - Behavioural theories, including competencies and stage model approaches

  - Economic approaches.

  - Sociological approaches.

  - Integrated approaches.

- All of these approaches offer some insight into what makes an individual act in an enterprising way. The integrated approaches offer potentially the most useful models for examining the process of enterprise. None has however yet proved to be helpful in predicting future enterprise or entrepreneurial success.

CHAPTER 4

The Culture of Enterprise

■ Introduction

Chapter 3 looked at enterprise from the perspective of the individual. Its starting point was that enterprise is recognised in enterprising acts: acts performed by individuals. It therefore looked at the attributes in those individuals that disposed them towards acting in an enterprising manner.

How does enterprise based on individual attributes, however, relate to the idea of an enterprise culture, a concept that is often mentioned? Are they contradictory or complementary? If there is such a thing as an enterprise culture, is it something more than just a collection of individuals who are themselves enterprising, or can the culture of a group, or society, itself be enterprising or influence the enterprise shown by its members?

This chapter looks at enterprise in the context of the environment in which individuals operate: at enterprise demonstrated by or in the larger group and the influence that can have on the behaviour of its individual members. It considers the influence of the group, society or culture of which the individual may be a part, and the extent to which that environment can itself be enterprising. It presents some of the cultural influences that can lead to enterprise being demonstrated by groups as well as by individuals and can produce enterprising groups even if the individual members of the groups may not themselves separately appear to engage in many enterprising acts.

■ Judgements on Enterprise

Before these aspects are examined in more detail, however, it will be helpful to consider some judgements often made about enterprise:

- Enterprise is a relative concept
- Enterprise is a good thing
- Enterprise is essential for economic advancement
- Enterprise has strong political and social connotations.

■ Enterprise is a Relative Concept

At any particular time some societies and some individuals are seen as more enterprising than others. For much of the second half of the twentieth century, the 'tiger' economies of the Pacific Rim were seen to be more enterprising than most Western economies, and they in turn were more enterprising than the communist bloc countries. Whether the Western economies were enterprising therefore depended upon whom they were compared to. Their enterprise was therefore relative.

Comparisons of relative enterprise are still made frequently. For example it is claimed that 'Britain is not as enterprising as it was in the nineteenth century' that 'the European Union countries demonstrate much less enterprise than the USA', and that 'more enterprise is to be found in the informal (black) economy than in the formal economy'. Whether such statements are true is a different matter.

Individuals can be judged to be enterprising or not be enterprising, which implies some sort of absolute judgement, depending on whether or not they engage in enterprising acts. In reality, we are making comparisons of one individual against another or against some notion of a 'standard' level of enterprise activity, although that standard will change over time and place. However, even in a so-called enterprising society, not every individual will be considered enterprising, yet the society as a whole may be judged to be so. If more individuals themselves show enterprise then the society could be said to be more enterprising.

■ Enterprise is a Good Thing

More enterprise is deemed to be preferred to less. This perception is based on certain assumptions such that a more enterprising person is happier than a less enterprising one, or that the enterprising person's state of self-actualisation is inherently more satisfying than self-actualisation by a non-enterprising one, or that a more enterprising person creates more utility, pleasure, or social welfare than a less enterprising one, or any combination of these.

The same views exist in respect of nations and societies. Enterprising nations are often viewed as being in a superior condition or moving towards a superior condition (however defined) than less enterprising ones. Why that should be is not always clear, but it appears to be connected with the view that enterprise leads to a higher standard of living, which is itself desirable. Indeed, enterprising people and enterprising economies have become synonymous with successful people and successful economies.

4.1 However...

It is said that a visitor to a Mediterranean country, impressed by the climate and its potential, got into a discussion with a local farmer who was sitting at the side of the road enjoying the sunshine and admiring the view. 'Why,' he asked the local, 'are you sitting here, when, with a little effort, this farm could be so much more successful. You could grow such a variety of crops here.' 'Why,' the farmer replied, 'should I want to do that?' 'Because you could invest in more land, grow even more crops and soon you could afford a large house with lots of features such as a terrace and swimming pool' 'Why would I want that?' 'Because you could then relax and enjoy yourself sitting on the terrace and enjoying the sun and the view.' 'And what do you think I am doing now?'

■ Enterprise is Essential for Economic Advancement

Enterprise may create happiness or a superior condition, but the means or process whereby this happens is rarely clearly articulated. It would appear that what is envisaged is that enterprise leads to economic growth, which in turn engenders more happiness. Whether economic growth does produce more happiness can be debated, but is beyond the scope of this book. It is however worth considering here the link between enterprise and economic growth.

There is a correlation between the nations that are generally regarded as enterprising and those that achieve significant growth (albeit often at a social cost). Hong Kong has demonstrated a capacity for economic growth, and is regarded as being enterprising by virtue of its thriving business activity, international trading links and considerable entrepreneurial activity; but what is the process by which enterprising behaviour leads to enhanced economic growth? One possible route is that enterprise generates entrepreneurialism, which generates growing businesses, which in turn leads to economic growth.

It is possible, presumably, for a nation to be enterprising but not to achieve economic growth, if enterprise can find outlets that are independent of economic achievement. It is also presumably possible to achieve economic growth without enterprise, at least in the short term, through the exploitation of mineral and other natural resources. Neither of these two conditions appears to be common.

That leads to the conclusion that enterprise and economic growth are linked, and that the mechanism for this is that enterprise produces entrepreneurship, which in turn expands the economy. This mechanism needs to be understood if all are to be convinced that a primary aim of government is to create an enterprise culture, or that enterprise and an enterprising society are something to be sought after. This is so, not least when the concept is perceived as ideologically based. All are agreed, undoubtedly, that the concept of enterprise has a variety of connotations – not just political, but also social and cultural.

▌ Enterprise Has Strong Political and Social Connotations

The term 'enterprise' has been applied and used to indicate aspects of a wider culture or value system as well as to describe the way an individual performs. Within Europe, for much of the twentieth century, the governments of the North-Eastern countries have been called communist. The economies of these countries were centrally planned in contrast to the market economies of the rest of Europe. The latter economies, with those of many other countries (most notably the USA), were often referred to as 'free-enterprise'. In this way the word 'enterprise' has acquired a political association. Now reference to 'free-enterprise' politics, 'free-enterprise' economies or 'free enterprise' countries conveys notions of freedom, liberalism, the dominance of markets and individual action and choice, for good or ill. Indeed, the concept of the 'enterprise culture' has been used politically in Britain (like Thatcherism) as a sort of independent variable which 'has had a considerable impact upon a range of other dependent variables; small business, self-employment, trade unions, manufacturing industry, the public sector, education, welfare and so on'.[1]

This may be a gross distortion of cause and effect, and an unduly simplified political analysis, but it is one nevertheless propagated at least in part by some people. But the restructuring of Britain in the 1970s and 1980s has been attributable to changes to which it has been convenient to attach such a handy label or slogan. In the process, the concept of an enterprise culture has assumed meanings incorporating dimensions such as 'individualism, independence, flexibility, anti-collectivism, privatism, self-help' and so on'.[2] Consequently, it has been argued that the former communist countries, if they wish to achieve economic growth, should restructure and develop these characteristics, which have social as well as politico-economic implications.

▌ The Influences on Enterprise and Economic Performance

Therefore, as well as the personal attributes and resources of the individuals who are being enterprising, external influences, social, economic and political, also have implications for enterprise. An obvious example is the 'tiger' economies of the Pacific Rim. They are thought by many to be very enterprising and among the most enterprising in the world today. They do not in general, however, have a culture based on the individual, and their success is seen to come from aspects of their society as a whole. They are therefore a prima facie case that an understanding of enterprise must include a view as to its socio-political context.

The importance of such a context is highlighted by a study carried out by the University of Groningen, covering nine countries (Brazil, Cameroon, Colombia, Indonesia, Japan, Kenya, Netherlands, UK, and West Germany) and almost 2700 entrepreneurs.[3] It gave some interesting indications of the values and motivations that differ between Western and Eastern countries and the values and motivations that differ between the industrialised and the less developed countries.

Among the findings were:

- Entrepreneurs in the industrialised countries more often started their businesses due to dissatisfaction (push factors) rather than ambition (pull factors). The reverse was the case in less developed countries.
- When determining choice of business activity, personal initiative plays a significant role in the highly individualistic West. Allowing oneself to be guided by the insight and initiative of someone else is very important in highly collectivist countries such as Japan and Indonesia.
- Entrepreneurs in less developed countries ascribe more importance to the business firm as a family institution. In the West, the firm is seen as the institutionalisation of work.
- In collectivist cultures, receptiveness to help and support from the environment is greater.
- Entrepreneurs in European countries are the most individualistic and display self-confidence in their entrepreneurial ability. Japan and Indonesia are the least individualistic (suggesting that individualistic and entrepreneurial behaviour are not, in this context, synonymous).

Other problems of cross-cultural interpretation are revealed by this study, in particular in ascribing differences in entrepreneurship to different cultural or political/economic environments. The authors comment that it is very difficult to disentangle the relative importance of the 'two environments, which, while they may be distinguished from one another, are interdependent'. They go on to say, however, that 'evidence is building' which suggests that entrepreneurship is primarily influenced by the politico-economic environment, which is, 'on the whole', more important than the cultural environment.

This is illustrated by considering the consequence for entrepreneurial behaviour in a less developed country, which may, typically, have an unstable and unpredictable environment. A business functioning successfully one moment can be faced with insurmountable problems the next. Businesses can be viewed as 'temporary projects' with people working on them and earning money on them as long as possible until a more attractive 'project' appears. In more economically stable countries, the continuity of the business, spanning many generations, can be of primary importance to the entrepreneur and the motivation is not just aimed at earning a living. Therefore it is argued that the concept of entrepreneurship acquires an entirely different meaning. 'The term 'business' must, under these conditions be interpreted as a 'project', and 'entrepreneur' must be seen as someone who, perhaps temporarily or part-time, provides leadership for a project.'

It is unsurprising therefore, if the studies show that the following conditions apply in less developed countries:

- The birth-rate of business is higher than in developed countries
- More businesses are started by entrepreneurs than are bought or inherited
- More entrepreneurs have had more than one business
- Risk avoidance behaviour is more pronounced (e.g. 'sell out today – who knows what tomorrow holds').

Therefore, in a less developed country, characteristics of business behaviour that might initially be regarded as culturally determined can have their roots in the economic facts of life.

Further illustrations that political and economic conditions significantly affect enterprise, entrepreneurship and economic success is provided by G. Hofstede in his book *Culture and Organizations*.[4] While concentrating on the importance of cultural influences on development, he states the need for a 'market' and a 'political condition' that allows development. He notes that the market circumstances for growth of the 'tiger' economies began only in the mid 1950s as world markets freed up:

The need for a supportive political context was met in all 'Dragon' Countries but in very different ways...with the role of government varying from active support to laissez faire. Labour unions were weak and company-orientated in all the countries and a relatively equalitarian income distribution meant that support for revolutionary social changes was weak.[5]

The impact of these influences on enterprise can be shown as in Figure 4.1.

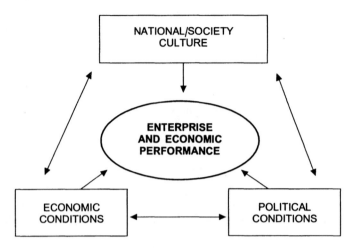

Figure 4.1   Impact of external influences on enterprise

■ National and Social Culture

4.2   Culture and learning

A Japanese friend once said that he could never ask a question in a class or lecture room unless, by so doing, he was obviously advancing everyone else's knowledge and understanding. Otherwise, he should not waste the teacher or his fellow students' time. He believed that problems of learning should be handled outside the group.

In the context of modern Western educational practice, such failure to participate and generate teacher feedback would be considered reticent and unenterprising.

What is the impact of culture on enterprise? This was analysed by Hofstede, who, although recognising the interdependence of culture, politics and economics, stated that 'Culture in the form of certain dominant values is a necessary but not a sufficient condition for economic achievement.'[6]

While culture has been further defined as the shared values that typify a society, Hofstede explains that, as almost everyone belongs to a number of different groups and categories of people at the same time, he or she will unavoidably carry several layers of what he calls 'mental programming' within himself or herself corresponding to different levels of culture.

4.3 Mental programming

Few will doubt the importance of the formal education system in shaping the attitudes and behaviours of individuals and groups, but in attempting to understand another country or culture it is difficult at times to question one's basic assumptions – deeply ingrained consciously or unconsciously over the years. The purpose of education is perceived differently from society to society.

An individualist society

aims at preparing the individual for a place in the society of other individuals. This means learning to cope with new, unknown and unforeseen situations... the purpose of learning is less to know how to do as to know how to learn... In the collectivist society there is a stress on adaptation to the skills and virtues necessary to be an acceptable group member. This leads to a premium on the products of *tradition*... the young have to learn *how to do* things in order to participate in society.

(Hofstede[7])

How can culture be described? Hofstede categorises a number of levels of culture:

4.4 Levels of culture

- A national level according to one's country (or countries for people who migrated during their lifetime).
- A regional and/or ethnic and/or religious and/or linguistic affiliation level, as most nations are composed of culturally different regions and/or religious and/or language groups.
- A gender level, according to whether a person was born as a girl or as a boy.
- A generation level, which separates grandparents from parents from children.
- A social class level, associated with educational opportunities and with a person's occupation or profession.
- And, for those who are employed, an organisational or corporate level, according to the way employees have been socialised by their work organisation.[4]

Hofstede also identifies and analyses five dimensions by which cultures can be described:

4.5   The five dimensions of culture

- Power distance – expresses dependence relationships in a country. It defines the extent to which the less powerful members of institutions and organisations expect and accept that power will be distributed unequally. For instance, there is only a small power distance in situations when subordinates would expect to participate in decision-making with superiors.
- Individualistic/collectivist – reflects the extent to which it is the interest of the individual or the interest of the group that prevails.
- Masculinity/femininity tendencies – defines the extent to which social gender roles in the society are clearly distinct. In masculine societies, men are supposed to be tough, assertive and focused on material success, and women are more modest, tender and concerned with the quality of life. Femininity pertains to societies where the social gender roles overlap.
- Uncertainty avoidance – defines the extent to which the members of a culture feel threatened by *uncertain or unknown situations*. This feeling is expressed through nervous stress and in a need for predictability (including a need for written and unwritten rules).
- Long-term orientation – defines a country in terms of its trade-off between short-term and long-term gratification of needs (long-term orientation emphasises values such as perseverance and thrift.)

Ultimately these dimensions reveal themselves in the values, preferences and behaviour of individuals and groups that they have acquired in the context of their families, their schools and their occupations. They are a measure of what we call national culture and which many perceive to be a determinant of the degree of enterprise in a country.

The earlier influences diagram (Figure 4.1) might therefore be amended to that shown in Figure 4.2.

The work of McClelland, who built a reputation for pioneering work in the field of achievement motivation, also helps to relate enterprise to culture. As noted in Chapter 3, he linked enterprise to the urge to achieve: 'Most people in this world can be divided into two broad groups. There is that minority which is challenged by opportunity and willing to work hard to achieve something, and the majority which really does not care all that much.'[9] He asked 'Is the need to achieve an accident, or is it hereditary, or is it the result of the environment? And further, 'is there some technique that could give this will to achieve to people, even whole societies?'[10]

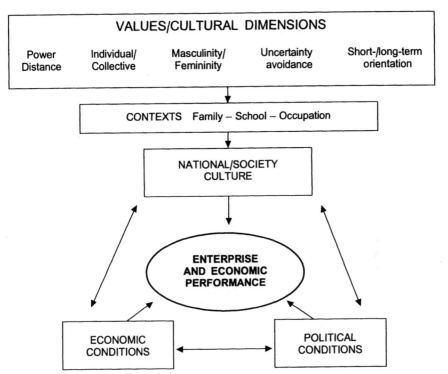

Figure 4.2   Influences on national economic performance

4.6   Cultural re-inforcement

The importance of cultural re-inforcement is seen in a study by McClelland in which he attempted to increase the achievement motivation of bright fourteen-year-old boys.

Boys from lower income groups did not maintain their improvements. Possibly it was because they moved back into an environment in which neither parents nor friends encouraged achievement or upward mobility. 'Negroes seeking to improve their condition frequently confront this problem ... faced by skepticism at home and suspicion on the job,' claimed McClelland on the basis of his work in the USA.[11]

An interesting contrast to the Negro situation may be the entrepreneurialism displayed by some immigrant groups, e.g. Hong Kong Chinese or Indians. If, and it is not always the case, immigrants are moving to seek betterment of their condition, it is also likely that entrepreneurial behaviour by members of their community will receive positive re-inforcement.

McClelland's is essentially a Western, individualistic view of motivation – the person being largely his unit of investigation. He points out that persons who are viewed as having engaged in 'outstanding' activities may be motivated by the need for power and/or the need for achievement. He demonstrates that the need for Achievement, its frequency in the popular literature of a country, and national economic growth, all correlate.

> A nation which is thinking about doing better all the time (as shown in its popular literature), actually does do better economically speaking. Careful quantitative studies have shown this to be true in Ancient Greece, in Spain in the Middle Ages, in England from 1400–1800, as well as among contemporary nations, whether capitalist or communist, developed or underdeveloped.[12]

It is worth noting that it is not a question of some people being motivated and others not being motivated, but that some are motivated by one goal and others by another. Overall, McClelland has found that while it is possible to change an individual's motivation (and performance), motivational change by itself is not enough if the environment in which he or she lives doesn't support, to at least some degree, his or her new efforts. This recognises the influence of the cultural and societal context of values and behaviour. In short enterprise and entrepreneurship happen in all societies. The form in which they happen, however, varies from society to society.

It is appropriate therefore to examine societal culture to consider how the concept of enterprise fits into it. Without such understanding, interventions to promote enterprise cross-culturally will, it is reasonable to deduce, be less effective, if not actually counter-productive. Interesting issues are raised by exploring the meaning and nature of enterprise in the context of cultural dimensions. One might question whether a 'high power distance' country is likely to be enterprising. In such a country, subordinates in organisations are more likely to accept inequality and hierarchy and, it could be argued, acquire attitudes inimical to entrepreneurial endeavour. Where individualism is counter-cultural, as in Japan (and children think of 'we' not 'I'), is enterprising behaviour inhibited – or can groups be as enterprising as individuals? It has traditionally been common to view attributes of the feminine gender as inherently less likely to lead to enterprising behaviour. Similarly, if a culture is uncomfortable with uncertainty and ambiguity, one might question if it can be as entrepreneurial as one that is comfortable coping in such situations. Equally, taking a long-term view may be felt likely to lead to caution and conservative behaviour. Intriguingly, little is known of how these different dimensions interact to re-inforce or negate each other.

Redding notes that

> other features older and deeper than modern policies have helped large Japanese and Korean organisations to...take a huge chunk of the world market... These extra features include societal norms supporting acceptance

of authority and discipline, a sense of the importance of the organisation in one's life and a consequent wish to belong to it an association of individuals with the collective good of the group and intense competitiveness on behalf of the nation via the company.

He adds that another societal feature critical to economic efficiency is the 'notion of trust', which explains 'why the Japanese and Koreans can handle very large scale organisations efficiently'.[13]

That some nations have achieved significant economic growth without exhibiting preconceived Western notions on the appropriate cultural dimensions should not therefore be surprising. Those Western definitions of entrepreneurial characteristics are themselves culturally biased.

4.7   Entrepreneurship and culture

At the top of Maslow's hierarchy...there is the motive of self actualization: realizing to the fullest possible extent the creative potential present within the individual. This means 'Doing one's own thing' (and) this can only be the supreme motivation in an individualistic society. In a collectivist culture, what will be actualized is the interest and honour of the in-group which may very well ask for self-effacement from many of the in-group members. As the interpreter for a group of American visitors to China remarked, the idea of 'doing your own thing' is not translatable into Chinese...the Chinese language has no equivalent for 'personality' in the Western sense. Personality in the West is a separate entity, distinct from society and culture: an attribute of the individual. The closest translation into Chinese is *Jen*...which includes not only the individual but also his or her intimate societal and cultural environment which makes his or her existence meaningful.

– G. Hofstede[14]

Hofstede's work reveals that successful nations (in economic terms) can exhibit significantly different scores in each of the dimensions he describes, suggesting that there are no easily defined 'right' or 'wrong' cultural conditions. Positive economic outcomes can emerge from a wide range of contexts.

Whether all such outcomes derive from enterprise in its conventional Western definitions is more difficult to assess. The collectivist tradition and culture is about subordinating personal to group interests, sharing, cooperation and group harmony (see Table 4.1). Is entrepreneurial behaviour exhibited by the group itself, by individuals working through the group or by breaking group norms? Or does the concept of 'entrepreneurial behaviour' need to be redefined in different cultural contexts?

Table 4.1   Key differences between collectivist and individualist societies

Collectivist	Individualist
Collective interests prevail over individual interests	Individual interests prevail over collective interests
Private life is invaded by groups	Everyone has a right to privacy
Opinions are predetermined by group membership	Everyone is expected to have a private opinion
Economy based on collective interests	Economy based on individual interests
Ideologies of equality prevail over ideologies of individual freedom	Ideologies of individual freedom prevail over ideologies of equality
Harmony and consensus in society are ultimate goals	Self-actualization by every individual is an ultimate goal
People are born into extended families or other in groups which continue to protect them in exchange for loyalty	Everyone grows up to look after him/herself and his/her immediate (nuclear) family only
Identity is based in the social network to which one belongs	Identity is based in the individual
Children learn to think in terms of 'we'	Children learn to think in terms of 'I'
Harmony should always be maintained and direct confrontations avoided	Speaking one's mind is a characteristic of an honest person
Purpose of education is learning how to do	Purpose of education is learning how to learn
Relationships between employer and employee are perceived in moral terms, like a family link	Relationships between employer and employee are a contract supposed to be based on mutual advantage
Hiring and promotion decisions take employees' in group into account	Hiring and promotion decisions are supposed to be based on skills and rules only
Management is management of groups	Management is management of individuals
Relationship prevails over task	Task prevails over relationship

Source: G. Hofstede, *Culture and Organizations* (London: HarperCollins, 1994) pp. 67 and p. 73.

Given the wide variations in societal understanding, perceptions, attitudes and behaviours, a unicultural interpretation of the meaning of enterprise and its development presents many dangers. Without recognition of such of differences, there will be difficulty in gaining global acceptance of enterprise as a positive concept. It will also be more difficult for business leaders to function effectively in other cultures as the drive towards globalisation accelerates. It is however clear that a supportive cultural environment for actions and policies to promote enterprise development and business start-up and growth is important, and that it can take many forms.

4.8   Different structures for enterprise

Not only are ways of doing business in Asia subtly different from those of the West but they are also different within the region itself.... The past 30 golden years have seen the emergence of three powerful systems of business, each represented by a particular kind of organisation:

- In Japan the large complex networked business, known as the *kaisha*.
- In South Korea the now internationalising *chaebol*.
- Elsewhere, in areas where business needs strong local knowledge and connections, the Chinese family business – that most unobtrusive and little-understood instrument of wealth creation and progress.

Each of these instruments for bringing together the components of economic behaviour has emerged as a distinct response to its circumstances. They are embedded in the cultures and development histories of their societies. They are not copies of Western forms and their behaviour does not follow Western rules or ideals. In simple terms, they exist for different reasons.

The main reason for the existence and driving logic of the large American corporation is return to shareholders, but that of the *kaisha* is to employ people. The *chaebol* has derived much of its dynamism from its contribution to the national development goals of Korea. The Chinese family business exists primarily to create and sustain family fortunes.

The outcome of these different routes to modern capitalism is that the Japanese form is a large, professionally managed and highly complex enterprise with wide ownership; the Korean is a huge family business run like a regiment; and the Chinese is a small family business networking to escape the limitations of its size and doing so successfully.

These different organisations compete on equal terms in world markets. Asia today contains some of the world's most competitive forms of enterprise which are able to hammer each other in world markets on equal terms. In doing so however, there is no logic which says they all have to have the same book of rules.

(Gordon Redding[15])

4.9 The history of regional difference

To understand the reasons for differences in enterprise and economic regeneration between different areas in England, Dodd[16] suggests, it is necessary to examine the relevant social history of the areas over many hundreds of years.

Compared with the North-East, the Black Country recovered well from major job losses and still has 50 per cent of its workforce in manufacturing. 'There is still plenty of metal-bashing and lots of foundries and it is still easy to get into all sorts of trades like pickling zinc.' Its history has a number of curious features. It was never conquered by the Romans because it was marshy, inhospitable and easily bypassed. From the thirteenth century its rich seams of coal near the surface gave it its character. For several centuries mining was carried on by groups of families. By 1665 there were 20 000 smiths within a ten-mile radius of Dudley, and an industrial culture appears to have been in full swing before the Industrial Revolution proper arrived.

It was observed that 'the Black Country was born, not as one area, but as a collection of separate entities of often fierce independence brought together on and about a unique coalfield, heaven-sent complete with an abundance of ironstone, limestone and clay' . . .

In contrast, Tyneside in the North-East also had coal mining but there that industry had a feudal feel about it, with enormous gaps between owners and workers, a relationship which might have been a carry-over from the employer and employee relationship that had existed in agriculture and tin and lead mining. The process of industrialisation in the North gave rise to relatively few small-firm operations in manufacturing and engendered attitudes incompatible with entrepreneurial behaviour. The high unemployment of the early 1980s, following the disappearance of many of the big manufacturing operations, was not therefore relieved by smaller operations, as happened in the Black Country, and self-employment is still below the national average.

■ Political Conditions

It has already been explained that it is generally impossible to separate the influences of political conditions from those of culture and economics. However, the island of Saint Martin in the Lesser Antilles does offer one example of a contrast in political styles and the different effects they appear to have on business enterprise.[17]

The island of Saint Martin is the smallest land mass in the world that is shared by two governments. It is only 37 square miles in area, but it is divided into two legal entities: Dutch Sint Maarten and French Saint Martin. Sint Maarten is 16 square miles in area and its capital is Philipsburg. It has a Netherlands Antilles constitution and has been self-governing since 1954. Saint Martin is 21 square miles in area; its capital is Marigot but the real administrative centre is Basse Terre on Guadeloupe. Guadeloupe is an overseas department of France and therefore Saint Martin is governed as an integral part of France.

In Sint Maarten there is relatively little government regulation of business. Starting a small business, for instance, is very easy, there is no need for a licence to do so and incorporation is simple, requiring only the assistance of a lawyer specifically appointed to pass deeds. There is no exchange control on currencies imported or exported, and bank accounts may be opened in any currency. There are no import duties and taxes generally are low, with tax holidays and other benefits in certain circumstances. There is an international airport with a 2000-metre runway which accommodates daily international flights and helps to boost the tourist industry. Further, to enhance tourism a number of casinos have been opened. The absence of all customs formalities makes Sint Maarten in essence a free port.

In contrast Saint Martin, the French part of the island, has inherited an abundance of regulations from its mother country. Rules made in France for France must be obeyed in Saint Martin. Some prices, as well as wages, are regulated. A new business venture must involve local participation. Foreigners staying for over twenty-one days must provide proof of departure as well as proof of citizenship (even though there is no longer any physical barrier, or even a border checkpoint, between the two sides of the island). The airport is tiny, virtually deserted and, because of red tape, there are no casinos.

The contrast between the two parts of the island is striking. Dutch Sint Maarten is a thriving business community with significant entrepreneurial activity, while French Saint Martin is largely rural and agricultural. Sint Maarten has not only achieved full employment for itself, but employs many workers from French Saint Martin and from other neighbouring islands such as the Dominican Republic.

These differences have been ascribed to the different government policies applied to the two parts of the island. On the Dutch side the attitude taken appears to be that it is dangerous to have the government in business and that government can best help business by staying out of it and by being a facilitator rather than a regulator. On the French side the attitude appears to be that government should intervene in the business sector for the purpose of keeping out potential danger. Rules are therefore established to protect business even if they to some extent hinder entrepreneurial activity.

Both sides of the island share a common history. The island was originally populated by Arawak Indians, who survived on local vegetation and seafood. They were then invaded by the more violent Carib tribes migrating from the Amazon basin, who were in turn followed by conquests from Spain, France, Britain and the Netherlands. As the Indians were wiped out the island was populated by slaves imported from areas such as Togo and Ghana in Africa.

Now, however, there are distinct differences in enterprise and economic performance between the two parts of the island. The reason for this appears to be the different political agendas: one side follows a policy of minimal economic intervention and minimal regulation, while the other has a policy of relatively heavy intervention and rules designed to protect business.

■ Economic Conditions

As with political conditions, the effects of economic conditions on enterprise are generally impossible to separate completely from those of other influences.

But for economic differences it may be illustrative to look at the economic conditions of the former Warsaw Pact or communist countries in North-Eastern Europe.

From the 1950s to the late 1980s these countries shared an economic system: one of central planning based on a communist ideal. Before that system was imposed, however, there had been considerable differences between their economies. A number of them had apparently been quite enterprising, with countries like Czechoslovakia and Hungary fully part of Central European economic life.

When they became part of the Soviet Bloc and its economic system the attitude to enterprise and entrepreneurship in all these countries changed. To a greater or lesser extent entrepreneurial behaviour was viewed with considerable suspicion – successful entrepreneurs were seen as anti-social, self-seeking and frequently as acting unethically, if not illegally. Disparities in income and wealth (and so behaviour likely to generate such disparities) made many reasonable people feel uncomfortable about enterprise and see it as a destabilising force in society, once they had grown accustomed to and comfortable with, an equality that is unusual in non-socialist countries.

4.10   Employment: the system and the individual

To comprehend the nature of the employment contract in 'communist' Eastern Europe it was said that you had to understand two 'facts'. The first 'fact' was that the system owed the individual a job. It was the system's clear obligation to provide paid employment for everyone. The second 'fact' was that it was the individual's duty to better him or herself, not by hard work which would return no direct benefits, but by doing as little as possible for the salary which was his or her right.

It has been argued that the collapse of the Iron Curtain came at least in part because the disparity between the economic benefits of the 'market' economies on one side and the central 'socialist' economies on the other could no longer be disguised. When it went, there was a desire by many on its former Eastern side to catch up with the West. Based on the perception that enterprise and an enterprise culture was a precondition for a successful market economy, attempts were made to introduce and encourage them. The political imperative of creating wealth in these transition economies, not least through attempts inculcating such enterprise into them, has however had another effect. It has brought into greater focus the issue of the cultural context of enterprise. Given the different nature of these nations after almost two generations of a particular political and economic system, one cannot ignore the differences in individual and group values, priorities and goals as compared with those in countries with different histories.

The Western cultural traditions they are trying to emulate have been rooted in individualism, and definitions of entrepreneurial characteristics emphasise individuality – founding by a single person, personal innovation, risk-taking, proactivity, persistence, creativity. Individualism is concerned with self-sufficiency, difficulty in coping with a structured pursuit of goals, personal goals that may conflict with those of one's group, a willingness to confront members of the group one belongs to, a suspicion of the world around. It is a culture where a person derives pride from his or her own achievements coupled with a desire for recognition. In contrast, as already noted, the more collectivist tradition and culture involves subordination of personal to group interests, sharing, cooperation and group harmony and, to that extent, an emphasis on the individual is counter-cultural.

4.11   The unwelcome entrepreneur

When the Central and Eastern European system was beginning to change in the early 1990s it was asked if this meant that the entrepreneur was now in the economic driver's seat. One reply from Poland, one of the earlier converts to the move towards a market economy, said that the answer was 'yes; the entrepreneur was driving' however; he or she had no driving licence, had no brakes, had no airbag, had not enough petrol to complete the journey and found the road ahead was filled by a big empty truck driven by a blindfolded union legislator.

To many people entrepreneurs were still not welcome. Neither politicians nor societies liked having to be grateful to anybody except possibly to God, and certainly not to bright and successful entrepreneurs. (It was wryly commented that this was surprising because God himself was surely an entrepreneur. After all had he not lost control of his enterprise shortly after he launched it?)

Although there were and are considerable differences between countries in Central and Eastern Europe, and although they had not all been centralised, socialised or collectivised to the same extent, it would seem that the economic system did affect enterprise and the attitudes it engendered are themselves now affecting attempts to reintroduce enterprise. The extent to which an economy has an enterprise culture has assumed a particular importance in understanding the prospects for the development of that economy. However, attempts to understand what an enterprise culture means and the process by which a culture develops has to be done in the context of the socio-economic conditions of the region under investigation. In short, we may speak of the 'cultural context of the enterprise'.

■ Other Examples of Influence

■ Religion

The three influences identified above were culture, economics and politics, a list which appears to leave out religion. However much less appears to have been written on the influence of religion on enterprise. There is the so-called 'Protestant work ethic', which appears to link an attitude to business with a religion; however it has also been commented that today it may often be more a 'go-to-work ethic' than a 'create-your-own-work' ethic. There is also a belief among some enterprise workers in Northern Ireland that there is a correlation between a readiness to engage in community enterprise and communities with a preponderance of members of one particular religion. However, because there may also be a correlation between the need for community enterprise and communities of that same religion, it could be that the explanation is not the influence of the religion. In general it is probably impossible to separate the influence of religion from that of culture, because they are so interlinked.

■ Community Enterprise

This chapter so far has considered enterprise primarily as it is manifested in private sector business, or entrepreneurship, and has looked at some of the influences on enterprise in terms of the effects they may have had on business formation and success. This was done primarily because that is the aspect of enterprise that has been most studied and it is therefore the most easy to analyse. However enterprise can be manifest in other ways, for instance in leisure, in cultural activities and in community enterprise.

Even business formation and entrepreneurship need not have profit for individuals as a major motivation. Businesses can be started for other reasons such as community benefit or cultural development. Also, businesses need not be started by individuals but can be started by groups. Much group enterprise behaviour has been variously known as 'community enterprise', 'community entrepreneurship' or 'social entrepreneurship'.

Three forms of business enterprise or entrepreneurship have therefore been distinguished: (a) the classical form of private or business entrepreneurship for commercial gain, (b) community enterprise or entrepreneurship for community economic benefit and (c) cultural entrepreneurship to influence cultural change or improve cultural standards.

It may be obvious that community and cultural enterprise are likely to influence each other. It is also very likely that private entrepreneurship will influence, and be influenced by the others. Private sector concerns have shown themselves to be responsive to local issues, especially when there has been community action to highlight them, and community and cultural initiatives

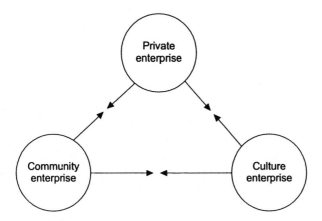

Source: O. R. Spilling, 'Enterprise in a Cultural Perspective', *Entrepreneurship and Regional Development*, vol. 3 (1991) p. 39.

Figure 4.3   The triangle of enterprise

have benefited from the involvement of enterprise skills of the private sector. This interrelationship is shown in Figure 4.3.

Community enterprise is of particular interest, because, as already noted, Western views of enterprise and entrepreneurship are perceived as largely the prerogative of individual, as opposed to group, behaviour. Experience, however, suggests that group behaviour can be affected by a 'community entrepreneur' and that, as a result, the actions of a group can be more enterprising than the individual attributes or resources within the group would suggest. Development of community businesses helps those involved to gain business experience, to develop personal knowledge and skills and to acquire a network that enables them to gain confidence in themselves and to tackle further opportunities. This is done in the relatively safe and low-risk context of group support and participation. (The concept of community enterprise is explored further in Chapter 5.)

■ Postscript

It has been said that, when decisions about potential actions have to be taken, a number of influences are at work. Krueger's model of these influences (see Chapter 3) includes:

- The perception of the attractiveness of the outcome of an action
- The perceived opinion of family, friends and peer group

- The individual's or group's views of their own competence
- The perception of the environment in which they operate – especially its receptiveness to the proposed actions and their likely outcomes.

Some of these influences are due to internal factors, but others are due to outside conditions. Broadly speaking, the outside influences can be ascribed to the cultural, political or economic environments, although the effects of all three are interlinked. Studies of enterprise in different countries show that they can all have an impact on enterprise.

Because of the interaction of these and other factors there is no single economic, political or cultural condition that universally best promotes and supports enterprise. Methods of increasing enterprise that work in one situation may not therefore transfer successfully to other situations and to other societies.

The link between enterprise and society is not easy to predict. C. Mason suggests that the observed differences in business start-up rates even within the UK are because

> the most important determinants of small business start-up rates are complex, interdependent and likely to vary intra-regionally, inter-regionally and internationally. Nevertheless the determinants will include an industrial structure biased towards small, independent economic units; employees engaged in problem-solving who have close contact with customers (so possessing technical and market knowledge); a concentration of technically progressive small firms; a high awareness of past small business activities; supportive banks and other financial institutions; the availability of help and advice; an affluent population and a social climate which favours individualism.[18]

A study[19] analysing regional variations in business births and deaths in the USA supports Mason's UK findings. Businesses showed significantly higher birth rates in regions that possessed greater economic diversity, more volatile industries, greater personal wealth, more experienced mid career people, as well as greater employment flexibility and population growth. Therefore, while the enterprise shown by individuals is influenced by their own internal attributes and resources, it is also subject to external influences. Culture and political and economic conditions have an important part to play.

Using a horticultural analogy (explored also in Chapter 12), one seeks to explain why some plants grow more than others and grow more in some areas than in others. It is possible to look for the cause both in the different qualities of seed and their inbuilt growth potential, and in the environment in which the seeds grow with differences in light, heat, soil, water and nutrients. Generally, maximising plant growth requires attention both to seed quality and to the growing environment. However, the interrelationship is complex, and the type of seeds and the steps taken to grow crops in one environment will not necessarily succeed in others. So, too, success in enterprise depends both on internal and external factors, and there is no single prescription which works in all circumstances.

Key points

- This chapter looks at enterprise in the context of the environment in which individuals operate, at enterprise demonstrated by or in a larger group and at the influence that can have on the behaviour of its individual members.
- The context for this is a recognition that enterprise is a relative concept, that it is frequently seen as inherently good, in particular because it is seen as essential for economic advancement, and that, because of this, it has strong political and social connotations.
- A number of studies have considered the links between culture and enterprise and have also included the influences of economic and political conditions. There is evidence that they can all affect the amount of enterprise, especially enterprise in a business context (i.e. entrepreneurship).
- It has been said that enterprise is influenced more by the politico-economic environment than the cultural environment. However, they are very interlinked, and culture can be manifest at a number of levels, including a national level, a regional and/or ethnic and/or religious and/or linguistic affiliation level, a gender level, a generation level, a social class level, and, for those who are employed, an organisational or corporate level. There are also a number of dimensions by which cultures can be described, including power distance, individualistic/collectivist, masculinity/femininity, uncertainty avoidance and long-term orientation.
- It is also clear that nations that are successful in economic terms can exhibit significantly different scores in each of these cultural dimensions, which suggests that there are no easily defined 'right' or 'wrong' cultural conditions. Positive economic outcomes can emerge from a wide range of contexts. Given the wide variations in societal understanding, perceptions, attitudes and behaviours, a unicultural interpretation of the meaning of enterprise and its development presents many dangers. It is clear, however, that a supportive cultural environment for actions and policies to support enterprise development, business start-up and growth is important, and that this can take many forms.
- As well as enterprise manifested in private sector business, or entrepreneurship, however, it can be also be seen in cultural and in community enterprise. Community enterprise is generally enterprise shown by a group, often in situations that appear to be the antithesis of an enterprise culture. Sometimes individuals acting in a group can demonstrate

enterprise in a way that acting individually they would not. The group can have a positive influence.

- In considering enterprise it is therefore necessary to consider external as well as internal influences. It is like growing plants: good seeds and good conditions are both needed for good results, but what works well in one situation may not work well in another.

CHAPTER 5

Other Aspects of Enterprise

So far we have looked at the ways in which the word enterprise is used in order to ascertain what people actually mean when they use the word, rather than just what a dictionary suggests it should mean. That has shown that, rather than a single, narrow definition, the word can have a whole range of meanings, although these can be broadly grouped either into a narrow definitional range in which enterprise basically means business and especially small business, or into a broader meaning of enterprise as the set of attributes that enable those who possess them to be creative, adaptable, innovative and responsive to change.

That set of individual attributes was explored further in Chapter 3, which looked at enterprise as something demonstrated in enterprising acts by individuals. Enterprise, however, is also influenced by the external environment in which individuals operate, and these influences were considered in Chapter 4. Before Part II in which enterprise is considered in the context of business, this part concludes with a look at some other aspects and implications of the way that the term is used. In particular, it considers enterprise in some of the contexts omitted from Chapter 2, in the context of some of the drawbacks potentially associated with it and in the context of some of the forces that may influence its future.

■ Some Enterprise Associations

■ Free Enterprise

Economic enterprise is said to thrive in a free, or market, economy. It was Adam Smith in *The Wealth of Nations* in 1776 who argued that the enormously complex task of deciding which goods and services to produce in an economy should be not be carried out by a central authority but should be delegated to individual buyers and sellers.[1] He did recognise that government nevertheless had a role in such a free market. It had the responsibility for the legal framework of laws to protect the right of individuals involved in the market and for mechanisms to maintain social stability.

Others more recently have been equally enthusiastic about the workings of the free market. Hayek[2] argues persuasively in *The Road to Serfdom* that socialist planning restricts individual decision-making and is invariably inefficient. Neither innovative technological changes nor changes in consumer preferences can be predicted with any accuracy, and consequently attempts to plan such matters are doomed to failure. The free market is the most flexible and responsive of economic systems and is always more efficient than deliberate economic decision making by the state. Free enterprise systems can lead to inequality, but it is argued that those with the best economic judgements of events reap the greatest rewards. Hayek regrets any attempt by centralised decision makers to legislate for equality, because it would restrict liberty and ultimately be ineffective.

These are the principal proponents of the line of economic thought that puts the emphasis on the individual in a system that is regarded as highly flexible and responsive to change and that provides the freedom to choose. This free enterprise economy, with its market-driven changes, is thus an attractive milieu for enterprising individuals to spot economic opportunities and exercise skill and judgement in the pursuit of economic rewards. By way of contrast, it can be seen that individual enterprise would be severely constrained in a command economy.

Much of the rivalry in this century between the so-called 'East' and 'West', between the first two 'worlds', can therefore be seen in terms of a conflict between the relative advantages of a market versus a command economy. In this sense the collapse of the 'Iron Curtain' in recent years is seen as a demonstration of the superiority of the market, or 'free' economy aproach. It has been hailed as the triumph of 'free enterprise'.

Capitalism, as practised in the nineteenth century, had been thought by Marx and others to promote the advance of the few and the economic enslavement of the many. Communism was the alternative that promised to end this inequality and to promote the benefit of the many. 'Bourgeois and Proletarians' is the heading of the first section of the *Communist Manifesto* and a note by Engels explains that by 'bourgeoisie' is meant the class of modern capitalists, owners of the means of social production and employers of wage labour, and by 'proletariat' is meant the class of modern wage-labourers who, having no means of production of their own, are reduced to selling their labour power in order to live. The *Communist Manifesto* specifically advocates the ending of the capitalist market and those states that have subsequently claimed to be based on a Marxist ideal have, by and large, had centrally planned, rather than market, economies. The apparent failure of this approach, and the abandonment of central planning in favour of the reintroduction of market forces, have been seen as a victory of 'free enterprise' over communism and as proof therefore of the superiority and rightness of the market approach.

That superiority may not always be so obvious, however, and it is not always so easy to replace a command economy with a free one. The recent apparent degeneration of the Russian economy into a 'mafia'-dominated mess indicates that the much heralded victory of Western market-dominated economics is not everywhere so clearly beneficial as may have been claimed initially.

The market approach has been identified with enterprise in this way and criticisms of a market economy approach have been portrayed as attacks on the ideas of enterprise. However, there are many variations of the market economy and much of the criticism of one variation is also intended to promote another. Nevertheless, some of this debate has been seen to be anti-enterprise. To see whether it is or not, it is necessary to distinguish between some different models of the market economy and their advantages and disadvantages.

The outward micro-economic manifestation of free-market thinking and behaviour is the perfectly competitive model. In this economic model there are very many firms in each industry producing largely homogeneous goods. No firm is large enough to influence the industry's price, firms and consumers have perfect knowledge, and firms will expand production until the cost of producing an additional item equals the revenue obtained from selling it. Under these conditions there is an optimal distribution of resources among competing ends. When markets are not in equilibrium, the price mechanism comes into play to restore equilibrium.

Among the criticisms of this model are the claims that in reality there are many matters that create and sustain imperfections in the model. Advertising allows firms to differentiate products, monopolistic firms dominate markets, labour markets do not 'clear' the unemployed, and inflation persists. According to one commentator, 'the major tenet of free market economics – that unregulated markets will of their own accord find unimprovable results for all participants – is now proved to be nonsense. It does not hold in theory. It is not true.'[3]

In spite of the claims that economic development in the USA is the 'product of the initiative and drive of individuals cooperating through the free market',[4] governments (the Kennedy and Johnson administrations in America are examples) have intervened to produce variations on the capitalist theme. Michael Thomas cites Keegan in concluding that there are at least three versions of capitalism: the American or liberal model, which draws heavily on the views of Smith and Hayek; continental European capitalism, which has active government involvement and embraces important interest groups that run the economy conjointly; and Japanese capitalism with strong state involvement, partnership and a focus on manufacturing prowess. In the European and Japanese versions, Keegan reports, the notion of 'community' is not seen as injurious to creativity or to the 'incentive to work'. He considers that the Japanese model, which emphasises loyalty and 'the value of long-term relationships between companies, their customers and suppliers, and *within* companies between the organisation, the employees, and the senior executives', is worthy of consideration.[5] Enterprise, of a more collaborative German or Japanese model, can indeed flourish in non-liberal (in the US sense) capitalist economies.

The economically sensitive, responsive, American-style capitalism presents many opportunities for enterprising individuals, but setting up and managing projects requires collaboration. Therefore the European and Japanese versions of capitalism can offer opportunities to do new things and to do so with the assistance of others. 'Markets, whether we like it or not', says Will Hutton, 'are embedded in a country's social system and values.'[6] Deviations from the perfect competitive model of 'free enterprise' are not therefore necessarily inherently contrary to enterprise. They may just be adjustments to produce a practical system that promotes the benefits of enterprise in a way that works in reality.

■ Enterprise and Dependency

It has not only been under communism that economic systems have discouraged enterprise, or at least discouraged what are perceived as some of the more beneficial sorts of enterprise. One way of defining enterprise is to describe it as the opposite of dependency, and yet dependency, it is argued, has been the result of some well-meaning attempts at economic stimulation. While governments have naturally been keen to ensure that their efforts benefit the worst off in society, as well as, if not even more than, those who are more advantaged, their efforts have not always been as effective as they might have wished.

One reason for this is encapsulated in the saying, 'Give someone a fish and you feed them for a day; teach them to fish and they can be fed for life.' In economic terms, however, it is often argued that teaching someone to fish is no help if there are no fish in the immediate area and that, in any case, it is a long-term strategy. What is often first needed is short-term relief, and governments often do seem to have the resources to buy in fish in the short term. However, economies are said to work when they create wealth and, if poorer regions are not creating wealth, then just putting in money, which is often the main resource to which governments can resort, is unlikely to change things.

Although governments do not like admitting to wasting resources, there is evidence that, even if economic development assistance appears to be carefully used, the result can be to build an attitude of dependency, not of enterprise. In Northern Ireland, for instance, a series of studies in the late 1980s showed that the effect of years of grant support for businesses, ostensibly to help those businesses offset a variety of factors reducing their competitiveness, had the effect instead of making them as profitable as their foreign competitors while remaining less productive. In other words the overall effect of the grants was to underwrite a lack of competitiveness. What could be said to be happening was that individual business owners were learning to be enterprising, not in improving business worth by better competitiveness, but in improving business worth by becoming better at accessing grants. That is enterprise, but like the stories of individuals in the so-called communist systems who became expert at getting the most out of the system while putting in the least, it is not the sort of enterprise that helps an economy to grow.

It can also be argued that strong government support of that kind can do more than just promote the rise of opportunistic 'grantrepreneurship'. It can also build a real dependency on that support. If there is a feeling that things are bad and that government ought to do something, and government then does intervene to do something, it reinforces the believe that sorting out the problem is the duty of government and should be left to it. Often the solution sought is inward investment: the attracting into the poorer regions of large industrial projects from outside to provide employment. That employment, however, is then dependent on the continuation of those projects and they are often the first to be closed by their parent companies in periods of economic retrenchment. Meanwhile, local businesses and prospective businesses, having become used to the availability of grants, tend to develop the attitude that if there wasn't a grant for something then they wouldn't do it. And even in local economic development initiatives local businesses and organisations become dependent on 'government' for ideas and drive. It was like a patient being put on a life support machine who, if the basic illness is not treated, becomes dependent on that machine for continued life. Enterprise, it could be argued, should be about taking your own initiative to improve your circumstances, not being dependent on others to do it for you.

5.1 Learned helplessness

Learned helplessness is a recognised health care problem in which patients learn to become dependent on external assistance and cannot do without it even when their original complaint is cured. Businesses, it would seem, can suffer from similar problems.

■ Clusters and Competitiveness

What then does actually promote industrial competitiveness? One answer comes from Michael Porter who, in his book *The Competitive Advantage of Nations*, seeks to overturn the traditional view on this subject. The prevailing theory, he suggests, has been that economies of scale, labour costs and interest and exchange rates are the strongest factors in determining competitiveness. He argues, however, that it is domestic rivalry and geographic concentration that provide the conditions necessary to build the expertise and innovation that really produce competitiveness. 'The presence of strong local rivals is a ... powerful stimulus to the creation and persistence of competitive advantage,'[7] and, again, 'nations succeed in particular industries because their home environment is the most forward-looking, dynamic, and challenging.'[8]

Companies achieve competitive advantage through innovation, including innovation in technology, in new ways of doing things, and in perceiving new markets or new opportunities in existing markets. Innovation is, however, linked to change and change is often unnatural, especially in successful companies. Conventional wisdom had argued that domestic competition was wasteful: that it led to duplication of effort and reduced the potential for economies of scale. Porter suggests, however, that it is domestic competition that provides the stimulus for innovation and that it is domestic competition that ultimately both forces domestic companies to look at export markets for their expansion and toughens them to succeed in them. When that domestic environment includes demanding customers and strong competition, together with appropriate support industries and the factors of production, there is the basis for international competitiveness. This is the cluster theory, and it has much in common with Mason's suggestions for the determinants of higher business start-up rates (see Chapter 4).

Porter's views are not primarily about the promotion of enterprise *per se*, but they do argue against the once conventional wisdom that economic prosperity is linked primarily to big businesses. If he is right then the conditions and attitudes that will give a nation a competitive advantage are those of an enterprise culture. National competitiveness and enterprise will be linked.

5.2   Network capitalism

While the examples of 'Third Italy' and Silicon Valley USA are often quoted as classic examples of clusters, equally impressive are the achievements of ethnic Chinese family businesses in many countries of the Association of South East Asian Nations (ASEAN). The ethnic Chinese have developed a formula for business which appears to have turned them into strong competitors on a world stage. Redding, writing of 'network capitalism', claims that

> their domains are OEM (original equipment manufacture) production, property, services, retailing, trading...This network capitalism of the ethnic Chinese is designed to respond to markets which companies from advanced economies would consider disorderly, volatile and very difficult to cope with.[9]

■ Community Enterprise

While Porter and others have concentrated on what best drives the macro-economy, others have looked at the micro end. While it is argued that an economy has to improve overall for real benefits to be felt, others have pointed out that this does not always benefit everyone within that economy. It is not a case in which a rising tide raises all boats when the results of improvements in the competitiveness of some businesses take too long to trickle down to others, if indeed they trickle down at all.

The creation of new enterprises or taking of new initiatives is perceived as a vital activity for any community hoping to have a thriving social and economic life. Some communities, however, appear to lack sufficient individual enterprising action to generate and develop new ideas that lead to improvement. Krueger notes that

> Economically disadvantaged communities often suffer from low self-efficacy. Communities suffering from poverty often reflect the symptoms of learned helplessness, a perceived inability to help themselves. People cannot lift themselves up by their boot straps if they perceive themselves as having no boots.[10]

The low levels of economic activity they have experienced, associated with high rates of unemployment, often result in a lack of confidence, a lack of relevant skills, a lack of resources and a lack of infrastructure. This can be a vicious circle of deprivation: there is a lack of business tradition, little enterprise, and an absence of entrepreneurs. There are therefore no role models and a lack of confidence is reinforced. That is the antithesis of an enterprise culture.

Community enterprise is generally enterprise shown by a group, and sometimes individuals acting together as a team or group can demonstrate qualities, command resources and engage in enterprising behaviour in a way that acting individually they would not. The reasons why group action occurs when individual action does not are interesting to surmise. No doubt issues of motivation, knowledge, skills (as well as of access to resources) and networks all contribute. Community enterprise is particularly recognised in community businesses, which have been defined in various ways but generally are business ventures that not only return to the community any surplus they create but also benefit the community in other ways such as by working on projects that enhance the environment or by developing skills of community members in their workforces.

Quite often the catalyst for effective community group action is an outsider or enterprising community member who mobilises, and releases, the latent enterprise in others. Such an individual is often referred to as a community entrepreneur. Such enterprises need not have an economic purpose, the purpose can also be social, e.g. to establish a refuge for victims of domestic violence or for drug users, leading to the term 'social entrepreneurship'. There is evidence, however, that the process of nurturing of community or social entrepreneurship is little different from that for individual entrepreneurs. According to Krueger, 'communities need to create a climate that enhances perceptions of feasibility and desirability.'[11]

Communities have also shown that they increasingly want other things as well as wealth, things which are not themselves wealth-creating, or at least not in the short term. Environmental worries are a case in point, and the rising perception of the importance of 'green' issues testifies to the strength of this concern. Many of the initiatives taken in this area, even if they are not business initiatives, are nevertheless also enterprising. They also are examples of community enterprise and can be the work of community entrepreneurs.

Various attempts have been made to define the concept of the community entrepreneur, and there is general agreement that it is about the use of personal networking, facilitation and resources accessing skills to improve a localised community in both social and economic areas. Community entrepreneurs facilitate community enterprise in the way that the more traditional entrepreneurs facilitate business development, although, whereas enterprise in the context of business is often seen in the start-up of new businesses, community enterprise is generally not applied to the start of new communities but to the revitalisation of old ones.

Communities are affected by many forces, including structural change, and they can, if action is not taken to counter the effects of those forces, die as a result. Often that structural change has an economic content, such as shifts in the pattern of industry or agriculture, but that does not mean that all the community needs is economic assistance. Community decline, for instance, can often be seen in rural communities where changing patterns in agriculture have reduced both the amount and the relative wages of agricultural employment. The result can be a move of some people, often the more able ones, to areas where there is more employment opportunity. Their departure in turn takes demand out of the local community, which loses the critical mass it needs to support local shops, schools and other facilities. A vicious spiral results.

Correcting this is not simply a matter of providing an alternative to the lost agricultural employment. It often requires a combination of local economic

Table 5.1   Autonomous and community entrepreneurs compared

The autonomous entrepreneur	*The community entrepreneur*
Aim for the growth of personal resources as the main personal goal.	Aim for the development of the community as the main personal goal.
Enhance own self-competence.	Help to build the self-respect and competence of others.
Mobilise resources to build their own enterprises.	Inspire others to start their own enterprises.
Put themselves at the top of the organisation.	Regard themselves as the coordinator in a loose federation.
See authority and society interest groups as hindrances.	See authority and society interest groups as potential supporters and resource providers.

Source: Adapted from B. Johannisson and A. Nilsson, 'Community Entrepreneurs: Networking for Local Development', *Entrepreneurship and Regional Development*, vol. 1, no. 1 (1989) p. 5. Reproduced by kind permission of Taylor & Francis, Publishers.

initiatives, of direct action to secure local services, of improvements to the local environment, of local cultural development and of local confidence raising. Community decline is not irreversible, and there are now many examples of successful community entrepreneurship in which the application of enterprise has built a better community.

There is therefore much in common between community and business enterprise. They both need a vision of what is possible, they both require the application of resources to achieve that vision, they both involve the acceptance of a level of risk and they both generally need personal drive to make them work. There are however some differences, as Table 5.1 shows.

■ The Drawbacks of Enterprise

> *All that glistens is not gold.*

Much of this book is based on the assumption that enterprise is essentially something of value, that it is a good thing. It may therefore be necessary to temper this implication by pointing out some of the pitfalls and the downside of enterprise. These can lie in the results of the practice of enterprising behaviour, in the way that a label of enterprise can appear to justify otherwise undesirable practices, and in the assumption that true enterprising behaviour is what should always be encouraged.

Enterprise, it has been said, is spelt R-I-S-K. It is important, when promoting enterprise, to remember that, inherent in enterprise and especially in enterprise in the business context, is risk: the risk of loss of career and of livelihood, of loss of money and resource, and of loss of reputation. While in an enterprising culture it may be expected that many new ventures will work and that, as a result, on average, things will progress, it must be remembered that individual initiatives, and the individual people behind them, will not all follow that average path. Some will fail. If however no one is prepared to risk that failure, which is a necessary condition for any venture, then nothing will progress. An economy is like an ecosystem in nature: organisations in it cannot stand still and survive, at least not for long. In a healthy environment there is both birth and death. If a living organisation does not continue to renew itself it will die, but not all renewal initiatives will work.

Just as enterprise does not ensure success, neither is it a magic cure-all. It can be an important element in economic, or other, improvement. However, the ways it is promoted can be both highly distorting and distorted. They can suggest that it is itself sufficient and can highlight selfish aspects only, as if they alone were what mattered.

5.3 Devalued enterprise

This is what angers people about the highly simplistic and distorted ways in which enterprise and the enterprise culture have sometimes been promoted and practised. They miss the human and social justice imperatives entirely. They turn 'enterprise' into a good-for-some part of a political and economic philosophy which is uncaring and divisive, synonymous with greed and self interest, and a subtle justification of the seeming inevitability of the coexistence of success and failure, richness and poverty, privilege and underprivilege. Others abhor this, and would point out that without social care, justice and cohesiveness, there can be no truly enterprising culture.

Enterprise has become one of the most devalued terms in the English language. A word that should embody all the complexities of risk-taking has come to stand as the legitimator of tax-cuts, breaking trade unions and denying there is any case for examining how companies are owned and managed.

By this definition, the genius of enterprise is essentially about individuals pitching their wits against the market. It is an individual who develops a new product, grows a company or cuts a deal. The structure and culture of the organisations in which these individuals strut their stuff are ignored. It is low-taxed, lightly-regulated, have-won-the-right-to-manage individuals who make the capitalist system tick...

Enterprise is in part an economic, in part an individual and in part a moral act. Companies have to reconcile the claims of individuals as social beings as much as assert the iron laws of the balance sheet – and these iron laws themselves change in different cultures and value systems. Enterprise is culturally determined.

Enterprise is as much a social and moral act as economic – but, until this is widely understood, economic success will be elusive. Early accounts of the rise of capitalism...stressed the congruence between Protestant values and those of successful capitalism. Religious non-conformism compelled the early capitalists to invest and not to dissipate their profits in consumption. The early Protestant sects were earning a place in heaven by their acts in the world, and so launching early capitalism.

(**Will Hutton**[12])

Now, however, things are being reversed and capitalism and enterprise are themselves in danger of becoming the religion that justifies the behaviour of their practitioners.

If enterprise can be mis-used in this way, do we want it at all? Is it a force for good, or for bad, or is it actually neutral with the potential goodness, or badness, lying in the way it is used? Some resist it because they see it as replacing clearer positive values with something that is only at best neutral. Attempts to introduce enterprise education into schools have been seen by its proponents as a long-needed attempt to help schools educate their students for a life in the 'real world'. Others, however, have resisted them as propaganda and as a preparation only for the nasty commercial world of business without introducing any positive elements such as consideration, tolerance or generosity. 'Do we really want our nine-year-olds to be adopting such a hard-nosed attitude – shouldn't they, during their ever-shrinking childhood, be thinking about saving the whale, rather than contracting to sell apples in the school tuck shop?'[13] While it can be pointed out that attempting to save the whale will itself require enterprise, there is still the potential danger that the application of commercial considerations will have the opposite effect.

■ The Future of Enterprise

Forecasting is difficult – especially when it concerns the future.

(Groucho Marx)

This book was written in response to an increasing emphasis in recent years on 'enterprise' in many areas of life but especially in the economic field. It is therefore relevant to consider whether that emphasis is likely to continue and whether the concept of enterprise, as described here, is likely to continue to be relevant. Despite the dangers of forecasting, this section therefore attempts to present some of the trends, ideas and concepts which may influence the future of enterprise.

■ Technology

The rate of development of technology shows no sign of slowing. One obvious result is to make older technologies obsolete and the industries dependent on them expendable. If technology changes, then businesses dependent on it must change too in order to remain competitive. Nowhere is this more so than in the computer and telecommunications industries. The technology changes have been profound, and this has assisted firms in their search for ever more flexible but cost-effective production methods. However, the impact of computers assisted by fibre-optic capability has been even more profound in revolutionising information processing. Personal computers, electronic mail, fax machines, mobile telephones and the Internet have transformed the provision of services such as marketing research, industrial design and advertising. Knowledge-based industries rely on information processing ability to confer competitive advantage. Therefore, the combination of computing capacity, a focus on knowledge, and fibre optics has, and will continue to have, a marked impact on the way we work.

No longer is it necessary to work in a fixed location under the direct supervision of a manager. The communications revolution has brought the possibility of global teleworking. Even small businesses can join in and offer something on a world-wide basis. Improved communications provide the opportunity for improved services with faster turn-round times, but faster responses also require more flexible organisations. Small business are then not only able to join in but can do so at an advantage with respect to their bigger rivals.

Advances in biotechnology are also having a major impact on our daily lives. Not only can food now be grown in formerly inhospitable areas, but microbes are being developed that destroy waste and toxins and medical advances are taking place on many fronts. Consequently people will be able to live longer in most parts of the world, which will have profound social and economic consequences.

■ Flexibility and Service

As was stated above, the possibility of and the demand for, flexible production and service is increasing. Large, inflexible production lines with their economies of scale, but also with their associated limitation that 'you can have any colour you like as long as it's black', are no longer the only way to meet customer demands. Customers can have, and now expect, variety as well as relative cheapness. Production must change to provide what customers want to buy, not what the business wants to supply. Businesses compete on flexibility and speed of response as well as on cost.

Smaller businesses can be more flexible in their approach and quicker to change to meet new conditions. Service industry, where flexibility, quality and speed of response are of primary importance, has a high proportion of small businesses. These combine organic, flexible structures with the decentralisation of decision making to those with knowledge and expertise. In addition, the need to solve specific client problems, or to customise products for market niches, will entail the use of temporary project groups to meet customer needs. The equipment used by problem-solving work groups will tend to be sophisticated, but employees will exercise a good deal of discretion in utilising it effectively. The organisations doing this will tend therefore to be smaller, more responsive, quality-conscious and much less bureaucratic than formerly. They may well employ a small number of core professional staff and contract out work that is very specialised or for which demand is uneven. They will both be enterprising themselves, and create the opportunity for the enterprise also of others.

■ Changing Lifestyles

It is not only the demands of the world of work that are changing, but also the way people feel that they can live their lives. It used to be the case that people expected to work for as long as they could and not to survive very long after that. Now, however, changed work expectations, combined with longer lifespans, mean that more people are planning for what amounts to second lives in which their styles of living will be significantly different from those of their first lives. They are therefore no longer planning on the basis of lifetime careers in one organisation, and are increasingly likely to have a second career in which they will be dependent on their own enterprise for their work and income.

■ Market Changes

Markets are also changing. Consumers want not only improved products and services but also want improved by-products from those processes. This is particularly noticeable, for instance, in the field of environmental issues. Businesses now have to consider the social, as well as the economic, consequence of their actions. Those that can't adapt will fail. There will therefore be openings for new businesses that can adapt and for service businesses to help the others to address, reduce or deal with the unwanted consequences of their actions.

Markets are also becoming more international. In a global environment in which businesses increasingly seek, and are encouraged, to establish overseas subsidiaries, who should adapt to whose culture? Should it be the business which wants to sell or the host country which wants the inward investment? There will be a need to think globally but act locally. That too will require enterprise.

■ Results

The result of all these, and of other, developments is change. Charles Handy among others has pointed out that organisations can normally cope effectively with rapid change so long as the change is incremental and developmental.[14] Organisations have much more difficulty in coping with discontinuous change, but this, according to Handy, is precisely what is happening in today's world. With this type of change, old ways of thinking and functioning are inappropriate and radical new reasoning is required.

In the economic sphere many of the more developed countries will continue to reduce their reliance on the mass production of consumer durables in favour of high-quality, high-volume customised goods, and services. In essence they can no longer compete in labour-intensive or skill-intensive sectors and must move to knowledge-intensive business. Added value will come from the innovation and knowledge base of people in organisations, not from their physical labour. Changes in markets require firms nowadays to offer 'quality, flexibility and innovativeness' along with the 'customisation of products' rather than low-cost, high-volume standard products'.[15]

For these reasons, and for others possibly including the management fashion for 'downsizing', many larger businesses have been actively reducing their direct manpower requirements. Charles Handy has spoken of the 'shamrock organisation' (see also Chapter 1): a structure with three parts, each of which has different expectations, management systems and methods of payment. One part is the professional core essential to the survival of the organisation, the second part consists of the subcontractors who will actually do much of the work, and the third leaf is the growing number of flexible and temporary workers and consultants who are hired for specific jobs as the need arises.

As a consequence, the traditional notion of the career is increasingly a thing of the past. Those in the core, with a 'normal' full-time career, will have to work very hard indeed and face the likelihood of burnout by their forties. Most will retire in their early fifties and leave their intensive brainwork to a younger generation. They can expect to live for thirty more years, but their source of income will have to change. A large number of people will have job histories characterised by part-time or temporary work assignments. Their earning power will be less than full-time careerists, and they will lack job security.

Other changes may incidentally help with the process of mid-career readjustment. There will be the subcontracting opportunities for those who want to take them up and, if individuals have the right mental preparation, then some of them may find that the necessary resources are provided by others. Redundancy payments are one obvious source of investment for new business ventures, and, in countries that have enjoyed a high standard of living for a period, inheritance of the assets accumulated by parents is an increasing factor. Also, it has been suggested that one reason for the recent considerable increase in the number of businesses started by women in some parts of the United States is the life-change occasioned by divorce, combined with the opportunity provided by the alimony payments.

Rapid and discontinuous change therefore seems likely to continue to have a major impact on the lives of people, organisations and society. Successful individuals in the world of tomorrow will need to be flexible in their attitudes, their acquisition of skills, and their knowledge base. Faced with ever faster environmental changes, organisations must respond, and people, their most flexible of resources, must be equally responsive. Specific knowledge is important for specific roles, but problem-solving, information search and analysis, and decision making will be crucial skills. People must be adaptable and be able to learn continuously. They must espouse a 'spirit of enquiry' and develop value systems that encourage 'inquiry, examination, diagnosis and experimentation'.[16] They must be enterprising.

In a situation of discontinuous change individuals, organisations and nations must develop the capacity to cope. In developing this capability, people who display enterprising attitudes, attributes and behaviours will be particularly useful. Individuals, organisations and countries must become more flexible, responsive, knowledgeable, mobile and proactive, and people who possess enterprising attributes such as boldness, innovation and confidence will not only profit themselves but will lead society in its drive to make necessary changes. The future, or at least a significant part of it, is therefore likely to be made by and to belong to the enterprising.

Key points

- A number of concepts have been attached in some situations to the word 'enterprise'. These associations include:

  - *Free enterprise* Capitalism, and particularly American-style capitalism, has been given the title 'free enterprise', and it has been hailed as the victor in the economic side of the 'cold war' between the Western Alliance and the Communist Bloc. However, there are other forms of capitalism than the American one, and, as shown in Chapter 4, enterprise flourishes in many of them.
  - *Dependency* There is a danger that, in trying to promote enterprise, initiatives which use means such as grants have instead promoted dependency. Learned helplessness is a recognised medical problem in which patients learn to become dependent on external assistance and can not do without it even when their original complaint is cured. Business can suffer from similar problems.
  - *Clusters and competitiveness* Michael Porter has shown that clusters of strong competing domestic rivals can develop strong international competitiveness. It is a truly enterprising culture that gives the clusters their effectiveness.
  - *Community enterprise* Community enterprise is the application of enterprise for community benefit, not for individual profit. Community and business enterprise therefore have a lot in common, but somewhat different objectives.

- Enterprise is frequently promoted as something positive. It does however have a number of real or potential drawbacks. Enterprise involves risk; there can be no guarantee that an enterprising act will succeed and, when it doesn't, there will be some loss. Enterprise is not the magic cure-all some people seem to want it to be. It can be an important element in economic improvement, but a distorted view of it and its benefits is sometimes presented, with the result that enterprise promotion is seen by some as just propaganda for a nasty world of shady commercial dealing.
- Enterprise does however have a future. The pattern of work and business is changing. More people will be working in and/or establishing their own small businesses. The reasons for this include technological developments, an increasing demand for flexibility and service, changing life styles and changes in markets. The result is that the future, or at least a significant part of it, is likely to belong to the enterprising.

Part II

Enterprise and Small Business

■ Introduction

Part I of this book explores the concept of enterprise, what it is and why it is the subject of interest. It shows that the word 'enterprise' has a range of meanings: from the narrow meaning of enterprise, referring to small businesses and the act of starting them, to the broad meaning of enterprise as a set of personal attributes and behaviours that can be demonstrated in a number of different situations and contexts.

The use of the word enterprise to relate specifically to small business is, however, very widespread, and it is the economic benefits that small businesses bring that are the prime reason for the wide interest in enterprise. Part II therefore looks at this aspect of enterprise in more detail.

The specific aspect of small businesses that distinguishes them from other businesses is obviously their size. Because of this they tend to have some features in common, but they are by no means identical. There are many varieties of small business, which differ for instance in their stage of development, in their business sector or in their type of ownership. These characteristics and variations are explored in Chapter 6.

Small businesses are not however just smaller versions of big businesses. They have a number of distinctive features that are not always obvious to the untutored observer. Those who wish to understand small businesses therefore need insight into the specific nature of such business. This is described in Chapter 7.

If small businesses are popular because they provide employment potential, growth businesses are particularly desirable because relatively few of them can create a relatively large number of jobs. Targeting them may therefore seem to be attractive, but it is not always possible. Chapter 8 looks at business growth: its meaning, components, motivations and environment.

Although the terms 'enterprise' and 'small business' tend to be used synonymously, there is still a need for enterprise in bigger businesses if they too are to survive and grow. The internal cultivation of enterprise within more mature businesses has been called 'intrapreneurship', and is the subject of the final chapter in this part, Chapter 9.

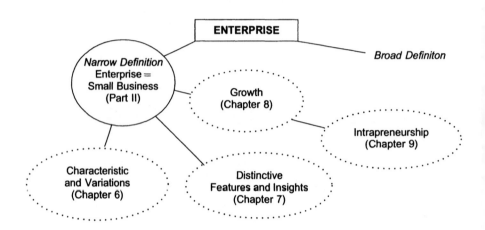

CHAPTER 6

Small Business Categories and Variations

This chapter seeks to explore further what is meant by the term 'small business'. Although small businesses have their size in common, and other features associated with, or dependent on, size, they are in many other respects heterogeneous rather than homogeneous. This chapter therefore considers some of the many different definitions of a small business. It considers small businesses at different stages of their development, in different sectors and under different types of ownership. It seeks to establish what they have in common, as well as the range of their diversity.

■ Definitions

6.1 Some official definitions of a small business

United Kingdom

DTI. In the UK for statistical purposes the DTI usually uses the following definitions:

Micro firm	0–9 employees.
Small firm	0–49 employees (includes micro).
Medium firm	50–249 employees.
Large firm	Over 250 employees.

Companies Act. Section 249 of the Companies Act of 1985 states that a company is 'small' if it satisfies at least two of the following criteria:

- A turnover of not more than £2.8 million.
- A balance sheet total of not more than £1.4 million.
- Not more than 50 employees.

A medium-sized company must satisfy at least two of the following criteria:

- A turnover of not more than £11.2 million.
- A balance sheet total of not more than £5.6 million.
- Not more than 250 employees.

Value Added Tax. The VAT registration threshold is a turnover of £48 000.

Small Firms Loan Guarantee Scheme. The scheme applies to businesses with fewer than 200 employees and with a turnover of not more than £3 million (manufacturing) or £1.5 million (other eligible businesses).

Corporation Tax. The Small Companies Rate of corporation tax applies to businesses with taxable profits of up to £300 000 and a marginal rate applied to profits between £300 000 and £1 500 000. Over that the full rate applies.

Bank of England. For the purposes of considering finance issues for small businesses the Bank of England focuses mainly on business with a turnover of up to and including £1 million per year.[1]

European Commission

At one time different European Commission programmes to help SMEs (small and medium-sized enterprises) had different definitions of SMEs. To avoid inconsistencies arising from this, the Commission decided, in 1996, to adopt a single definition, namely:

Maximum	*Medium-sized*	*Small*	*Micro-enterprise*
Number of employees	250	50	10
Turnover (million ECU)	40	7	
Balance sheet total (million ECU)	27	5	

There is no single, clear, precise and widely accepted definition of what is a small business. Different definitions exist, often because of different purposes such as support policy application, taxation or legislation. Many people, however, feel that they know what is meant by a 'small business'. It is one that has few employees, a low turnover, little or no formal structure and is usually managed by one person, who is also the business owner. It is these characteristics that make a small business behave the way it does, and many feel that the key point at which a growing business ceases to be small is when it has to change its organisational and control system, from the loose and informal to the structured and formal, if it is to continue to be effective. However, most definitions use the size of the business as its distinguishing feature, presumably because that is easier to measure. Definitions vary widely in the way they define the size of a small business. Some use turnover, which can however change over time with inflation, but most go for employment, which, as already indicated, also happens to be the benefit which very often provides the rationale for small business support. Even when employment is used there are different definitions. The EU definition of an SME (small and medium enterprise) used to be one that employed fewer than 500 employees, but the limit is now 250 (see box above). The USA Small Business Administration uses 500 as the limit for its remit. Elsewhere the limit is often set at 200, which many take as being closer to the size that forces a change in organisational structure. Some use 100 as the limit, and there are small business agencies which use 50.

There are also definitions that, in effect, seek to subdivide the category that others describe as small by separating those businesses that are merely 'small' from those that are even smaller. As well as the EU definitions quoted above there others such as:

Self employed	1 person in the business
Micro businesses	up to 19 employees, or up to 9
Small businesses	20 to 99 employees, or 10 to 99
Medium businesses	100 to 500 employees.

Small may also be employed as a relative term, rather than an absolute one. A 200 person business may not be small in terms of the absolute definitions given above, but if it is a shipyard then it would be very small compared with the average for its industry sector. One definition of a small business is therefore simply a business with a scale of operations significantly below the average, or below the minimum size usually necessary for efficient operations, in its industry.

The above definitions are almost entirely quantitative, but there are qualitative ones. Small businesses do tend to share a number of qualities. They are generally businesses that serve only local customers and have only a very limited share of the available market, that are owned by one person, or by a small group of people, and are managed by their owners who deal with all management issues usually with little other help; and they are independent businesses not parts of, or owned by, larger companies.

A definition based on only one of these qualities would be in danger of excluding some businesses that others would regard as small. A number of qualitative characteristics should therefore be included. One attempt to do so is a definition of a small business as one which possesses at least two of the following four characteristics:

- Management of the business is independent. Usually the managers are also the owners.
- Capital and ownership are provided by an individual or a small group.
- The areas of operation are mainly local, with the workers and owners living in one home community. However the market need not be local.
- The relative size of the business within its industry must be small when compared with the biggest units in the field. This measure can be in terms of sales volume, number of employees or other significant comparisons.[2]

Most of the definitions of a small business given above are, however, in effect only attempts to provide a proxy for what is the essence of 'smallness' in business units. Smallness is about being autonomous yet having limited resources of manpower, time, skills, expertise and finance, and therefore having to be dependent on external support. It is about having to cope with greater uncertainty and about carrying greater risk while having few opportunities for risk spreading. It is also about:

- the influence of ownership on entrepreneurial behaviour;
- having greater individual authority;
- managing a total activity and carrying total responsibility;
- being closer to customers, and being potentially more flexible and adaptable;
- managing networks of suppliers, customers, and financiers;
- paying greater attention to business opportunities;
- taking a strategic approach while also having close and informal control structures and communication channels; and
- creating a 'can-do' culture.

These are the things that being small means and that present challenges and opportunities different from those in larger businesses.

The Stages of (Small) Business Development

However they are defined, small businesses exhibit considerable variety. In considering them, and in particular in trying to establish their needs and the issues facing them, it can be helpful to try to distinguish groups or categories of them with common characteristics. One of the commonest ways of categorising businesses has been by the 'stage' of their development. However, it is important to recognise that the use of the term 'stage' in relation to the business development process does not mean that businesses develop in discrete phases with clear boundaries between them. Separating the development process into stages is rather like dividing the spectrum of visible light into colours. Traditionally there are said to be seven, but in reality there are not seven distinct colours but a continuing gradation through the colours. We can say that one area is green compared with another area which is yellow, but we cannot say precisely where one changes to the other. Dividing the business development process into stages is helpful, in that there are issues at the heart of each stage that differ from the issues central to other stages, but, while we can indicate broadly the stage of development of a business, we cannot say precisely when it moves from one stage to another.

Like distinguishing colours in the colour spectrum, the number of areas ascribed to the process is a matter of interpretation. However, unlike the colour spectrum, the order of the areas is not necessarily fixed. While a 'pre-start' stage cannot follow 'start-up', and 'termination' has to be the end, businesses do not have to progress through every possible stage between; they can be static, they can grow and they can decline in any order, they can do them more than once, and they can reverse their steps. There are many models of the different stages and the sequence in which they occur, but the reality is that very few businesses actually follow the models. Many of the models, in the way they are presented, imply steady growth, for instance by presenting a steadily rising line on a plot with axes of size and time. Growth, however, is not the norm, and where there is growth it is generally achieved through a number of discrete steps, rather than by a steady, even progression. It is also important to recognise that these models do not explain what is happening inside a business: they only describe its situation, and they present symptoms not causes. Therefore they do not help in predicting what will happen next to a business.

■ The Stage Model

Because the development process is not divided by natural boundaries, there is no single, generally accepted development model. Many different ways have been suggested for segmenting the development of a business. One of the most used is the Churchill and Lewis model (see Table 6.1 overleaf).[3]

Other models, however, have additional stages that come either prior to or after the Churchill and Lewis stages. A model proposed by the Forum of Private Business, for instance, does not stop at maturity, but includes the stages of 'decline' and 'termination', while the Krueger model (see Chapter 3) recognises that the commencement of trading is not itself the beginning of the process and that there are stages before the formation of a business which, while not strictly stages in the development of that particular business, are nevertheless relevant to an understanding of its inception. These prior-to-business-start stages can include:

Table 6.1 – The five stages of business growth, according to Churchill and Lewis

- *Existence* – staying alive by finding products or services and customers.
- *Survival* – establishing the customer base, demonstrating viability.
- *Success* – confidence in its market position, options for further growth.
- *Take-off* – opting to go for growth.
- *Maturity* – the characteristics of a larger, stable company.

Source: N. C. Churchill and V. L. Lewis, 'Growing Concerns: The Five Stages of Small Firm Growth', *Harvard Business Review*, May–June 1983, pp. 31, 32, 34, 40.

- *Culture*. People are more likely to think of starting a business, and that business is more likely to survive, if the underlying culture is one that will help to nurture awareness and interest as well as ideas and embryo businesses.
- *The Idea*. Before they can proceed to start-up, people need to have the idea that they can start a business and have a product or service idea around which the business can be formed. This is the stage where they are not only aware that business start is possible, but must feel that it might be appropriate for them.
- *The Pre-Start Phase*. The process whereby those thinking of starting a business progress from the business idea to the stage of actually starting the business.

A fuller list of stages might therefore include the following (these stages are described in more detail later in this chapter):

Model X: the list

- Culture and awareness
- Idea – both the idea that a business is possible and a product/service idea for it
- Pre-start/preparation
- Start-up/inception
- Growth and expansion
- Static – including survival, consolidation, comfort and maturity
- Decline
- Termination.

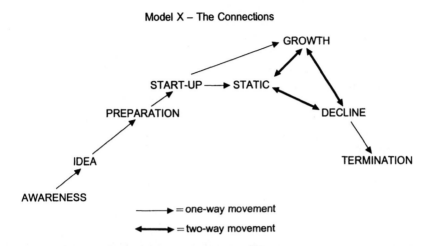

Figure 6.1 **Business paths from conception to death**

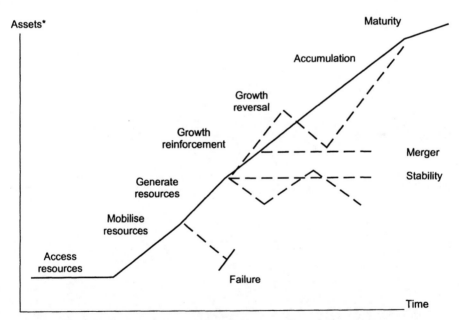

* Firms, as they grow, accumulate assets, both tangible 'fixed' assets and intangible assets such as expertise and reputation. Assets are therefore used here as an indicator of growth.

Source: E. Garnsey, 'A New Theory of the Growth of the Firm', *41st World Conference of ICSB, Stockholm* (June 1996) p. 4.

Figure 6.2 **Growth process as reflected in possible growth paths**

To show the possible sequences of these stages, Model X can be presented diagrammatically, as in Figure 6.1.

As well as showing both pre-start and termination phases, the model also recognises the dynamics of business development. Despite the straight lines of most models, businesses very rarely progress steadily onwards and upwards. The diagram in Figure 6.2 recognises this by showing possible paths for a business, not only in steady growth, but also in a phase of growth reversal, in stability with possible oscillation, in a merger with another business and in early failure. This model also shows the dominant problems that have to be addressed by a business. It is therefore, in effect, presenting the precursors, or stimulators of physical change, rather than the change itself. These precursors or stimulators are, however, very hard to measure, compared with qualities such as turnover or numbers of employees, and are therefore much harder in practice to use to describe a business. Nevertheless, their presentation can provide useful insights.

The diagram in Figure 6.2 can be extended to show a cohort of firms, for which, at any stage, there are possibilities of closure, steady state, merger or independent growth. The presentation in Figure 6.3 gives some impression of the number of different paths that can be followed in reality, and is very different from the single development line of some models.

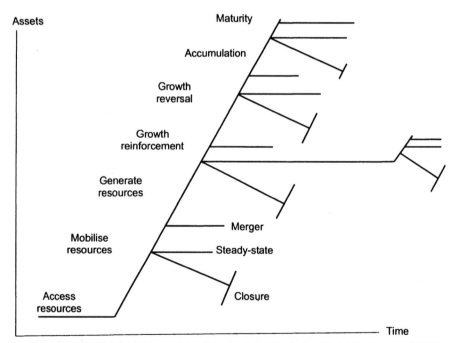

Source: E. Garnsey, 'A New Theory of the Growth of the Firm', *41st World Conference of ICSB, Stockholm* (June 1996) p. 18.

Figure 6.3   Diverse trajectories of a cohort of businesses

Another variation is to draw a parallel between Maslow's hierarchy of needs and the stages of business development:

Maslow's hierarchy	Business development	
Self-actualisation	Maturity	Leader
Recognition	Expansion	↑
Belonging	Growth	Manager
Security	Survival	↑
Survival	Start-up	Entrepreneur

While the stage model approach may have its drawbacks, it helps nevertheless to divide small businesses into different categories to make them easier to examine. The possible stages in this approach are therefore considered in more detail.

■ Culture and Awareness – The Supply of Entrepreneurs

What all the listed stages of business development, apart from 'culture/awareness', have in common is that they are all concerned with people who might be or already are, in business. To use a horticultural analogy, they all deal with plants: with sowing the seeds of plants, with growing plants, with pruning plants, with flowering plants and even with dying plants. The 'culture' or 'awareness' stage, however, deals with the preparation of the ground: the preparation of a medium which will encourage, feed and support the seeds and growing plants. Chapter 4 has shown that the surrounding human society or culture is important for business growth, just as the condition and type of the soil is important for plants.

The influences on new firm formation can be many and varied. Krueger's model of entrepreneurial potential, described in Chapter 3, illustrates some of the antecedent influences on enterprise. An alternative presentation, which represents the same framework but also highlights some of the specific factors that may be influential in a business context, is shown in Figure 6.4.

This model illustrates the variety of possible antecedent factors that may be relevant to the 'culture' or 'awareness' stage. This stage can be subdivided to show the progression from no particular interest in enterprise through awareness and potential interest to actual new business formation. This is illustrated in Figure 6.5. Both Figures 6.4 and 6.5 also show the link between enterprise culture in a business sense, and the wider, or 'education', definition of enterprise, in that the latter is a necessary precondition for the former.

This model is goes beyond the simple culture/awareness > idea > pre-start > new business model by indicating further gradations within the spectrum.

INFLUENCES UPON THE ENTREPRENEURIAL DECISION

Antecedent Influences upon Entrepreneur

1. Family and religious background.
2. Educational background.
3. Psychological makeup.
4. Age at time(s) of maximum external opportunity and organisational 'push'.
5. Earlier career experience.
6. Opportunity to form entrepreneurial groups.

Incubator Organisation

1. Geographic location.
2. Nature of skills and knowledge acquired.
3. Motivation to stay with or leave organization.
4. Experience in 'small business' setting.

Entrepreneur's decision

External Factors

1. Examples of entrepreneurial action and availability of knowledge about entrepreneurship.
2. Societal attitudes toward entrepreneurship.
3. Ability to save 'seed capital'.
4. Accessibility and availability of venture capital.
5. Availability of personnel and supporting services; accessibility to customers; accessibility to university.
6. Opportunities for interim consulting.
7. Economic conditions.

Source: Arnold C. Cooper, 'Technical Entrepreneurship', *R & D Management*, vol. 3 (1973) pp. 59–64.

Figure 6.4   Model of new Enterprise Formation

Another illustration, which also includes possible stages within culture and awareness, is presented in Figure 6.6. It also shows the importance of the opportunity provided by the educational system.

■ Pre-start – Idea and Preparation

Businesses do not arise fully fledged from even the most positive of enterprise cultures. A time of preparation is still needed first. The preparation may include identifying a suitable opportunity (the idea), acquiring the necessary knowledge and skills, and locating the contacts who will help. Continuing the horticultural analogy, it is the stage of planting and germination of seeds. The growing medium is important, but seeds are also needed to produce plants and those seeds have to have the ability to take root and to put out leaves. In business terms, negotiating this stage requires both a willingness to start it and some ideas of what might best be done in it.

Krueger (see Chapter 3) has argued that a willingness to start comes from the credibility gained for the proposed action because of its perceived desirability

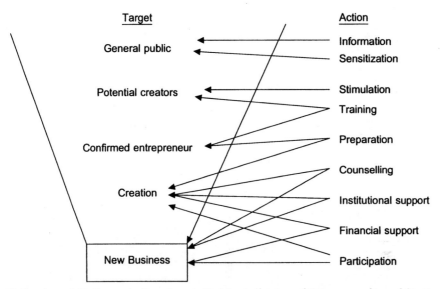

B. Garnier and Y. Gasse, *An Experience in Training in the Area of Entrepreneurship and Starting a Business in Quebec: The Project 'Become an Entrepreneur'*, October 1986.

Figure 6.5   Vickery's Model

and perceived feasibility; in other words from a recognition that there are rewards that can be gained from starting a business and a desire for those rewards, together with a belief that the rewards can be achieved. It may also be relevant to add that this presupposes that the possibility of engaging in the action in question has already occurred to the person concerned.

If these conditions are met and there is a desire to proceed then it is helpful to know how. Various suggestions have been made about the key components of the ideal pre-start process. The formula produced by Peterson and Rondstadt

Stage	What	Where
Stage 1	Basics	Primary school
Stage 2	Awareness	Secondary school
Stage 3	Creativity	College level

Break for job experience, training, gaining experience, contacts, etc.

Stage 4	Start-up	In business
Stage 5	Growth	In business

Figure 6.6   Another Model

Entrepreneurial success = New venture Idea

+ Entrepreneurial know-how

+ Entrepreneurial know-who

Source: R. Peterson and R. Rondstadt, 'A Silent Strength: Entrepreneurial Know-Who', *The 16th ESBS, efmd IMD Report* (86/4) p. 11.

Figure 6.7   Entrepreneurial success

(Figure 6.7) summarises some of the key components that are needed for start-up success, components that by implication might then be assembled in the pre-start stage.[4] It is also however important to recognise that the pre-start process can be very long. The pre-start stage can be defined as ending when a business starts and starting when there is an intention at some time to prepare for that eventuality.

A traditional view of enterprise has been based on the assumption that some individuals are inherently more enterprising than others. Because of that predisposition towards enterprise, it was assumed that, given the right stimulus, they were more likely to try starting a business. There could then be virtually no pre-start stage in the sense defined above. Another view of enterprise, and of enterprising behaviour, is considered in Chapter 3. It is based on the attributes and resources that an individual may possess. Attributes may include self-confidence, diligence, perseverance, inter-personal skills and innovative behaviour. Resources may include finance, experience, knowledge, skills, a network and a track record. It is suggested then that it is the interaction between these factors that produces a rational response, on the basis of available information, when the possibility occurs of a business start-up.

6.3   Starting a business

Given a suitable trigger, the likelihood of start-up is a function of the attributes and resources possessed by the individual, or individuals, concerned, plus the perceived opportunity and the availability of assistance.

It is acknowledged that there is inertia in individual behaviour and that it may take a discontinuity in work, or in life, to trigger a review of an individual's situation. Whether this review will lead to an individual trying his or her own enterprise will then depend on the attributes and resources he or she has accumulated and his or her perception of the opportunity and of environmental factors such as the availability of grants. The acquisition of those attributes and resources, if it is done with a view to a possible business start, is the pre-start stage. It is generally perceived as a stage of individual, or small team, preparation. If the culture stage can be seen to relate to the concepts covered in Chapter 4, the pre-start stage relates to the concepts in Chapter 3.

An individual, or a team, can be helped to acquire the components for a start-up. There are many ways in which this can be done, but the following paragraphs illustrate some of the possibilities.

☐ *The Idea*

The 'idea' can cover both the idea of starting a business and the idea for a particular business to start. The former comes from the issues just explored. The latter can come from a number of sources, but usually from one's own experience. This is one list of sources of ideas common in small businesses (Table 6.2).

Table 6.2   The self-employment spectrum

Form or approach	Platform	Springboard
Turning a hobby into a business	Long-standing passion	Personal connections
Becoming a professional consultant/trainer	Specialised knowledge	Professional contacts
Acquiring an existing business	Managerial and marketing skills	Financial resources
Taking on a franchise	Organisational ability	Financial and marketing resources
Creating a business of your own	Enterprising spirit	Market place
Matching personal and market potential	Personal knowledge and potential	Knowledge and potential of yourself and others
Developing your vision	Personal charisma and inspiration	Economic and social need/potential

Source: Reprinted by permission of Sage Publications Ltd © from R. Lessem, 'Getting into Self-Employment', *Management, Education and Development* (Spring, 1984) p. 31.

☐ *Know-how*

Know-how covers a number of areas of knowledge, all of which may be needed by the owner-manager of a small business if that business is to be successful. This know-how has been shown to have (at least) four dimensions (Table 6.3).

Table 6.3   The four dimensions of management development

Functional knowledge and skills	*Generic management knowledge and skills*
The technical knowledge and abilities appropriate to the business. The main know-how typically of the 'butcher, the baker and the candlestick maker'.	Planning, organising, managing time, negotiating, coordinating resources, solving problems (not functionally specific).
Business and strategic awareness	*Personal competencies*
Understanding the bigger picture, conceptual skills, analysis, synthesis, creativity.	Results orientation, initiative, interpersonal skills, enthusiasm, perseverance, commitment, leadership.

Source: Based on R. E. Boyatzis, *The Competent Manager – A Model for Effective Performance* (New York: Wiley, 1982).

Small business training is often the means offered for increasing small business know-how. Despite the plethora of courses sometimes offered, it is important to recognise the potential barriers that can make small businesses averse to conventional forms of training, and some of the possible counterbalancing incentives (Table 6.4).

One skill often overlooked is communication – the ability to relate to and exchange appropriate information with the people who matter to the business, including staff, suppliers, customers, funders and advisers. It has been suggested that the traditional components of pre-start training, namely finance, accounting/book-keeping, marketing/selling, etc., are secondary skills and that the core skill is communication. Communication is necessary in all aspects of small business development and is of particular relevance in building up and using an appropriate personal network of contacts.

☐ *Know-who*

The phrases, 'It's not what you know, but who you know' and 'The old boy network' reflect a sometimes popular, but essentially negative, perception of certain social networks. Yet those who have examined small firm networking are convinced of its importance for the success of enterprise.

Credibility is established through personal contact and knowledge of the skills, motivation and past performance of the individual – the bankers call this the 'track record'. Since for an embryonic business there is no trading track record, investors must look to their previous relationship with the individual, whether it be commercial or personal. Thus, for example, a previous employer may agree to be the first customer, a friend may allow use of spare office space, or a relative may be prepared to lend money with little real hope of a return in the short or even the medium term.[5]

Table 6.4 Barriers and incentives to training

Barriers	Incentives
Cost implications	*Value*
• Time is the most valuable and precious resource and time spent on training is considered to be a cost not an investment • Time training is time not working • Much training is not relevant • Much training is not effective	• Courses of real current relevance that require minimal time off the job, and have identified early benefits
Attitudes	*Funding available*
• Bad experiences of formal training, e.g. school • Failure to perceive the need and the potential benefits • A belief that the benefits will not last	• Grant assistance available to help with the cost
	Content
Lack of relevance	• Trainers with business credibility • Training itself promotes further training • Process counselling will be accepted but not expert consultancy
• No desire to improve or grow the business • Want solutions to yesterday's problems today • Not prepared to look ahead	*Promotion*
Promotion of training	• Peer business managers will be believed • Influencers will be listened to, but not 'officials' • Mail shots don't work • 'It's about increasing profits' • Through networks of contacts.
• The word 'training' is a turn-off • Suggestions of paternalism • Government initiatives are distrusted	
Apprehension	
• Too many courses on offer • Too many agencies • They may be sold something they don't need • It's an admission of defeat • Exposes oneself and one's business.	

Advice and guidance are often seen as the benefits of a network, and they may be the traditional base upon which many small firms support agencies have been built. But while they may be important characteristics of an active network they are not the only ones.[6]

Information. Entrepreneurs use their social network to signal their intentions, and to gather information about potential opportunities.

Sponsorship and Support. Family and friends will not only provide introductions into appropriate networks, but will also offer emotional and tangible support.

Credibility. Membership of the network gives added weight to the evaluation of skills. Family and friends can provide credibility in areas unfamiliar to the entrepreneur.

Control. Membership of the network, and assistance from it, requires certain standards of behaviour. Owner-managers who do not conduct their business in a way that is acceptable to the community will quickly find themselves, and their businesses, isolated.

Business. There are market networks of customers, suppliers and partners as well as production networks of subcontractors, consultants and service suppliers. In addition, there are networks of firms that may work together on projects on a basis of collaboration. This structure can provide all the components necessary for a project without the need for 'vertical integration'.

Resources. Friends and family can also be a sources of resources for a new small business, and many businesses are assisted by the informal venture capital market that they access through their networks.

These networks are complex, but relatively user-friendly and informal systems for the exchange of information. They have been described as 'creative communication in the business milieu'. They are not rigidly bounded and exclusive, and individuals often belong to more than one network. In general they facilitate the economic cooperation that is a feature present to at least some extent in all markets.

Networks involving small firms have a number of particular features. They are usually based on personal contacts, not official links, they are informal and are not openly advertised. They are flexible, being built up and maintained, specifically to suit the purposes of their members. It is often these networks that give their member entrepreneurs the potential to react fast to new developments. Having 'know-who' competency or networking skills can therefore be essential for success in dynamic environments.

□ *And The Result*

Possessing or acquiring some or all of the possible components of the pre-start stage does not however guarantee that a business will be started. The decision still has to be made actually to do it although this is often triggered by an external event. It has been suggested that the decision is essentially a choice about the balance of risk. While the chances of success increase as relevant attributes and resources are built up the costs of failure can also increase as personal financial commitments build up. It has therefore been suggested that there is a window of opportunity when the balance between benefits and costs is at the optimum, typically when people are in their thirties or early forties.

■ Start-up/Inception

The typical small business start-up is a 'new business venture; in temporary, small or unusual premises; nearly always financed from within, plus bank borrowings and with little or no long-term borrowing. Usually small in terms of employment, often with only family members involved'.[7]

Table 6.5 presents an analysis of a start-up business. The reasons for starting the business may vary, but the main values driving the firm will be those of the founder(s). The basic skills of the founder will also determine the functional emphasis and management will be by direct supervision. The main efforts will hinge around developing a commercially acceptable product or service and establishing a place for it in the marketplace.

The result will normally be one operating unit, operating in a single market with limited channels of distribution. Sources of funds will be haphazard, and will place heavy demands on the founder, his/her partner(s) and friends and relatives. With the high level of uncertainty the level of forward planning is low.[8]

Table 6.5　An analysis of a start-up business

Aspect of the business	Description
Key issues	Obtaining customers Economic production
Top management role	Direct supervision
Organisational structure	Unstructured
Product and market research	None
Systems and controls	Simple book-keeping Eyeball contact
Major sources of finance	Owner's savings Owner's friends and relatives Suppliers and leasing
Cash generation	Negative
Major investments	Premises, plant and equipment
Product/market	Single line, limited channels and market

Source: Reprinted from M. Scott and R. Bruce, 'Five Stages of Growth in Small Business', *Long Range Planning* (1987) vol. 20, no. 3, p. 48. ©1987, with kind permission from Elsevier Science Ltd, The Boulevard, Langford Lane, Kidlington, OX5 1GB, UK.

□ *Needs*

At the stage of start-up the small business can have many needs. This is one list:

Capital
To be close to the family.
Customers
Suppliers
Employees
Premises
Company formation – a business name, stationery, management
    procedures
Infrastructure
Management skills – provided externally (consultants), or internally
    (training)
Information and advice
Confidence.[9]

□ *Barriers*

As well as facing the needs of start-up businesses, which are in the main an inevitable aspect of the process in which they are engaged, such businesses can also face a number of distinct barriers:

- The resource/credibility merry-go-round. This refers to the problem of how to acquire credibility in order to get the resources necessary to prove what you can do (Figure 6.8).

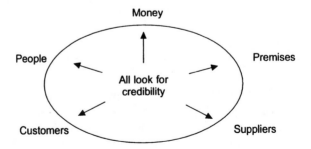

Source: S. Birley, personal communication (1987).

Figure 6.8   The resource/credibility merry-go-round

- High entry or survival barriers. The barriers to entry into business will depend on the amount of investment, technology, or labour skills required or on the availability of niches or of growing markets. Then, once started, the business may find that there may also be barriers to survival. High survival barriers occur when there is intense competition, saturated markets, excess capacity and changing technology or product quality requirements.
- The burden of government bureaucracy. Ignorance is no defence when dealing with the legal requirements of officialdom. There are penalties if forms are not returned, or are returned incorrectly, but full and proper compliance can be costly, even if only in the time it requires, and this is proportionally more costly for small businesses than for big ones.
- The business plan. Business plans are often not appropriate. When asked for a plan the new entrepreneur feels irritated, because producing it takes him or her away from the real work, frightened because he or she is not sure what it means, and confused about how to plan at all when things change daily.[10] (See also Chapter 7.)

■ Growth or Expansion

The growth or expansion of a small business is for some, its most important aspect, because it is that which produces the economic returns of significantly increased turnover, exports and jobs. Growth certainly has its problems, but is not necessarily quite as fraught or as taxing as start-up. Many of the issues of start-up can be the same for growth, such as who are the most influential people, and the risk involved in moving from a known state to an unknown one, but growth also has its particular and distinctive needs.

□ *Definitions*

Growth or expansion has been defined as characterised by the movement of the business into bigger premises, taking on more staff, significant increases of turnover, taking on a new product line or lines, buying another business, etc. The growth stage can itself also take different forms or be subdivided into different phases:

Growth Where a distinction is made between growth and expansion, the growth stage is defined as the first significant increase in sales, revenue and/or employees after start-up. The business is likely to be established, but still small. It should be profitable, but all the cash generated will be used to finance the increases in working capital needed for growth.

Expansion   Expansion has been seen as the more controlled increase in market, size, etc. after the first growth. One difference will be in the rate of increase in size. For a two-person business to take on two more employees there will be a 100 per cent increase in size and complexity, even if the absolute increase is small. For a ten-person business to take on two the absolute increase is the same, but it is only a 20 per cent change, which is much more easily absorbed.

Gazelles   Birch noted that a small proportion of all small firms create a disproportionally large portion of the net new jobs. He called these businesses 'gazelles', possibly because of their propensity for sudden leaps upwards that outpace the rest.

□ *Needs*

The needs at this stage include courage by the owner to take the risk again, capital to do it, customers, suppliers, employees, space, transport and infrastructure, and management skills and tolerance by his or her family.[11] To these can be added the possible need for a transition in the business, for ensuring product quality, for managing the risks of growth, and for continued product and/or process innovation. If growth and expansion are seen as separate stages, their needs and possible crises, in more detail, can be described.

Growth needs

- Ensuring resources
- Delegation and coordination by top management
- An entrepreneurial management style
- A functional and centralised structure
- Possibly some new product development.

Growth crises

Crises are likely to be caused by the reaction of other, larger, competitors and the demands on time and resources made by expansion into new markets or products. Liquidity can be a major problem, especially if the business over-trades and growth gets out of hand. Optimism may be high and businesses can be unaware that there are risks in growing, as well as rewards, and that care is therefore still needed, especially in controlling the flows of money.

Expansion needs

- Financing growth
- Maintaining control
- Delegation by top management
- A professional and administrative management style
- New product innovation and market research
- Moving beyond simple control and accounting systems to budgeting, monthly sales and production reports for delegated control.

Expansion crises

Good management is necessary to maintain expansion, and internal politics can be an important issue when the demands of expansion may indicate the need for professional 'middle' management, who may not have the same commitment or outlook as the owner. Top management must then adjust to a new role, and can become distant from the detail of the business, which can be a source of crisis. Another possible source of crisis is the failure to look outside the business to maintain a competitive advantage through a differentiated product, instead of just concentrating on production and selling, as may have been the case at earlier stages. Longer-term funds will be necessary, possibly through new equity partners, so that the founder loses absolute control, which can be a painful process.

□ *The Longer Term*

It is traditional to see growth/expansion as coming after the stage of start-up. However, it is probably more normal for it to come after a static period or even after a decline. Although it is often portrayed as the natural progression from start-up, growth is not actually the norm for small businesses. Similarly, it is often hoped that growth will be followed by more growth, but the trend of a businesses development is rarely a steady consistent increase in size. If there is a period of growth in a business then it is realistic to expect it to be followed by a time of consolidation before growth may be resumed. However, if the growth is mismanaged then it can be followed by decline and even termination.

□ *Backing Winners*

Recent research has indicated that it is the relatively small proportion of small businesses that do grow that are responsible for much of the long-term job creation in the small business sector. Therefore many people would like to be able to pick those businesses that are going to succeed in this way and to devote resources to them to speed up and enhance that success. This aspect of growth businesses is therefore considered further in Chapter 8.

▌ Static – Survival, Consolidation, Comfort ▌ and Maturity

A static stage in small business development may not sound very exciting, but it characterises the state of most small businesses. Once they have started their own business, electricians, plumbers, chimney sweeps and consultants, for instance, rarely grow, and many other one-person businesses are the same: static is the normal state for them.

Because, by definition, the static stage is not one that produces results in terms of more start-ups, more jobs or more other benefits, it is often ignored. Growth is a much more attractive stage in those terms, but in many cases it is in the static stage that the growth businesses of the future are to be found. Growth does not often follow immediately after start-up. But even if a static business is not a growth business of the future it can still perform a useful function. Together, static businesses provide significant employment. They also can be an essential part of the social fabric, they can provide choice and diversity, they can provide the necessary infrastructure support for other growth businesses and they can be useful role models. They should not be ignored.

Like the separation of growth and expansion it is possible to distinguish more than one type of stage during which a business, once started, does not grow. *Survival* has been the name given to that period following start-up during which a business may not grow but is nevertheless working hard to stay still, struggling to establish itself as a viable business. Once established, a business may then have a period of building resources, of *consolidation*, before the next move. Because a business shows few signs of growth for a long period, this does not mean that it will never grow. In many cases the growth of a business has been likened to that of bamboo, which can lie dormant for many years before suddenly shooting up in one season.

There is a large group of businesses whose growth is limited by their owners' ambitions or by their market niche. This stage has been labelled *comfort* or *maturity*. There may be many reasons why a business does not expand, such as the desired lifestyle of the owner-manager, the limits of his or her management capability, or even peer pressure not to get too far ahead. In general, however, this phase of development is characterised by a business which has taken up its share of the markets, has filled its capacity or which for any other managerial, political or social reason remains at the same size either in physical or economic terms.

A categorization of static businesses can now be summarised:

- *Survival.* Survival is the stage which comes after start-up. Typically, a 'surviving' business has the potential to be a viable entity, but needs to work at it. It is probably a one product or service business, but is concentrating on short-term issues of survival rather than the longer-term ones of future growth potential.

- *Consolidation.* After surviving the struggle to survive or to grow, most businesses need a period of rest to build up the reserves they need to move forward. This may not be a conscious decision or a deliberate strategy. What was happening may only be obvious in retrospect, when subsequent growth can be seen to have been built on the contacts, the credibility and the expertise accumulated at this stage. A period of consolidation following a period of survival may be one during which even businesses that do eventually grow show few indications of their potential.
- *Comfort.* For a business that does not move on to growth, 'consolidation' can easily merge into 'comfort': the stage at which a business is doing enough to survive at least into the medium term and is providing enough profits to maintain the owner's desired standard of living. There may be little incentive to do anything different.
- *Maturity.* Maturity is generally seen as coming after some growth, and indeed there may still be slow continued growth. The businesses concerned, however, are no longer in the first stages of their existence. They may be passing the peak of their products' life cycles, or they may be on the verge of moving out of the definition of a small business because their management structure is facing a transition phase in which personal contact and word of mouth have to be replaced by more formal systems to cope with a larger organisation and more decentralisation. The onset of maturity may therefore be a transition, either onwards to bigger and better things, or sideways towards an eventual decline.

☐ *The Issues*

In general, the needs at this stage are for encouragement and incentive, either to prevent decline or to encourage expansion. The motivation of the owner is critical. A firm can be adapting and changing while staying still in terms of turnover or employment, but in the long term staying static is not a good strategy. It must always be presumed that competition will change or increase and in that case not to try to grow is to invite decline.

The needs of these businesses include:

Needs of survival businesses

- Control of the business
- Generating revenues sufficient to cover all expenses
- Supervision of the work
- Both entrepreneurial and administrative management

- Simple structures, systems and controls
- Little product or market research.

Needs of mature businesses

- Expense control
- Increased productivity
- Niche marketing, especially if the industry is declining
- Watchdog top management
- Product innovation – to replace products towards the end of their life-cycle
- Formal systems for objectives and budgets
- Further long-term debt or bridging finance
- Succession planning.

The succession planning issue possibly summarises one of the key dilemmas at this stage of the business. The entrepreneur behind the business has probably built it up from its inception, and has a keen sense of achievement and ownership. Now it is being suggested that he or she considers who should succeed to the management of the business. This might be advisable because the business needs it but for the owner concerned it means contemplating giving up the thing that may be the most important part of his or her life.

☐ *The Longer Term*

As already explained, the static or survival stage can be seen as the norm for most small businesses. It is not therefore usually a stage on the way to something else, but an end in its own right. It can of course therefore be preceded by start-up, growth or decline, and be succeeded eventually by growth, decline or termination. It is important to realise that, while this stage is described as static, it may only be so in the short term, and that often in the longer term not to move forwards is to risk moving into decline, when others take the market as a result of one's passivity. Survival is not compulsory and there is a natural tendency towards regression. There is no superior power that will intervene to force all businesses to survive and so ultimately, they must progress or die.

■ Decline

Decline is another of those stages of business development sometimes ignored by government agencies or support organisations when planning assistance. However, decline need not always lead to termination if the problems of the business can be addressed. Helping in the decline stage may therefore result in more surviving businesses or jobs than would otherwise be the case.

☐ *Definition*

The business is losing its market share, profitability, management skills and the ability to sustain itself at a previous high level.

☐ *Where From and What Next*

Decline can come after any stage from start-up onwards. If nothing is done then it will in all probability be followed by termination. If it is arrested then it can be followed by a 'static' stage. If it is cured then a 'static' or even a 'growth' stage is possible.

☐ *The Issues*

The needs of the business are:

- Confidence
- Finance
- Tolerance of the family
- Customers
- Suppliers
- Employees
- New management and leadership
- A strategic review and plan for a new direction, because the decline may be as a direct result of a market or other relevant business environmental change.

■ Termination

Businesses, as Table 6.6 shows, do terminate. In any healthy, living ecosystem there are both births and deaths. Individual business deaths may be deemed regrettable, but some are to be expected in the best of economies. It would be unhealthy to have none, and the policy should therefore to be to avoid the unnecessary ones but not to prevent them completely.

The terminology of termination requires care. The word 'failure' is often ascribed to the termination of a business. A business may cease to exist or otherwise change its identification for a number of reasons. A business can terminate if it is sold and its operations are absorbed into another: the operations of the business continue but its separate legal existence disappears. It can terminate when it chooses to cease to trade because those concerned see a better opportunity elsewhere, or it can terminate if it is closed when the owner retires. These are all terminations but they are not all failures. If VAT statistics are taken as guide, a business decline and subsequent VAT deregistration may be

Table 6.6   Business survival rates: percentage of enterprises surviving after 1, 2 and 5 years

	After		
	1 Year	*2 Years*	*5 Years*
France	84	62	48
Germany	86	70	63
Ireland	91	70	57
Italy	87	66	54
Portugal	76	56	47
United Kingdom	87	62	47

Sources: France: INSEE and ANCE; Germany: IfM; Ireland: Department of Enterprise and Employment; Italy: INPS Data-Bank; Portugal: MESS-Portuguese Enterprise's Demography; United Kingdom: Department of Trade and Industry. Reproduced from *The 3rd Annual Report of the European Observatory for SMEs* (Netherlands: EIM Small Business Research and Consultancy, 1995) p. 87.

treated as a termination, and even as a failure, even if the business is actually still trading. (The implication of this for small business statistics is considered further in Chapter 7.) Some of the varieties of termination are shown in Figure 6.9.

☐ *Definition*

Termination can be any closure of a business, but the term 'closure' can be ambiguous. It might therefore be more accurate to define it as the ending of the separate legal identity of a business and its ceasing to trade as a separate entity.

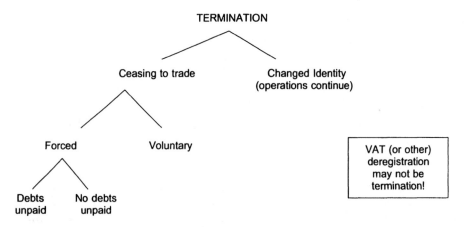

Figure 6.9   Types of business termination

☐ *The Issues*

The need is for excellent legal advice to indicate the best way to handle employees, customers, suppliers and finances.

☐ *Intervention*

It is not necessarily a waste of resources to help a business to terminate. Compared with a bad termination, too late and with many debts, a properly conducted and orderly termination can save resources. It can avoid unpaid creditors with the consequent risk to other businesses. It can save ideas for adoption elsewhere. It can help people to learn and try again instead of being put off ever running their own business again. Assistance can be in the form of advice in how to do it well.

■ The Variety of Small Business

The stage of development of the business may be the system most used for distinguishing different types of business, but there are many others that, although sometimes bewildering in their variety, can help to define the distinctions between different types of businesses and their characteristics.

■ Industry Sectors

The average size of businesses can differ widely in different industry sectors. Where the purpose of classifying a business as small or large is in relation to its place in its industry, and the influence it might have on that industry, it is important to pick a definition that recognises the average size of businesses in the relevant sector. For instance, in relation to other businesses in the same sector, a 10-person window cleaning business would be very large, while a 100-person car manufacturer would be very small. Examples from Europe show some of the ranges; thus in 1995 the average employment in a coalmining business was 924, in a railway business 996, and in a communication business 376, but in a travel agency 12, in a retail business 4 and in an estate agency two.[12]

■ Ownership and the Motivation of the Owners

Another key distinguishing feature among different small businesses can be the type of ownership of the business and the motivation of those owners. There will be a lot of difference between a business started by a sole owner who wants enough income to support his or her lifestyle and a business currently of the same size started by a group of investors with a view to maximising its future value.

☐ *Legal Structure*

In the UK a number of terms are encountered for possible forms of business structure:

Sole trader   Operating as a sole trader is the simplest form of business. An individual can start a business in this way with the minimum of fuss. In this situation, however, there is no legal distinction between the assets of the business and those of its owner. Such people are 'self-employed' and subject to income tax.

Partnership   A business can be established as a partnership of a group of individuals doing business together. However, the business does not have a separate legal identity, and each partner is jointly and severally liable for any liability incurred by the partners acting for the business. The liability of the partners in unlimited, except in the case of the less common (in the UK) 'limited partnership'.

Company   A business can be established as a company. The company then has its own separate legal existence independent of that of its owners. If it is a limited company, this limits the liability of its owners. This limit can be achieved by shares, in which case the business has shareholders who together own the business and can receive dividends from its profits in proportion to the number and type of shares they hold, or the limit can be by guarantee. A business limited by guarantee is controlled by its members, who each agree to guarantee its liabilities up to an agreed amount (often £1 each) but who cannot benefit from the profits of the business.

Cooperative   Cooperative businesses are governed by different legislation from companies. They have to be registered as cooperatives and they have the benefit of limited liability. A cooperative is owned and controlled by its members, who may for instance be a group of workers or people living in a local community, who want to use the business for the benefit of themselves and/or the community. This can be reflected in the memorandum and articles of association of the business. A workers' cooperative is a business owned and controlled by the people working in it, an approach which can lead to greater involvement and responsibility.

Community business   A form of business also sometimes encountered is the community business, which is often set up specifically to assist disadvantaged communities. This, however, is not a separate legal form of business but an intention of the owners of the business to use the returns from the business for the benefit of the community in which the business operates. Many cooperatives are community businesses.

□ *Family Business*

One distinct type of business that is often small is the family business. In the days when craft businesses and farms were almost the only businesses in existence it was almost the universal practice for them to be passed on through generations of the same family. It now widely accepted that small firms make a major contribution to many economies, but it is less well known that the majority of small businesses are family businesses.

A family business does not mean a separate form of legal structure, but instead refers to any business owned primarily by members of a family, who operate it for the present and future benefit of at least some members of that family. Family businesses therefore are ventures in which a family body exercises considerable managerial and financial influence and control on the current and future operations of a business. This can happen where, for instance, more than half the voting shares in a business are owned by one family, where a significant proportion of the senior management of the business are drawn from the same family, or where one family group is otherwise in effective control of the business.[13]

This can produce a permanent, solid family atmosphere and *esprit de corps*, which can often encourage both a closeness among staff and long-lasting relationships with customers, suppliers and other contacts. Family businesses can as a result often build a reputation for excellent service. However, they may also have their problems: family relationships and goals can be in conflict and can be superimposed on business practice, and these incompatibilities can lead to managerial difficulties.[14] There are therefore special issues that are unique to family businesses and that need to be understood by those offering advice and guidance.

Staff in family firms can have a 'sense of belonging' and strong commitment to the goals of the organisation. When the owning family are justly proud of the venture their enthusiasm and commitment can enthuse non-family staff. This sense of togetherness is a powerful asset in that it focuses the energies of all involved on customers and on the need to serve them.

This commitment can produce a flexibility in terms of working practices, working hours and remuneration. Family members do what is necessary to get a job done. There is little demarcation over duties, and many family members are reluctant to take money out of the business. Some of this flexibility rubs off on non-family members, and this allows the family firm to respond rapidly to changing technological, sociological and economic conditions. In the turbulent environment that firms face nowadays this is a considerable advantage.

Family firms are normally free from stock market pressure to produce quick results, because they are not quoted on the market and have no institutional shareholders. They can, as a result, often take a longer-term view. They are not forced to vacillate, and can pursue a consistent long-term strategy. This long view is reinforced by the permanent nature of their management teams. Permanent managers allow behavioural norms to emerge and a recognised way of doing things to develop.

Decision making in family firms is centralised, because important decisions are generally the preserve of family members. Centralisation produces quick decisions, and this can be a considerable advantage when reacting to market opportunities in a changing world.

However the pre-eminence of the controlling family, centralised decision making and long-standing management teams can result in static thinking. It can make it less likely that new ideas which are essential for long-term development will emerge, and family firms are often reluctant to use outside advisers preferring the counsel of the family when exploring business matters.

Another difficulty is the conflict that often emerges between family members, in particular fathers and their children. The father often recognises that he has to let go of the reins and develop his successor, but the business is such an important feature of his life that he fears that the 'loss' of it will damage his self-image and bring his competence into question. Such behaviour can be resented, and tension can build as a result.

Rivalry between siblings can also create difficulties. Conflict can reach such a level of seriousness that it has an impact on 'every management decision and magnifies the jockeying for power that goes on in all organisations'.[15] Where multiple family members have an interest in the business they may all expect equal treatment but, in the nature of things, this is rarely possible. Also, they may have different expectations such as short-term riches or long-term growth. As a consequence, various family members may set about gaining power and influence by means of 'internecine' warfare that is often to the detriment of the business.

Conflict is inevitable in organisations, and it must be managed, but its management presents special problems for family-run businesses. Because the conflict can be intense, and because it is transposed from the business to the personal or family arena, it is often suppressed and not resolved. Therefore open discussion and the challenge of ideas which can help progress in a changing world, are avoided. In addition, when disputes do occur, the anger and resentment that occurs is also transferred to family life, and this makes it difficult for family members to break out of a self-defeating cycle of conflict. All this can make rational business decision-making exceedingly difficult.

In family businesses there are often family concerns that override business sensibilities. Incompetent family members may be retained in post as a favour to shore up deteriorating family relationships, and promotion for otherwise eligible non-family managers may be blocked as a result. Business logic and rationale may thus take a back seat in favour of family preference. There is some evidence that this is especially likely in second-generation family businesses. Attempts to improve the business by recruiting professional managers bring other problems: such managers may find that they can never achieve the measure of recognition and control, such as promotion to the board, that their expertise and contribution merit.

Managing the transition of power and control can often be a difficulty in family businesses, especially the transition from one chief executive to another.

There is evidence that this is rarely planned in family firms, and that the transition is, as a result, frequently traumatic. This may contribute to the failure of many family businesses to survive to the third generation. This seemingly unprofessional behaviour can come about because owners:

- will not face up to their limited lifespan
- may unconsciously care little about what happens when they are gone
- may resent their successor
- may have an aversion to planning.[16]

The result of the combination of advantages is often a business that has initial staying power, but which does not last beyond the tenure of the founder. For instance, recent US data[17] suggests that:

- Only 30 per cent of family businesses reach the second generation.
- Less than two-thirds of those survive through the second generation.
- And only 13 per cent of family businesses survive through the third generation.

Family businesses are however common: a survey of 8000 of the largest businesses in the UK[18] found that over three-quarters were family-owned. They are relatively long-lived: 60 per cent of those in the survey had been established for over 30 years, compared with only 35 per cent of their non-family counterparts. And their management have longer tenure: over two-thirds of the family businesses had been under the same management for eight years, compared with only one-third of non-family businesses.

Today also it is natural for the owner of a business to want to pass it on for the future benefit of his or her own family. There are many such businesses. What is different now, however, is that the ideal model many people have of a business is one based on the larger limited-liability business run to maximise its value for the shareholders. The requirement of keeping ownership, as well as key management positions, in the family can often run counter to such a goal. This can give rise to many problems of control and of succession.

☐ *Owners' Motivations*

Another aspect of ownership that can distinguish businesses is the motivation of the owners. These have been divided into three broad categories:

Life-style   A life-style business is the description often given to a business run by an individual because it not only facilitates, but is also part of, the lifestyle that individual wants to have. Examples of lifestyle businesses are frequently to be found in art or craft businesses where the owner lives to practise that craft rather than only practising that craft in order to live.

Comfort zone   A comfort zone business is typically one that provides its owner with sufficient returns for the level of comfort he or she wants in life. Unlike in the case of the lifestyle business, the basis of the business is less important than the level of benefit it can provide in return from a reasonable amount of effort. In some places the comfort zone business has been characterised as the 'BMW Syndrome'. This is where the level of comfort desired includes the possession of recognised symbols of success. Once that level of comfort is reached, however, there is little incentive to build the business further.

Growth   The 'growth' business is the one that approaches closest to what to many is the ideal business, namely one where the owners wish to manage the business to maximise its earning potential, especially for the future.

☐ *Other Types*

A further classification often used to distinguish among categories of business is that of craft, manufacture, service, technology, or agricultural. However, while these categories are in common use, there are no fixed definitions of them. Confusion can therefore arise in their use. For instance the distinction between 'craft' and 'manufacturing' is not clear, and there would appear to be some overlap, while in mainland Europe the category 'craft business' depends more on size and ownership than on the type of handcrafted manufacturing associated with a UK craft business.

■ The Implications of Being Small

Small businesses have assumed an importance in many people's minds, largely, it would seem, because of their employment creation potential. They are classified as small by their size, whether that is measured in terms of their worth, their turnover or their employment. There are, however, many differences between the businesses in those size categories, but there are many aspects, apart from just their size, that small businesses tend to have in common and where they differ from big businesses. It is for these reasons that they often need to be treated differently.

Some aspects of small businesses that require particular insight if misunderstandings are not to occur are considered in the next chapter. It is, however, relevant to consider here some of the aspects of small businesses that make them different. These differences can be grouped under the headings of culture, influence, resource and ambition. They encompass some of the crucial differences between small and big businesses for which distinctions of size are only a proxy. They are the reason for a separate analysis and consideration of small businesses as a category distinct from big business.

■ Culture

The culture of a small business is tied in with the needs, desires and abilities of its owner. It tends to focus on independence; flexibility, both from preference and necessity; closeness to the customer and supplier; individual and personal, rather than system, control; working with networks of contractors; tolerating uncertainty; and the shorter-term view rather than the longer one.

For many people the culture of a small business epitomises enterprise. It can, however, be argued that, while starting a small business may be enterprising, running it need not be. In the case, for instance, of an inherited family business. running it may be what the person concerned has been expecting and preparing to do possibly from birth, and involves little that is new or innovatory. Nevertheless, businesses, and particularly small businesses, are frequently referred to as enterprises, which emphasises this aspect of their culture.

■ Influence

Small businesses have very little influence over, for instance, their environments or their markets. Their small size may enable them to respond more quickly to changes in those environments or markets but, unlike their bigger counterparts, they have little influence that would enable them to change them. Their job creation potential, especially when combined with groupings to promote combined lobbying, may give them some political influence, but it is unrealistic to assume that they will individually be able to able to change their markets in the ways they might wish.

As well as their final markets, the intermediate markets or distribution channels of small businesses are also beyond their control. Again, bigger businesses may be able to dictate terms to distributors, or may be able to acquire their own distribution channels through 'vertical integration'. But not the small businesses: they are at the mercy of their distributors, and also their suppliers, to a very considerable extent.

■ Resource

It is almost invariably the case that small businesses lack resources. Most of them are started, at least financially, on a shoestring and few get richer after that. Most therefore do not have easy access to the financial reserves necessary to carry them through a lean period or to utilise a sudden opportunity for expansion.

But it is not just finances of which they are short. They are usually short of management, both of management time and of management skills. As has already been mentioned there is often only one person, the owner, in a management role, and this role will embrace all aspects of managing the business. This means both that the amount of management time that can be focused on a problem is very limited and that aspects of management expertise are also likely to be missing, because the single manager is unlikely to be fully conversant with marketing, production, financial, technical, legal and human resource aspects of business.

In the business world, therefore, small may mean poor, but not always. There are examples of small businesses that do make very large profits, and others that, if not wealthy in themselves, have, by virtue of their technology, markets or other intangible assets, been very attractive propositions for prospective buyers.

■ Ambition

In terms of their behaviour, however, the biggest difference between small and big businesses is likely to be that which results from the ambition of their owners and managers. As indicated above, the larger the business is the more likely it is to be run by a professional management trying to maximise its value. The converse is that the smaller the business is the more likely it is that it will be run by an owner-manager with an aim based on personal benefits rather than on maximising business results.

■ In Conclusion

Small businesses are very diverse, and this chapter has looked at their variety by examining a number of different classifications. There is no one best way of classifying the different types of small business. Which is most appropriate in a particular circumstance will depend on what form of analysis or prescription one is engaged in.

Key points

- There is no single definition of what is a small business. Most definitions use the size of the business as the distinguishing feature, as indicated by either asset value or turnover, or, more commonly, by employment. The upper limit in employment terms can however vary from 50 to 500. It is, however, important to remember that 'small' is often used as a relative term, and what is relatively small in one industry may be relatively large in another.

- However they are defined, small businesses exhibit considerable variety. One of the commonest ways of categorising businesses has been by the 'stage' of their development, even though there are no clear boundaries between the stages. There are many models of the different stages of business development. These can help in identifying the different issues, such as needs, barriers and crises, that businesses face at different stages of their development, but they do not help in predicting what will happen to the businesses.
- Other key differences between small businesses can include the type of ownership of the business, the motivation of those owners, and the different legal forms of a small business.
- However, despite the many differences between different types, or stages, of small businesses, they do have a number of key aspects in common, and many of these aspects distinguish them from big businesses. These aspects include issues of culture, influence, resource and ambition. For many commentators it is these aspects that are the crucial difference with size, and even the description 'small' is only a convenient distinction to stand as proxy for the real differences.

CHAPTER 7

Distinctive Features of Small Business

The differences in the administrative structure of the very small and the very large firms are so great that in many ways it is hard to see that the two species are of the same genus.... We cannot define a caterpillar and then use the same definition for a butterfly.

(Dame Edith Penrose[1])

In seeking to understand how small businesses behave, it is easy to fall into one of two traps by comparing them to big businesses. Small businesses are not big businesses writ small, and concepts, theories, practice, forms of behaviour and interventions that apply to big businesses and their management will not necessarily apply on a small scale to them. Neither is every one an embryonic big business that, as a caterpillar turns into a butterfly, will eventually metamorphose to a big business. Many will always remain small.

Understanding both small businesses and their place in an economy requires therefore more than an understanding of business in general. It requires (a) an appreciation of the significant differences between small and big businesses, (b) a knowledge of specific small business issues and (c) insight into the ways of small business. This understanding is needed by those who have not had the experience of running a small business themselves, and by those who have experienced little else. The former may see the economic wood, but they may also fail to appreciate the nature of at least some of the trees of which it is composed. The latter have been accustomed to the small business milieu and therefore find it hard to see the larger picture. The difference can be especially important for those who might wish to intervene in the field of small business by offering direct or indirect support. Failure to comprehend crucial aspects of small business behaviour, constraints and issues can often be the cause of much misunderstanding. This chapter therefore looks at some of these key areas of difference between small and big businesses and some of the pitfalls that those without insight may stumble into.

■ The Nature of Small Business

■ The Distinctive Characteristics of Small Businesses

Many commentators, including Gibb,[2] have identified differences between the behaviour of small and big businesses, differences manifest in a range of characteristics. Some of these have already been indicated in Chapter 2, where the meaning of 'enterprise' was explored. Others are as follows:

☐ *An Absence of Functional Managers*

Often the management of a small business resides with one person. The advantage of this can be that an overall view of management, including production, finance and marketing, is taken instead of a conflict between the different specialities. On the other hand, knowledge of such specialised functions may not be evenly developed and in some areas may be severely lacking.

☐ *On-the-Job Learning*

Many small business owner-managers have acquired most of their business knowledge on the job. They will often have been in the job a long time and will therefore have a deep experience, but not necessarily a broad one, or an objective and informed view. The business systems employed are likely to be of their own devising, based on experience, and are unlikely to be changed unless experience also suggests it is necessary.

☐ *Investment and Resources*

Money invested in the business is often personal money, not that of impersonal investors. There can therefore be a reluctance to spend this money on anything except the bare essentials, for short-term obvious returns. More formal investment appraisal methods are not seen as being as useful as a 'feel' for what is right. Similarly, the time needed for formal 'training' or review is seen as both an unaffordable distraction from the real work of the business and as earning a return that is more theoretical than practical. Change, where it occurs, is likely to be the response to short-term need rather than the result of long-term strategy.

☐ *Discontinuities*

There are thresholds and discontinuities in a small business that do not occur in a bigger business. In a bigger business, for instance, increasing capacity by 10 per cent in a key department to cope with a 10 per cent increase in turnover may be relatively straightforward. In a small business however there may be only two people in the department, who are already fully loaded. Extra capacity is still needed, but taking on an extra person would be a 50 per cent increase and may not be justified by the likely extra return. This same is also true of getting a second machine when one is just unable to cope.

☐ *Owner's Identification With the Business*

However dedicated he or she may be, the professional manager brought in to run a business will not identify with that business to the extent many business founders do. 'The business is the ego', as Gibb points out, 'and therefore even objective criticism of the business is taken personally'. The implications of this include the fact that:

- A business 'consulting' approach, which attempts to analyse and list what is wrong with a business before suggesting corrective actions, will be rejected because it is perceived as a personal criticism. Instead, a 'counselling' approach, which seeks to help the owner himself or herself to identify some of the issues, stands a better chance of being accepted and producing change.
- Perceived social status or acceptability may be linked to business success. Indications of business problems will therefore be played down or hidden.

☐ *Values*

The values embodied in the business will be those of the owner-founder and can be revealed in the products or services supplied, growth orientation, quality standards and employee relations. Where these differ from those of advisers, the input of the latter is likely to be rejected and, indeed, small business proprietors often lack the confidence to discuss problems with professionals. For these reasons, an owner's support network is likely to be based on personal friends and contacts, rather than on the formal support network.

■ The Influences on a Small Business

A small business will be subject to many influences. It is not however always obvious what these influences will be or what will be the interplay between the different influences. The relative strengths of the influences of different groups of people are indicated in a diagram produced by Gibb to indicate the layers of small business support networks (see Figure 7.1). One implication of this is that the closer, and more personal, layers will always have a much stronger influence than the outer, and more official, layers.

The totality of influences on a small business is often not appreciated. For instance, if assistance is made available to encourage small business development, it may be designed to add a positive influence, but it is unlikely to work if it does not outweigh other existing negative influences. If friends when consulted are negative in their advice then it will be far more influential than any positive input

Source: A. Gibb, 'Towards the Building of Entrepreneurial Models of Support for Small Business', paper presented at the *11th National Small Firms Policy and Research Conference* (Cardiff, 1988) p. 14.

Figure 7.1   The layers of the small business support network

from government agencies. It can be helpful to portray the possible influences on a business as being of three types: those that may influence the business to be more competitive, those that may influence it to be less competitive, and those that may influence it to stay where it is. The latter can be the most powerful. Trying to make a business more competitive can be likened trying to move a heavy weight up hill. Gravity may tend to drag it back, friction and inertia tend to keep it where it is, and only the push applied uphill will tend to move it in the desired direction. (This analogy is pursued further in Chapter 8.)

It may also be relevant to compare the prime influences on, and sources of advice for, small businesses with those of big businesses. The most powerful influence in a small business is often the ownership. This is often one person or a small group who take an active role in the business. They are much more influential on the business than the shareholder owners of a bigger business who, because they are external and disparate, have less immediate impact. In contrast,

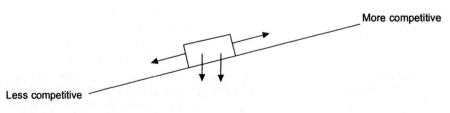

Figure 7.2   The influences on a business

however, suppliers and customers, although they are external, can have a much bigger influence on a small business than a big business. Some reasons for this are that a small business generally has less market influence in pricing or advertising than a big business, and is likely to have fewer customers and to work more closely with them. Other external influences on big businesses can include trades unions, public bodies and pressure groups. Small businesses, in contrast, are less likely to be unionised, are more likely to try to ignore regulations and are a less rewarding target for campaigns.

Inside a small firm the owner-manager is often all-powerful. While in a big business the chief executive can be very powerful, he or she still has to answer to a chairman and board, and to work with professional senior managers who often have expert knowledge relevant to their particular departments. In big businesses a unionised workforce can have the influence of their combined strength exercised through the union structure. Also, generally, in big businesses professional sources of advice are used. The small business owner-manager, in contrast, has fewer such sources of influence and will instead be more likely to listen to his or her own inclinations, to rely on his or her own experience and to seek advice, if that is needed, from a personal network of contacts. The small business owner-manager, in comparison with the manager of a larger business, often has less general professionalism but more flexibility and knowledge of his or her particular niche.[3]

■ Models of Small Business Success

There is an aspect of thinking about small business that has not been much commented upon but that nevertheless probably affects many peoples' thinking on the subject. It is the model of business success that people have in their mind when they talk about small businesses and consider how well they are doing. Such a model probably falls into one of two categories:

The Business Professionals' Model Many business professionals (which term could include business commentators, advisers and academics, as well as professional employee business managers) have as their model of the successful, or 'perfect', business: one that is achieving its highest potential in terms of growth, market share, productivity, profitability, return on capital invested or other measures of the performance of the business itself. Professionals may not be conscious that they are adopting this model, because they may fail to see that there is an alternative, but whether it is consciously adopted or not, the result is that a business is often judged by how close it comes to what a 'perfect' business might do in particular circumstances. Small businesses often score badly in such comparisons.

The Small Business Proprietors' Model   Many owner-managers of small businesses do not however have the same model as the one just described. Their main concern is whether the business is supplying the benefits they want from it. These benefits are often associated with a lifestyle and an income level to maintain it. If, as already noted, that is achieved satisfactorily then there is no need to grow the business further. Business success for them is therefore being able to reach a level of comfort ('satisficing') rather than achieving the business's maximum potential.

This difference of appreciation may be linked to the different ways in which persons making the appreciation are linked to the business concerned. Even if the 'professional' is employed as the chief executive of a business, he or she probably still sees the business simply as a business, and can compare it therefore with an ideal. It, and its success or failure, may be very important to such persons, but they can and do see those aspects of their life that are not involved with the business as being completely separate. For the small business owner, however, the business is such a crucial part of his or her life that the business and non-business parts of life are not considered separately. The business is therefore seen in terms of life as a whole and therefore subject to more than purely business considerations. The model of a 'perfect' business that the owner has is therefore one that best fits with desired personal goals and values. The stress of further business improvement may be too high a price to pay for a better business if it detracts from other aspects of life, and continuity of employment for well-known employees may be more important than increased efficiency.

The implications of having these two different models is that the professionals may see a business as under-performing in terms of its potential as a business, while the owner may see it as successful in terms of what he or she expects from it. In such cases the owners will not automatically share a professional's agenda of pursuing continued business improvement if that is of a form that is unattractive to them.[4]

That does not mean that there will not be scope for further improvement, but it will have to be improvement that also increases the returns desired by the owner from the business. Professionals advising small businesses will be puzzled and ineffective unless they understand this. There is room for their assistance, but they must look at both the negative impact of business improvement on the owner's requirements as well as the positive impact, and ensure that the positive outweighs the negative. The 'professional' business model assumes that growth in a business is almost always automatically positive in its effect: the owner's model may not share that assumption. This means that in the extreme case, which is not uncommon, it may be in the owner's perceived best interests to close the business completely, and that obviously doesn't lead to the business performing better. Such a closure is not a failure, but would be counted as such on the 'professional' model.

One area where this lack of appreciation of two models is very significant is in business accounting. Traditional accounting focuses on the money and therefore has a key place in businesses, because a lack of money is the ultimate reason for business failure. It therefore needs to be watched closely, and traditional accounting provides the methods and disciplines for doing this. However, traditional accounting is often linked to business audits and then to reporting on business success or failure. Here the traditional approach is based on the 'business professionals' model or at least on a similar way of thinking. It appraises a business in terms of its financial or other tangible returns and not on any other requirements a business owner may have. Provided that is realised and accepted by the auditors no problems should emerge. However, its very universality of usage means that the traditional method is usually taken as the whole picture, which leaves many business owners feeling that they may be perceived as having failed but not understanding why.

If this 'two model' concept is correct then it suggests that relatively low productivity in small businesses may sometimes be due, not to a failure of management, but to a different vision of management and of what management should be trying to achieve. The 'may' is because there is undoubtedly a considerable amount of management failure in small business, and by no means all of it is due just to differing agendas by the various stakeholders. It may however be hard initially to distinguish between satisficing and a mere lack of competence.

■ Models of Business Failure

Just as caution is needed in evaluating the success of a small business, care must also be taken when considering so-called small business failures. Again the problem is one of interpretation and of a propensity to assume that a business closure and a business failure are the same thing.

Most people studying small business will at some time have heard of statements such as 'one in three small firms go out of business during the first twelve months' or 'three out of five new businesses cease to trade within three to five years of starting'. Although statistics, such as those quoted in Table 6.6, indicate that such statements are misleading, some claims go further and say that 'one small business in three fails in the first three years' or that 'three fifths of these businesses fail within three to five years'. Those are different things and appear to be quite wrong. The reason that the two sets of statements are different is that there is a difference between business closure and business failure.

Just as there are different models of what constitutes the success of a business, so too there are different models of what constitutes its failure. It may seem that the closure, or termination, of a business and it ceasing to exist as a trading entity is prima facie evidence that the business has failed, but that assumption presupposes that the purpose of the business could only be achieved if it continued to exist. That would be the case if the purpose of the business was to maximise the returns from its activities but would not necessarily be so if its owner had other aims in mind for it. If for instance a business is started to provide an income for someone until a pre-planned retirement, and if it does so and is then closed when that retirement time arrives, then the business will both have succeeded in its purpose and been closed. Alternatively, if a business is started as an investment and is then sold for a profit, but the new owner transfers the process to an existing business and closes down the bought business, then again the business has achieved its purpose and been closed.

This issue was considered in Chapter 6. It is, however, relevant to point out here that instances of business closure are often wrongly described as business failure. Statistics on business failure should therefore be treated warily. The corollary to this is that there are some businesses that do fail, as least in terms of failing to meet their founders-owners' objectives for them, but that don't close. Such a business may still be kept in existence, for instance, either for possible revival in the future, or because it continues to fulfil at least some needs, or to deliver at least some benefit to its owner. The benefit may only be a sop to the owner's pride, but it may be enough to prevent the termination of the business's existence. In such cases, business failure may not lead automatically to business closure.

▌ Control, Management and Organisation in Small Businesses

☐ *Top Down*

In a small business the dominant position of the entrepreneur can create a person-centred culture. Consequently the strategy, or absence of one, of the business will correspond to that of the entrepreneur. This top-down approach can be attractive in a stable environment, if the entrepreneur articulates a vision that motivates others. Increasingly, however, even in small businesses, it is intelligent employees, more than the entrepreneur, who are in touch with the latest technological, economic and sociological developments. Considerable decision making discretion, even at the strategic level, may have to be delegated to these individuals, but entrepreneurs are notoriously reluctant to share their power. In a world of discontinuous change that is a drawback.[5]

☐ *Decision Making*

In general, the decision making process in small businesses will be less formal and more personalised than in larger ventures. In a rational approach objectives are set, alternatives are investigated and economic evaluations are made of alternatives. In a large business the distance from top to bottom, and the consequent number of layers and communication steps, may mean that the message, and the rationale behind, it can be distorted. In small businesses the omnipresence of the owners can mean that everyone in the business can hear a clear articulation of the goals and objectives. However, the smallness of the business, and the lack of managerial skills of its owner, can also mean that goals are not articulated at all. Clear objectives facilitate rationality, but rational economic decisions depend on having access to often large amounts of information and the employment of sophisticated quantitative techniques to make sense of it. The lack of resource in small businesses, and their heavy reliance on information gleaned from personal contacts, are unlikely to encourage rational evaluations of alternatives. The information available to decision makers in small businesses will be even more inaccurate, incomplete and time-bounded than in other organisations.[6]

□ *Organisational Structures*

Most work in large organisations is highly specialised, and much of the brain-work is removed from operational tasks. However, an extensive division of tasks, especially at management level, only makes sense when there is a large volume of work; it is no use employing experts if they are underemployed. By definition, a small business does not have a large volume of output and work must therefore be done by generalists. Furthermore, organisations tend to perpetuate the fruits of their learning and standardise regularly recurring activities; however, this is sensible only when environmental conditions are stable. In the turbulent environment so characteristic of the small business, change is the order of the day and problem-solving is a higher requirement of organisations than efficiency.[7] As a result of these factors, small firms tend to have simple, flexible, non-differentiated structures and flexible work practices, to possess general-purpose rather than specialised machines and to exhibit few of the features so characteristic of bureaucracies. The general nature of employee skills and flexible production capabilities means that much more of the creative aspects of production can be easily delegated to operators. Faced with an order from a customer, operators and their managers are more likely to plan operations jointly.

□ *Control*

If the all-pervasive control mechanisms of large organisations are absent, how do managers in small businesses exercise control? Decision making can be considered to take place at three levels: strategic, management and operational. In the bigger business these will each happen at different levels of the organisation and involve different people. In small businesses they are, as often as not, all done by the same person with no formal or recognised boundaries or hierarchical split between them. There is therefore a lack of clarity about the type of decision being taken, with little distinction in thought between strategic and tactical decisions. Once a decision is taken, control through standardisation, performance measurement and bureaucratic structures are often absent in small businesses. Instead the presence of the owners, or their representatives, will mean that control is exercised by direct supervision. These individuals are never far away, and the numerous work-related discussions that take place will confirm the position of managers in an overseeing role. This does however often lead to much speedier decision making and shorter reaction times, which in turn can mean an improved competitive edge.[8]

Differences Among Small Businesses

We have now considered some of the ways in which small businesses can differ from bigger businesses. But just as it is wrong to assume that small businesses will behave and respond like big businesses, it is also wrong to assume that all small businesses will behave and respond identically. It can be helpful to understand the varieties of small business, some of which are considered in this section.

■ Family Businesses

Family businesses are significant because there are so many of them and it is therefore important to recognise those unique aspects that arise with regard to the involvement of family members in their ownership, management and staffing. These aspects have however already been considered in Chapter 6 and do not therefore need to be repeated here.

■ Community Businesses and Cooperatives

Community businesses and cooperatives also have been mentioned earlier, in Chapters 4 and 6. Community businesses are often cooperatives, and vice versa, but need not be so. The essence of a community business is that the benefits accruing from it, such as employment, profits and the development of skills, should go to the community in which it was formed. Profits, for instance, are not distributed to shareholders but are recycled for community benefit. As was indicated in Chapter 6 a cooperative is a particular form of business that is often owned by those who are employed by it when it is sometimes referred to as a workers' cooperative. In some countries, such as Spain and Portugal, there are good examples of the success of cooperatives, and in Ireland there are some very successful producer cooperatives, especially in farming, dairying and other food industries.

In many cases in the UK, cooperatives were formed by earlier owners, who gave the business, or sold it cheaply, to its employees, often for reasons of Quaker values. Other, later foundations have been the result of attempts to provide employment for or by unemployed or otherwise economically disadvantaged groups, or have been formed by professionals as an alternative to partnerships, or else have been 'new wave' businesses started by groups of people with a sense of community. In the UK there are however very few of them – only about 1500 in 1991, employing about 10 000 people – and their potential there can best be described as still rather unproven.

Both cooperatives and community businesses are frequently, but not always, small businesses. They can suffer from particular problems, which arise from the attempt to combine market and social issues. Restrictions on profit distribution can make it hard to raise capital, because the returns may not be sufficient to attract external investors. Reactive reasons for foundation can result in defensive, rather than aggressive, business strategies and there can be an ambivalence about active competition in the market place. Management can be strong, where it is organised on private sector lines, but sometimes these businesses can be adversely influenced by ill-conceived attempts to develop new structures for work organisation and new approaches to the management function. In dealing with community businesses and cooperatives it can therefore help if these issues are understood.

■ Understanding Specific Small Businesses Issues

■ The Transition Out of Employment

The pre-start-up stage of small business development has been described in Chapter 6, and it has its own particular issues to understand. Despite the emphasis that has been put on the benefits of small business, the predictions of increasing numbers of people who will not have the option of lifetime employment, and the varieties of help available to ease the business start-up process, moving from employment to self-employment can be traumatic. Business planning (see below) can help to indicate the physical and financial provisions necessary to establish a business, but not the mental changes necessary.

Especially if the change is an enforced one, for instance when it is occasioned by redundancy, the range of mental adjustments that have to be made can be considerable. One study[9] identified six phases in the process of leaving employment:

Immobilisation	The change in status shocks and overwhelms to the extent that understanding, reasoning and planning are not possible
Minimising Change	The first reaction to change is to try to minimise it and to try to carry on as if it hadn't happened
Depression	When the reality of change can no longer be avoided depression sets in, change has happened, but is neither desired nor understood
Acceptance	Eventually however the reality of change is accepted, the turning-point has been reached

Testing	Previous attitudes and assumptions are released, new concepts, methods and ways of coping are tested
Meaning	As this progresses, stereotypes are abandoned, new possibilities emerge and success can be possible in the search for a new meaning.

If the process of leaving employment is continued into starting one's own business, then other changes have to be made. Lessem[10] suggests that they include:

Employee to employer	• You become the giver, not just a receiver • You set the standards, not just adhere to them • You accept responsibility for other people's jobs • Money becomes important
Salary to profit	• You need to spend before you receive • Income becomes uncertain • Your family cannot be kept at arm's length
Evaluator to decision-maker	• You need to consider the options, evaluate them, and then make tough choices
Specialist to generalist	• You need to call on technical, marketing, financial, administrative, people and management skills, and possibly all of them from yourself.

■ Business Planning

Before launching any new venture, the first step is to draw up a business plan.

(Introduction to a business factsheet on business plans)

Business plans are another area in which the appropriate approach for larger businesses is not necessarily also appropriate for small ones. The orthodox view that a business plan is essential for anyone starting a small business is, to some people, so obvious that it does not need to be proved. Others however believe that, at least for some businesses, a formal written business plan in the recommended format would be a waste of time. To understand each point of view it is necessary to look more closely into the limitations of plans and what benefits business planning and plans can offer.

I only did it for the bank, and a year later it was obvious that the bank had not looked at it.

(A successful businessman describing his first business plan)

I had to present a business plan for my grant application and now, actually, I find it very useful. At the end of each week, if the sales are above the projected levels, I get a lot of comfort because it means that the business is actually succeeding. If I didn't have that reassurance I would have a lot of sleepless nights worrying whether the business was a good idea.

(Owner of a newly opened small shop)

Owing, at least in part, to the way it has been presented, many of the people starting a business often see the business plan primarily as an obstacle – one that they have to address somehow, because it seems to be a compulsory part of the process. Professional advisers have told them that they should do it and may have indicated that its completion is a precondition for further help. They may have been provided with some guidance on how to do it and given examples of suggested layouts. They may not, however, have been persuaded that it is anything but an unnecessary chore. They don't see it as a helpful tool (some would say the most helpful tool) for the venture they are about to undertake. This is especially hard to appreciate if all a potential funder appears to require in a plan is financial projections (cash flow, profit and loss, and balance sheet) and a CV, when it is the assumptions underlying the projected figures that really matter.

Therefore, for the person starting a small business, the basic question to be answered in relation to the business plans is not actually how to do it, but why. What use really is a business plan to a small business? Only when this is understood may the question of 'how' be relevant.

If the question 'why' is honestly addressed, it will appear that there are some new business starts for which a formal written business plan may not actually be essential. To some advisers that is heresy, which may be why business plans can get a bad reputation. If the assumption is made that they are essential then there is a temptation to assume that others share this view, and so the reason for it does not have to be explained. Advisers then address the question of how to do it, while those being advised still do not see why. If there is no good reason why then the result is unlikely to be helpful. This is compounded when it is the possession of a business plan, rather than the process of its preparation, which is seen to be the key.

It is generally accepted that there are two ways in which the preparation of a good business plan can be of very real and direct help to a new business.

☐ *'Selling' the Business*

The simplest application of the business plan to understand may be its role in 'selling' the business, i.e. putting across its merits. Potential funders of the business often need to be persuaded of its worth. A business gets financial support because the providers of the assistance think that they will themselves benefit from providing that support. Banks seek to get paid for an overdraft or loan (interest); grant givers seek a contribution to the achievement of their aims (often improvements in the economy). They don't have to help a business. It is like a supplier–customer relationship: both have to benefit for it to work. In this case, however, the funds have to be provided some time before the benefits can be delivered, and the funders have to be able to trust the recipient to do that. In such circumstances, the business plan can be an essential tool for persuading funders that if they provide the funds then the business will be able to deliver the benefits and will survive long enough to do so.

The business plan is in effect the sales document for the business, and an understanding of the benefits the funders seek can be helpful in its preparation, for the following reasons:

- Government agencies want a lasting contribution to the economy, by means such as increased business and exports and more jobs. They may use terms such as 'viability', 'additionality' and 'admissibility' – so that is what the plan or sales document has to convey.
- Banks want interest on their capital, and eventually their capital back, so they will want to see how the business will be able to afford this.
- Venture capitalists want to see that their investment in the business will increase in value and can ultimately be realised.

☐ *Managing the Venture*

The plan is nothing: planning is everything.

(Napoleon)

The more important use of the business plan, or rather of the process of preparing it, is that it can help the business owner to see that all relevant aspects of the potential business are addressed and allowed for. Further, the subsequent monitoring of events against the projections can show where action is needed, if any, to keep the business on course. Can someone, in a new business, in a venture and in a field that is to some extent new to them, allow for everything without thinking it through, and probably putting it on paper?. Are they prepared to invest their savings in the business without analysing the risk? Can they do that without going through the analysis needed for a plan? The answer to these questions may be yes, but they may need to think about it. The process of producing the plan can assist in focusing strategic thinking; and the plan, when completed, can provide a benchmark against which to measure subsequent performance.

☐ *When a Business Plan Does Not Help*

From the above it will appear that if someone starting a business does not need to raise funds, and understands what he or she is about to do, and the process of doing it, then a written business plan may not be needed. That at least is the view of some small business commentators, although it is a controversial one. They believe that strategy is often in the head of the small business owner, and he or she may see no need to write it down. All that is required is that the person starting a business has some idea of the goal and the route to be taken to it. In these circumstances, asking an aspiring entrepreneur for a formal business plan can actually be detrimental to the business. In deference to the apparent expertise, and therefore presumed superior knowledge, of the person making the request for the plan, the emerging entrepreneur may try to produce one in line with a prescribed format. If he or she does not understand what a business plan means, or the logic behind the format, then the plan may be a bad one and the time wasted on it may be considerable.

☐ *Demystifying the Business Plan*

> *Whereas anyone can make a plan it takes something quite out of the ordinary to carry it out.*
>
> **(General Sir Frederick Morgan)**

It may help to understand what a plan is and what it is not:

> *What a plan is* Planning is an essential part of the process of getting positive results. It is the working out of how those results can best be obtained. It is a means of communicating your thoughts on this to others.
>
> *What plan is not* A plan is not holy or magical, it is not a forecast, a means in itself, a pious hope or fixed and absolute.

☐ *Professional Help – A Word of Caution*

Why don't businesses get someone else to prepare plans for them? Others can help, but they should not do it all, unless the sole reason is to get a grant. Getting someone else to prepare it all will not give the business an insight into the issues to watch and an understanding it of what will make the business work best. Apart from possibly securing a grant or a loan, a plan someone else prepares without the owner-manager and his or her involvement will at best probably give the business nothing and could actually do worse. Generally, the process of preparing the plan is much more valuable than the plan itself. What, however, if all the business wants is a grant or a loan? The business should invest the minimum of resources required to produce a plan with acceptable wording.

7.1   The failed plan

Sue and Mary were two partners who started a business with financial backing from their parents, who put up their houses as security. Because they were too busy setting up the business, an adviser prepared most of their business plan for them, including the financial projections. The business looked attractive and the bank supported them. Probably because of their personal appeal and enthusiasm they even won a small business start-up award. Unfortunately, however, the partners had never understood cash flow forecasts and the adviser's business plan only served to disguise this. Almost inevitably they lost control of their cash flow, and the business collapsed. The parents of one of them lost their house as a result.

☐ *Summary*

Everyone plans in some way or other, but not always on paper. Properly used, a business plan is a help, not an obstacle. A lot of nonsense has been talked about it and it has in some cases been promoted as the answer to almost every business ill. A formal written plan is not the essential starting point of every successful business but there have nevertheless been many businesses that suffered because they were not planned properly, and plans are often essential for securing the support of others.

■ Small Business Finance

To some extent small business financing issues vary from country to country. In many former communist countries in Central and Eastern Europe, the banking system recently has been very undeveloped and unreliable and, especially when this is combined with the need to charge very high interest rates in times

Table 7.1   Debt structure by country (percentage of total borrowings)

	Britain	France	Germany	Italy	Spain	Overall
Overdraft	42	23	17	32	14	29
Short-term loans (under 2 years)	9	18	20	20	45	20
Medium-term loans (2 to 5 years)	13	32	20	15	19	18
Long-term loans (over 5 years)	19	11	36	19	20	21
Leasing and hire purchase	17	14	7	13	3	12
Total	100	100	100	100	100	100

Source: P. Burns and O. Whitehouse, *Financing Enterprise in Europe 2* (Milton Keynes: 3i Enterprise Centre, 1995).

of high inflation, the result has been that businesses there rarely use bank financing. Even in Western Europe the use of bank financing varies from country to country. This is shown by a recent survey that produced the results shown in Table 7.1.

In many countries there are claims that small businesses are particularly disadvantaged, because finding appropriate sources of funding for them is harder than it is elsewhere. In almost every country there are claims of disadvantage because finding funding is harder for small businesses than it is for bigger ones. There is no doubt that the difficulty of financing small businesses is one of the most frequently heard complaints. The reasons why there is this difficulty include the following:

- *Small businesses are not a good risk*. Suppliers of business finance, when they exist, want something in return for their money. Usually this is a financial return, either interest or dividends, plus some way eventually of getting the initial investment back. If the finance sought is a development grant then returning it may not be an issue, but there will nevertheless still be an expectation that some benefits will be delivered, such as job creation or other economic benefits. In all cases, if the money is to be provided in advance of the returns, which is inevitably the case, then there needs to be some indication that the return will come, and that the businesses will survive to deliver it. Although the often quoted very high failure rates for small businesses are not always what they seem to be (see earlier in this chapter), a large proportion of small businesses do fail soon after start-up. Small businesses are therefore more vulnerable than larger ones, and will need to provide potential investors with some evidence that in their particular case they will not fail.

- *New small businesses do not have a track record.* It is said that business financiers generally assess a business on three aspects: the management, the management and the management. For a new business with no trading history, and with untried management, it is very difficult to provide satisfactory evidence that they will not only survive but will also do well enough to provide investors with the returns they seek.
- *It is not cost-effective to provide small amounts of money.* Any commercial source of funds will want to check the business, its backers and its proposals before investing. This is sometimes known as 'due diligence'. The cost of these checks will have to be recouped from any eventual income from the investments made. It is therefore not cost-effective to check requests for small amount of money, because the cost of checking will not be significantly lower than for larger amounts yet there will be less interest out of which to recoup it. (However some steps can be taken to reduce the costs of small amounts of assistance. An example in the USA is the Wells Fargo Bank, which has stopped monitoring many of the small businesses to which it has advanced loans because the cost of monitoring was more than the bad debts it incurred.)
- *Small businesses can be equity averse.* There is evidence that many owners of small businesses can be averse to sharing the equity, and therefore the ownership, of the businesses with anyone else. Investors, however, often like to take some equity because it gives them some control over their investments.
- *Grants produce dependency.* Because of their potential contribution to economic development, grants are sometimes considered to assist small business development and in particular to fill the so-called funding gaps that are perceived. Without care in their use, however, grants can easily freeze out whatever other sources of funding there are and can build a culture of dependency on free money.

The sources of finance that are generally used by small businesses, especially when they are very small and are in the early stages of development, are the owners' own savings or the resources of kind family and friends. The result is that the typical pattern of small business funding can be as depicted in Figure 7.3, which is based on American experience.

■ Small business growth

The growth patterns of small businesses differ from those of big ones. Small size means growth is more likely to be incremental than steady, because taking on an extra unit of capacity is a much more significant increase. Not all small businesses grow, and even for those that do, growth can be slow. It has been

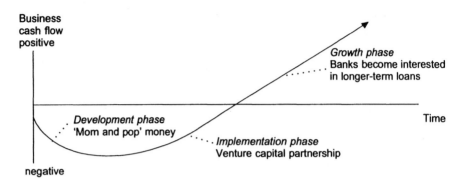

Source: Based on personal contacts relaying US experience.

Figure 7.3   Early stage small business finance

pointed out that 'seven lean years' between start-up and growth is not at all unusual. Despite this, however, small business growth is the subject of considerable interest because, by definition, it is those small firms that do grow that create the employment that many want to see. It is because of this interest that the next chapter has been devoted specifically to growth issues.

■ Small business support networks

Small businesses are inherently suspicious of others who seem to want to interfere in their businesses, including those who may be doing it for the best of motives. Government small business advice centres are for instance under suspicion in case anything said to them might find its way to other arms of government such as the tax and regulatory authorities. This means that government support initiatives have to find ways of overcoming such reservations if they are to be effective. Support organisations run by businesses are more likely to win clients' confidences. In the England the Business Links system has therefore been established, supported by Personal Business Advisers. (See Chapter 12 for more on specific support interventions.)

■ Small Business and Social Engineering

Small businesses are seen as having the potential, through their existence, to address issues of disadvantage, such as unemployment or underemployment and a lack of community leadership and management development. Small businesses are not however primarily about addressing social problems, but nevertheless this potential is an important dimension for some interested parties, and social engineering and targeting social need can provide the justification for such interventions as the provision of grants. This can lead to a confusion in objectives between funders and business owners, unless the basis for the relationship is clear from the start. In the context of social issues it is also sometimes relevant to recognise that small business is much more compatible with the black economy than big business. A thriving black economy can be prima facie evidence for the existence at least of elements of an enterprise economy. Moves to legalise unofficial small business can therefore help to reduce the negative effects of illegal trading (see also Chapter 10).

■ Small Business Statistics

There has been considerable interest in recent years in small business statistics, largely because of the work of Birch and others in highlighting the contribution small businesses make to employment and to economic development. Two questions in particular have been raised: first, what is the size of the overall contribution of small businesses to job creation, and second, does the major part of this contribution come from all small businesses or from only a few of them? The questions are very relevant to the targeting of government intervention to promote employment, but the answers are not always clear. The first is about the validity of Birch's work and its application to other countries such as the UK and the second is about which small businesses create most jobs. Exploring issues such as these highlights a number of problems in small business statistics, which may require some insight if they are to be interpreted properly.

■ The Validity of Birch

Birch first indicated in 1979 the significant role that small businesses play in the creation of employment. His original work concluded that 81.5 per cent of all net new jobs formed in the USA between 1969 and 1976 were formed by firms with fewer than a hundred employees. Armington and Odle, on the other hand, subsequently looked at job creation results for 1978–80 using a database specially created by the US Small Business Administration (SBA) and found that less than 40 per cent of net new jobs were created by businesses with fewer than a hundred employees. They had no explanation for the difference from Birch's figures, but speculated that Birch may have made errors. Subsequently, Armington and Odle have been cited as experts who found Birch to be in error, but, according to Kirchhoff, what is less commented on is that their subsequent research validated Birch and showed that percentages calculated in their way were cyclical.[11]

Sixteen years after Birch, Kirchhoff stated that, 'it seems safe to say that, on average, firms with less than 100 employees create the majority of net new jobs in the US economy.'[12] Others however still disagree. Davis, Haltiwanger and Schuh, in their book *Job Creation and Destruction* based on the Longitudinal Research Database constructed by the US Census Bureau, state that they 'found no strong, systematic relationship between employer size and net job growth rates'.[13] There is therefore no single agreed verdict on the validity of Birch, who was in any case only looking at the situation in the USA. Nevertheless, right or not, his work was, to a very large extent, the trigger for much current interest in small businesses.

Subsequent careful work in both improving and examining the SBA's database appears to have shown that fluctuations in the economy of the USA reveal themselves mainly through job changes in larger firms and that small businesses are consistent net creators of jobs. Taking the period 1976–88 as a whole, it is now estimated that businesses with fewer than twenty employees provided 19.4 per cent of total employment, but about 37 per cent of net new jobs. In the UK a similar analysis has been carried out with broadly similar results. One analysis indicated 'that during the 1987–9 period, 54 per cent of the increase in employment was in firms with fewer than 20 workers'.[14] In the UK, however, all components of employment change are of lower magnitude than in the USA, and job change in the latter is more strongly influenced by births and deaths, especially of large businesses, whereas in the UK job change 'is more influenced by expansions and contractions'.[15] Nevertheless in both countries there are arguments that small businesses do make a disproportionally large contribution to net job creation.

■ Which Small Businesses Create Jobs?

If small businesses create significant proportions of net new jobs then governments and others trying to increase employment will be particularly interested in them. However, there are very many small businesses, and support would be spread thinly if it went to all of them. Indications that within the small business population it is a relatively small proportion of each year's cohort of businesses that create a disproportionate share of the jobs over time have had a particular appeal. In the UK Storey has frequently asserted that 'out of every 100 small firms, the fastest growing four firms will create 50 per cent of the jobs in the group over a decade'.[16] The implication of this was that, if support could be focused on those four businesses, or on the few businesses that had the potential for such growth, it would be applied much more effectively than if all 100 businesses were to be supported. These high-growth businesses are the sort of businesses that Birch called 'gazelles'.

Storey's statement needs to be examined with some care, however. He himself points out that the data it is based on are rather old, but he does indicate that other data, in particular from Northern Ireland, produce fairly close results. He also acknowledges that the data refer only to manufacturing businesses and then only to new ones.

There is also another issue. Despite the way it is sometimes interpreted, Storey's statement does not mean that 4 per cent of small businesses create

50 per cent of the jobs. What Storey says is that if 100 businesses are started in year t, in the year $t + 10$ only 40 of those businesses may have survived and just 4 of those surviving businesses will between them employ as many people as are employed by all the other survivors put together. However, that also means that half of the employment in the survivors will not be in those four businesses, and nor will the employment during the intervening 10 years in the 60 businesses that did not survive to the end of the period. Storey's own table[17] indicates that all of the 4 high-growth businesses at the end of 10 years employ more than 25 people (one × 25 to 49, two × 50 to 99, and one × over 100), yet he also indicates that businesses with fewer than 20 employees created 'between 78 per cent (1985–7) and 85 per cent of total new employment' from small businesses.[18] It is very hard to compare these figures directly with the 10-year cohort figures and to say how many of them are due to the early stages of growth of the 4 per cent high-growth businesses. For instance in any one year there will be the following:

Jobs in Storey's 4 per cent of the businesses which started ten years earlier

---

plus

An equal number of jobs in the other surviving businesses which started 10 years earlier

---

plus

Jobs in businesses which started fewer than 10 years earlier (not all of which will survive the 10 years but are nevertheless employing people in the interim)

---

plus

Jobs in businesses started more that 10 years ago (some of which will be the 4 per cent businesses from the earlier cohorts but some of which will also be the other businesses which are nevertheless growing).

Without comparable figures for all these groups, comparisons cannot be made. It would be expected from a Pareto analysis that a relatively small proportion of small businesses that grow significantly would have a disproportionate share of the total employment over time. Nevertheless, the major part of the employment in small businesses appears to come from the other small businesses employing fewer than 20 people, not from the fastest-growing 4 per cent.

■ Dynamic versus Static Analysis

One of the reasons why Birch's original findings were surprising was that they were contrary to previous research and thinking on job creation. They were also based on a dynamic analysis, while the previous research was carried out using static analysis. Such static analysis is carried out using classified data in the form published by government statistics agencies. Such publications will, for instance, list the number of businesses in given size ranges and the number of jobs in them at the end of each period. However, for a given business size range, the difference between the number of jobs at the end of one period and the number at the end of the previous period does not give the number of jobs created in that period by businesses in that size range. The reason why can be illustrated by considering a business employing 70 people which over a period grows by 50 per cent and therefore at the end employs 105 people. At the beginning it would have been classified in the 1 to 100 employee size range, but at the end it is in the 100-plus size range. The effect is thus to reduce by 70 the number of jobs in businesses in the 1 to 100 size range, and increase by 105 the number of jobs in businesses in the higher size range. The static statistics will therefore show a reduction of jobs in businesses in the lower size range and an increase in the higher size range. The reality however is that the net increase came from a business that was in the lower size range. In the reverse situation, however, the shrinkage of a business initially in a higher size range will appear at the end of the period as a reduction in that size range, because *either* the business will still be in the size range but with fewer jobs *or* it will have left the size range and all its jobs will appear to have gone. A lower size range will then correspondingly appear to have grown. Static analysis assumes implicitly that the net inter-class movement of businesses is negligible, which may not be the case.

■ Cohort Analysis

Cohort, or dynamic, analysis, in which a class of subjects is tracked as it changes over time, will avoid the problem of static research analysis. It will also reveal other interesting features of growth. Dynamic analysis of US small businesses has, for instance, indicated that survival rates of businesses improve exponentially with, for a group founded at the same time, a smaller proportion of the original number terminating in each successive year. It has also shown that less than half of the surviving businesses show any growth in the first six years, but that between six and eight years of age the number of businesses that show growth leaps increases significantly: a result that confirms suggestions of the 'seven lean years' of business development and indicates that observing business survival and growth over a lesser period may be misleading. In taking only new business starts and looking at their employment after 10 years, Storey may therefore be missing from his 'high-growth' business those businesses that do not start to grow until after seven years or so.

■ Summary

It would appear that there is now clear evidence that small businesses do create a disproportionate amount of new employment. Different researchers vary in their estimates of how much, and there appear to be variations over time and between different countries. There is however some confusion on whether this is mainly due only to a small proportion of that small business population. Some figures seem to indicate that it is, but overall it would appear that most of those jobs come from the very small businesses in the smallest size ranges and not from Birch's 'gazelles'.

■ In Conclusion

Without insight into what is happening, objective observation, it has been suggested, might lead us to conclude that revision causes exams. Without some understanding of the way small businesses behave, and of the factors that influence them, the actions they take may be misunderstood and the wrong conclusions may be drawn about the way they will respond to a stimulus. People who work with small businesses generally do so to achieve a change, either in individual businesses or in groups of them. It is therefore important that they treat them as small businesses, and recognise that they will behave in ways that will not only differ from large businesses but will also differ from one small business to another. Assuming that all small businesses are homogeneous and that they will react in the same way as big businesses is a recipe for failure.

Key points

- Small businesses are not big businesses writ small, and concepts, theories and practices that apply to big businesses will not necessarily apply on a small scale to small ones. Neither are they all embryonic big businesses that, as caterpillars turn into butterflies, will eventually metamorphose into big businesses. Many of them will always remain small. Understanding small businesses therefore requires not only an understanding of businesses in general but also an insight into the ways of small ones.

- The characteristics of small businesses that differ from those of big businesses include limited investment and resources, little functional management, on-the-job learning and the owner's identification with the business. The implications of the latter include the necessity for a business 'counselling' approach rather than a 'consulting' one, and the perception that social status or acceptability may be linked to the success of the business. Also, the values embodied in the business will be those of the owner-founder. Small businesses do however, have many benefits such as meeting many of their owners' needs and the ability to survive market changes by rapidly responding to new customer requirements.

- It is not however always obvious who or what will influence a small business or what the interplay will be between different influences. Often at an early stage close families and friends can have more influence than professional business advisers. As well as positive and negative influences on a business there will also be influences that encourage a business not to change. A positive influence may therefore have no effect if there is a stronger contrary influence.

- In considering small business success there are two main models. Many business 'professionals' have as their model of business success one that involves the business achieving its highest potential. On the other hand, many owners of small businesses have as their main concern whether the business is supplying the benefits they want from it such as a lifestyle and an adequate income level. Care must also be taken when considering so-called small business failures. Not all business terminations are necessarily due to business failure, nor do all businesses that in reality have failed necessarily close, yet the statistics sometimes presented do not recognise this.

- Just as it is wrong to assume that small businesses will behave and respond like big businesses, it is also very wrong to assume that all small businesses will behave and respond identically. Small businesses in different industry sectors have their own particular characteristics, as also do businesses of different ages and different sizes and family, and cooperative and community businesses.

- Other particular small business issues include the problems of the transition by an individual out of employment into self-employment; the difference between the view that a business plan is essential for starting a successful small business and the reality that many businesses do start without formal plans; the problems of small business finance; small business growth and small businesses and social engineering.

- A further potential minefield is the area of small business statistics, where again insight may be needed if they are to be interpreted properly. The original work of Birch, which indicated the job creation benefit of small business, has been challenged but has subsequently been found to be largely correct in both the US and the UK. This has highlighted problems in the completeness of the data, the different relative impact of cyclical fluctuations on large and small businesses, and the research method difference between dynamic and static analysis.

CHAPTER 8

Business Growth

■ Why Growth?

In recent times there has been a substantial shift in interest and emphasis in the field of small business towards a focus on the growing business in particular. This shift has been evident in policy-making, in the application of small business support, and in related research and commentaries. Fast-growing small firms have been described as 'gazelles', 'fliers', 'growers' and 'winners', and the targeting of effort towards them has been described as 'picking', 'stimulating', or 'backing' winners.

Why has this interest developed? It is likely that, just as the earlier emphasis on small businesses in general arose from a recognition of their contribution to the economy, this focus comes from a similar desire to maximise that contribution. Birch's study, and other subsequent studies, had claimed to show that the major proportion of net new jobs are created by small businesses. Governments and others saw that there could be economic benefit in supporting small businesses. More detailed analysis showed that many small businesses did not grow and therefore, once established, did not create more jobs. It was suggested that it was a relatively small proportion of small business starts that did subsequently show significant growth and were responsible for much of the main employment benefits over time. The argument, therefore, was that if small business support resources were limited, which was invariably the case, then the way to maximise results was to apply those resources where they would be most effective. The small business sector is huge and varied, and if support has to be rationed, and if growth businesses produce a disproportional large share the desired jobs, then the logical thing to do is to concentrate that support on growth businesses in order to secure the best return. (But see also the contrary indications in Chapter 7, under 'Small Business Statistics'.)

Associated with this line of argument have been other reasons to look favourably on growth businesses:

- There is a belief that to base support primarily on employment creation can be distorting. Instead, support should try to promote competitiveness in the economy, which should then in turn lead to jobs. Competitiveness embraces notions of innovation, dynamism, efficiency and the winning of greater market share, in particular in export markets. All these are associated with growth firms, which presumably grow because they are competitive. Promoting growth businesses therefore promotes competitiveness and ultimately wealth creation.
- There is a recognition that simply increasing numbers of small businesses may not increase total employment in small businesses because of displacement effects. Those businesses that do survive may only do so at the expense of others.
- There is also a realisation that new businesses have high casualty rates. Many of those that do start do not survive, and do not therefore contribute anything lasting to the economy. Effort applied to helping them is therefore wasted.
- Indigenous businesses are seen as crucial for regional development, because they have the local roots that inward investments do not have. If a suitable indigenous business base does not exist however then it has to be created from growing small firms.
- The UK economy is thought to suffer from the absence of a population of efficient and resilient medium-sized businesses that could provide a backbone in the manner of the German *Mittelstand* – globally competive, usually family-owned, medium-sized businesses, often quoted as key to the success of the German economy. If such a 'backbone' is to emerge then it must come from small growth businesses. (Views on this vary, however. Levy notes that the 'distribution of manufacturing employees between small, medium and large firms' is not greatly different between the UK and Germany.[1] An alternative analysis contends that within the UK population of businesses there are more 'make-weights' and 'punchbags'. A recent study of 600 manufacturing companies in the UK, Germany, the Netherlands and Finland concluded that the UK had as many world-class firms as the other countries, but a significantly higher proportion of companies that lagged badly in many key aspects of performance.[2])
- Growth businesses are inherently attractive to suppliers of funding and other business services, because the prospects for financial returns are greatest and because of the feeling of success through association.

> *We have also begun to recognize the importance of the 'gazelle' [rapidly growing businesses] phenomenon within the small business, as well as the middle size and large company universe. In fact, mobility across firm size is almost more interesting than firm size per se. I would say the number [of gazelles] is somewhere between five and ten per cent. In my last look, four per cent of the firms were doing seventy per cent of the growth. So it's four, five, six seven per cent. You can take it as far as you want. Rank all firms by the growth index we have developed and start peeling them off the top. Four per cent at 70; five per cent at 77; ten per cent at 87.*
>
> **(David Birch[3])**

The trend towards concentrating support on growth businesses, pursued by the UK government among others, does not command universal support. Inevitably it results in relatively less support for small business creation. Many would see new businesses as potentially a vital element in a vibrant economy, even if they don't grow, since they produce a variety of products and services on which the economy and the growth businesses in it depend. It is also argued that new businesses are the seedbed for future growth businesses, and, even if only a small proportion of the businesses in the seedbed do grow, the bigger the seedbed the more seedlings that may grow. Moreover there is evidence that the size category of businesses in which net job creation is greatest, over a given period of time, is the employment of up-to-twenty-people category, because it contains the greatest number of businesses, including almost all new starts.

This debate, and its implications, is an important one for those who seek to enhance the small business contribution to economic development. It is therefore the subject of this chapter.

■ Some Statistics on Growth

Overall, small businesses can be divided into are three broad groupings. First, there is a high proportion of small businesses that have a short life. Then there is a second large group of businesses that, although surviving, remain small. The third group is by far the smallest: it consists of those businesses that achieve rapid growth in employment. These groups have been referred to by Storey respectively as 'failures', 'trundlers' and 'fliers' and by Birch as 'failures', 'mice' and 'gazelles'. The following empirical data help to put the last, the fliers or gazelles, into context.

On the basis of a study of manufacturing firms in the UK Storey[4] (as already explained in Chapter 7) claims that 'over a decade, 4 per cent of those businesses which start would be expected to create 50 per cent of employment generated'.

The Northern Ireland Economic Research Centre (NIERC)[5] studied the performance of manufacturing firms from 1973 to 1986 and also found that almost 10 per cent of surviving firms created 43 per cent of employment. (Applying Storey's assumption that 40 per cent of firms survive ten years, one can again conclude that 4 per cent of the original firms generated 43 per cent of employment.)

Other findings help to confirm the view that in the UK a small number of businesses have a disproportionate impact on job creation. The US experience is broadly similar. For example, a study of new firm growth in Minnesota found that 9 per cent of new firms formed in the 1980s provided over 50 per cent of employment after two to seven years.[6] While there are particular criticisms that can be made of these findings (see Chapter 7) the general picture is probably reasonably accurate: it is that a relatively small proportion of all small businesses contribute the major part of the small business contribution to net new jobs. But this is scarcely surprising, because it is consistent with Pareto's law (or the 80/20 rule), and of course not all small businesses aspire to or are capable of growth. Their owners form and grow the business to a point where they are satisfied or from where they can go no further.

However it is important to note that demonstrating that, in any cohort of businesses, a few will create most jobs, is not the same as demonstrating that, in any one year or combination of years, the greatest overall net job creation comes from the fastest-growing businesses. Indeed the up-to-twenty employee size range appears to be the category that generates absolutely and relatively the greatest number of net new jobs (see also Chapter 7).

■ The Meanings of Growth

Before examining growth issues further it is logical to consider what is meant by growth, in the context of small businesses, and what observers or business owners interpret as the desirable aspects of growth. Storey, in presenting the statistics given above, makes it clear that, in common with others, he is using increases in employment as a measure of growth. Growth in a business can however also be defined as greater turnover or increased profitability, but, while these measures may all be seen as desirable, they may not even be positively correlated. Some analysts may in addition interpret growth in the context of a broader product range, or an increased number of patents or of customers, none of which necessarily imply greater turnover, profitability or employment.

People with a financial interest in small businesses often want to increase the value of their investments by growth in shareholder value, which implies a growth in business earnings and net assets, which themselves may be achieved by growth in turnover and/or profitability (or the potential for it). Employment, therefore, for them is not necessarily a growth goal, but may be a byproduct of it. For government support agencies a straightforward growth in employment

Table 8.1   Yardsticks for business growth

Share value	Return on investment	Market share
Net worth	Size of premises	Exports/import substitution
Profit	Standard of service	New products/services
Employment	Profile/image	Innovations, patents, etc.
Turnover	Number of customers	

may however be the requirement, or at least an overall improvement in the economy, that is most likely to come from a growth in exports, or a replacement of imports, and which may lead to a growth in employment.

It is important therefore to understand that, while growth may be seen as a desirable process or goal, it will mean different things to different people. For most people, growth in employment will generally be the primary goal. For those managing economies and balances of payments, growth in export turnover, or in import substitution, is critical. For shareholders, profitability as a means to enhance dividends and share value is likely to be predominant. The individual small business owner however, as noted previously, may have one or more of a number of aspirations. These might include being a major local employer, creating wealth, building a large income, being seen as innovative or providing jobs for the family. Many of these will be derived from, or be facilitated by, growth in aspects of the business.

While researchers frequently measure growth in terms of employment, its potential to mean different things to different people means that care must be taken in describing it. Unless its meaning in a particular situation is clear, misunderstandings may arise. It may also be necessary sometimes to remember the distinction made between growth and expansion that was described in Chapter 6. Some of the yardsticks used for measuring growth are indicated in Table 8.1.

■ The Components of Growth

Growing a business is not easy. The natural tendency of a business, like any other system subject to natural decay, is to regress. It takes energy and effort to prevent that and instead to grow. The easiest way to understand the effort needed is to look at the needs of a growing business and the things that must be done to address them.

Under almost every definition of growth, growing a small business needs resources, especially funding; it needs management delegation, coordination, systems and control; and it needs more sales, which may in turn come from new products or markets. These issues have already been described in Chapter 6 but they are repeated here as the starting point for a wider look at the implications of growth.

Understanding growth however requires a regard, not just for these internal needs of a business but also for the totality of the influences on a business. Such influences can be external as well as internal and can oppose, hinder or help growth. They are illustrated in Figures 8.1 and 8.2; see also Table 8.2.

One benefit of establishing the totality of influences on a business is that it helps to put any single influence in perspective. Without it there is a tendency to overestimate the effect of any particular influence. If, for instance, it is considered that R&D can help to build competitiveness and that a grant scheme will encourage R&D, then it might be thought that such a grant scheme would be a positive influence on a business. However, it is important to recognise the strength of the influences keeping the business where it is, which are likely to be much stronger than the more dubious incentive of the grant. This has been likened to pushing a heavy object: friction tends to keep it where it is, unless the pushing force is sufficiently large, while attempts to reduce the frictional resistance might be more effective than attempts to increase the amount of external push.

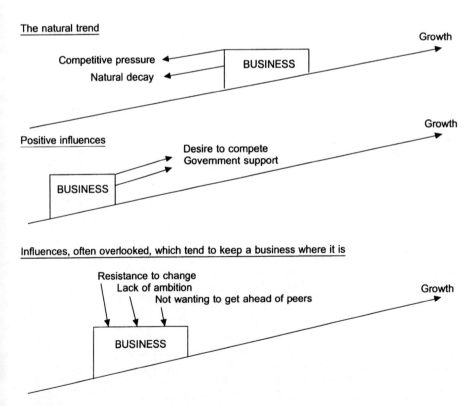

Figure 8.1   Influences on a business

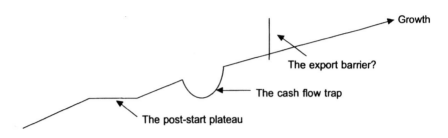

Figure 8.2   Nature of the path to growth

Growth, or its absence, can however be attributable to a wide variety of factors. There is no comprehensive theory to explain what firms will grow or how they grow, but various explanatory approaches have been used. Of course, whatever approach or combination of approaches one favours, seeking to distinguish between what is necessary and what is sufficient for growth has been and is likely to remain an unattainable goal. Indeed most of the research work in this area 'fails to provide convincing evidence of the determinants of small firm growth as a basis for informing policy-makers',[7] and again, 'Given the significance of employment created in rapidly growing small firms, it is surprising that theoretical and empirical understanding of the characteristics of these firms remains somewhat sketchy'.[8]

Table 8.2   Some of the influences on a business

	Internal	*External*
Positive influences	Owner's desire to increase profitability and/or to prove him or herself Impetus of earlier growth	Stimulus of competition Encouragement of others Favourable tax incentives Encouragement and support from small business agencies
Negative influences	Bounce back from earlier uncontrolled growth Lack of ability of the owner and/or management team	Adverse tax, interest and exchange rates Improvements in the competition Product obsolescence
Influences which can encourage a business not to change	Owner's lifestyle and the consequent need for the present level of return but not for more Inertia and the difficulty of mobilising the resources needed to do more Limits on internal capacity to plan, coordinate and supervise	Peer-group pressure

8.1 Previous academic approaches to understanding small business growth

[There] has been a considerable body of literature embracing very different approaches to understanding the growth process. This can be broadly divided into five categories as follows:

- Approaches exploring the impact of the entrepreneurial personality and capability on growth including the owner manager's personal goals and/or strategic vision.
- Approaches seeking to characterize the way the small organization develops and influences, and is influenced by, the owner manager.
- Approaches broadly embraced under the term 'business' which focus upon the importance of business skills and the role of functional management, planning, control and formal strategic orientations.
- Approaches which are more macro in scope and which usually have their academic base in industrial economics. These include sectoral approaches pertaining to regional development, a focus upon specific industry sectors or sub-sectors, for example, high-technology firms.

There are obvious overlaps between these approaches.[9]

In the context of small businesses, what are the main influences? Three in particular are examined here: the influences of the entrepreneur linked to his or her personality, behaviour, attitude and capability; the influences due to the business itself, related to its structure and goals and to the performance of its management; and the influences of the external environment such as the business's industry, region and other strategic issues.

The Entrepreneur – Motivation and Aspiration

The first approach focuses on the entrepreneur himself or herself. Personality and behaviour are believed to be causal factors for or against growth-orientated achievement. This is understandable. It is a characteristic of small business that decision powers are centralised at the level of the owner-manager, so his or her personality, skills, responsibilities, attitude and behaviour will have a decisive influence on business strategy.

Typical of the analysts using this appraisal is Kirchhoff, who develops a 'dynamic capitalism typology'[10] to explain the relationship between innovation and firm growth. The typology divides firms into four categories: economic core, ambitious, glamorous and constrained growth. Each category has its own broad growth profile.

'Economic core' businesses are low on innovation and on growth. They are the largest single category, but fast-growing firms can leap out from the core; an example is Wal-Mart, the world's largest retailer, where the most significant growth came after over thirty years of operations. 'Ambitious' firms achieve high rates of growth with one, or a few, initial innovations. Growth comes from a gradual buildup of market share. However, growth cannot be sustained without additional innovations (usually in the product or service or in its marketing). With additional innovations, firms become 'glamorous'. Microsoft is a good example. Glamorous businesses, according to Kirchhoff, can have experienced periods of 'constrained growth'[11] for two broad reasons. First, growth may be self-constrained growth owing to the owner's reluctance to relinquish ownership and control to generate the necessary resources for growth and, second, it may be constrained where businesses are genuinely limited by a lack of resources. They can often be highly innovative, but still unable to secure early-stage capital.

Kirchhoff concludes that 'what is interesting about these four classes of firms is that they do not depend upon industrial sector, business size, age nor location.'[12] This typology, he continues, 'identifies the firms' behaviours that indicate the true ambitions and goals of the owners and defines their contribution to economic growth. Aspiring entrepreneurs need to realistically assess their personal ambitions and where *they wish to be* in this typology.'[13]

This is a clear attribution of business growth to entrepreneurial motivation and competence, as exhibited in a willingness to innovate. It is probably reasonable to assume that the motivation to grow is likely to be the '*sine qua non*' of growth. Yet for many business owners the growth of their businesses is not an objective. Growth is associated with many unattractive circumstances. These may include having to find work for others, loss of management control, reliance on others, sharing responsibilities and decision making, perhaps relinquishing some ownership stake, and unnecessary risk (although there is evidence from the UK and USA that survival and growth are positively correlated).

A desire to spend more time with one's family or to engage in other forms of social and leisure activity are also valid reasons. Professional and social issues combine very often, as is noted in the significant amount of literature on the family business, which recognises the influence of family in respect of growth and the issues of ownership. Often growth is rejected where it might lead to a conflict of interests.

Businesses exist that have a no-growth aspiration. They were described earlier as 'lifestyle' businesses, and in almost every case they are established solely to provide a satisfactory level of income. They are very often home-based, sole-trader operations employing no more than one additional person. Statistics[14] reveal that well over half of all UK business owners in the late 1980s had no plans to grow. In addition there is a clear association between firm size and the desire to grow.

Even among those entrepreneurs who seek growth, significant numbers would appear to seek only moderate or limited growth. They may reach a stage or plateau, described as a 'comfort zone', at which the owner is satisfied with his or her condition and the costs of pursuing continued growth exceed the expected benefits. These perceived costs will dominate over any material or psychological gains that might be expected from growth. As more than one owner has remarked, 'The problems grow geometrically while the firm grows arithmetically'.

The motivation of the owner is undoubtedly a very important ingredient in the (no-) growth process and, of course, the motivation can change over time as the business develops and events external and internal to the business occur. It is a dynamic situation. Firms can appear to be in a steady state for many years and then begin to grow rapidly. Growth is not necessarily a continuous process for many firms, which is an important consideration for those who rely on recent past performance as a predictor of future performance. One possible reason is a need to establish the business – to build strong roots – before moving on and upwards. Similarly, as noted in Chapter 7, it is revealed that the majority of firms show no growth for their first six years, while more than 50 per cent of surviving firms show growth after six years. Indeed, rapid growth appears to begin after six to eight years of trading.[15]

■ Other Entrepreneurial Characteristics

It will also be apparent that the will or motivation to grow by no means guarantees growth. So a growth model that focuses on the individual entrepreneur as the key to the growth process must also take into account aspects of the individual other than motivation, such as traits, behaviour and resources. These factors will influence the entrepreneur's ability to achieve growth, as well as his or her will to do so.

Storey[16] has reviewed a number of empirical studies that examine which characteristics of the entrepreneur, including motivation, are related to growth. The conclusions drawn however do not permit the development of a profile or model of the growth-achieving entrepreneur in terms of the subsequent performance of the firm. There is some suggestion that the more significant variables, in addition to motivation, are education, age and management experience, all of which are positively correlated. (Motivation, in this instance, however, refers only to why the business was established – not motivation to grow.) Interestingly, there appears to be some evidence that businesses founded by groups are also likely to grow faster than those founded by single individuals.

Another characteristic of the entrepreneur that has also been studied is his or her willingness to accept external equity. As finance from an external source is usually needed to permit rapid business expansion, accepting equity involvement and sharing ownership removes a growth constraint. Alternative funding sources can be used, but usually not without increasing the business's gearing. It is reasonable to impute, therefore, that a willingness by the entrepreneur to share ownership and so decision-making and control is key to the growth of some businesses. When the concept of the entrepreneur is extended to embrace his or her management style and strategic management practices, including the development and use of networks, conclusions are no simpler to reach. For example, there is an increasing tendency to link the business's growth with the quality and quantity of the personal and organisational networks that the entrepreneur develops.

Some studies support the contention that a greater use of external sources of information, advice and other resources results in faster growth, particularly for high-technology business. It is logical to assume that, as the entrepreneur's resources are often limited and he or she has to gain some control over his or her socioeconomic environment, networks play a more crucial role for the small business that seeks growth. Moreover the nature of networks appears to change as the business develops, which is to be expected also.

However, work on management style and networks is subject to criticisms which are frequently mentioned. To be useful, such studies need to distinguish cause and effect and also to distinguish whether the factors being studied actually cause growth or merely facilitate (or hinder) processes determined by other influences.

■ Conclusion

The conclusion reached by one Third World study[17] is instructive. It tested three groups of personal entrepreneurial competencies: first, those perceived to pertain to basic personality, e.g. assertiveness, determination, initiative; second, those relating to business management styles, e.g. efficiency orientation; third, those classified as business skill indicators, e.g. systematic planning. It was however concluded from this that personality variables are not useful predictors of business performance. The personality-orientated competency measures represented in the data did not relate consistently, it was claimed, to the various measures of business performance for the respondents.

It is reasonable to conclude, therefore, that what the entrepreneur 'is' (traits) is less important than what he or she 'does' (behaviour), because the latter effects change. The link between what one 'is' and what one 'does' is clearly largely undetermined. To quote Gibb and Davies, 'different types of entrepreneurial behaviour are required in different marketplaces to achieve growth and different traits, skills and competencies will be needed depending upon levels of uncertainty and complexity in the market.'[18]

In conclusion, it is reasonable to deduce that the entrepreneur's (or business leader's) ambition and desire to grow is critical. In addition, the skills of the entrepreneur are particularly important in the early stages of growth. The ability to broaden and adapt to changing circumstances is likely to be of major importance in removing obstacles to growth. Different types of behaviour may be acquired in different market situations and different personal competencies are likely to be needed to deal with the different levels of complexity and uncertainty in the business environment. It is important that entrepreneurs are willing to delegate and, by implication, that employees must be capable and willing to accept that responsibility. It is also a truism to say that an inability to manage growth, despite a motivation to do so will prevent growth. It is undoubtedly the case that many firms fail to grow because of a variety of barriers including those of a technical, marketing, and financial nature but not least those which are managerial (which may in fact be at the root of some of the former barriers). How management factors can help or hinder growth at different stages is captured in Figure 8.3.

Storey's research stresses the critical importance of the attitude and quality of the initial manager(s) whom the entrepreneur recruits. Such a finding would reinforce the importance of the management team to growth achievement and of the owner's ability to build such a team. These issues of management are explored further in the next section.

■ The Business

A second approach to explaining growth is to look at the characteristics of the business itself. These characteristics can be divided into two categories, chosen because they are firm-specific:

- The firm's structure: ownership, legal form, age and size
- The firm's management skills and performance, including its access to resources.

■ Structure

Storey[19] reviewed research from eleven studies on one or more of the elements in this category. His conclusion was that little is known about the impact of ownership. It is not known, for example, whether a second or subsequent owner is more likely grow a business, nor is it known if an individual with more than one business is more likely to succeed in growing one or more of them, nor whether a business begun by a team is more likely to grow.

On the legal form of the business, it would appear that a limited company is more likely to be a grower as compared with a sole trader or partnership. This should not be surprising, because most businesses convert to limited company status at some stage in their development and are frequently under various pressures to convert as they grow.

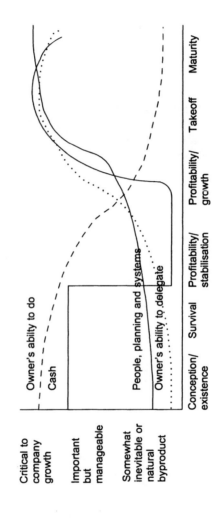

Source: N. C. Churchill, 'The Six Key Phases of Company Growth', in 'Mastering Enterprise', *Financial Times*, February 1997, p. 3.

Figure 8.3   Management factors and stages

Most studies also conclude that younger firms grow more quickly than older ones. It is important to note, however, that one reason for a correlation between age and growth is that it is easier to achieve a doubling in any growth parameter if the business is smaller to start with. Few large businesses would try a 100 per cent increase in employment at one stroke, but that is just what a one-person business does when it takes on a second worker. Additionally, many businesses will initially grow rapidly to reach the 'critical mass' needed to service their market efficiently, but subsequently 'plateau'.

Overall the general findings about the firm's characteristics and growth are of very limited value for policy purposes. As with information about the entrepreneur, either the causal relationship is unclear or no meaningful basis for policy intervention has been identified. Indeed none of the structural factors identified indicates, with adequate clarity, anything about the ambitions or goals exhibited by its owners and managers.

■ Management

The second category of firm-specific characteristics relates to management performance. Many would argue that the motivation and ability of a firm to grow rests with the owner and his or her management team. Such an approach recognises that growth is related to a business's performance in the marketplace, and in particular to its ability to make rational (profitable) decisions about its products and/or services in the context of market development.

In short, a condition of growth is the ability of management to plan and implement the firm's growth in both strategic and operational terms. It is instructive to note that an European Observatory for SMEs annual report[20] identifies four weaknesses of smaller businesses:

- High mortality rates
- Weak market orientation due to lack of strategic marketing approaches and to operating in small segmented markets
- Low productivity of labour leading to high unit wage costs
- Low equity/debt ratio and difficult and costly access to financial markets.

All of these weaknesses can be related to management inadequacy (as indeed can almost all aspects of small business performance). Even difficulty in raising finance can be attributed to a 'failure' of management adequately to search for sources, build networks, prepare suitable business plans or share ownership and control.

Evidence concerning the impact of a selection of firm-specific factors attributable to the performance of the management team is summarised by Storey.[21] These factors are: management recruitment and training, workforce training, technological sophistication, market positioning, market adjustments, planning, new product introduction, customer concentrations, exporting (information and advice) and external equity. The list of factors reflects research that has been done, and is not necessarily an exhaustive list of management-related issues.

Unfortunately, as before, the findings are not conclusive. It seems to be counter-intuitive that proper practice in many of these factors, which conventionally constitute good management, are yet not correlated with growth in businesses. It is however, suggested that three aspects of management did appear to be the most closely linked with growth, as opposed to size (an important distinction). These are market positioning, new products and management recruitment:

☐ *Market Positioning*

A key decision for any business is the definition of its market and where it perceives itself to be in relation to its competitors. While it is difficult to define precisely, market positioning has to do with notions of who the customers are, competitive advantage, product and service range and the role of quality, service and price. These are important issues for management to clarify – otherwise, the business's ability to take corrective action if things go wrong will be limited. It would appear that the ability to know of and take advantage of market positioning (i.e. to determine one's niche) is related to growth success.

☐ *New Products*

Related to market positioning is the development and introduction of new products. There is some evidence, but it is by no means conclusive, that new product introductions are associated with faster growth. Introducing new products is usually seen as part of the process of innovation, which is itself in much of the literature seen as the engine driving continued growth. Innovation is often limited however to development by absorption of new techniques. Indeed, definite conclusions in this area are difficult to find from empirical studies, although views similar to those of the OECD are commonplace, such as 'a businessman's attitude to using new technologies to ensure or increase competitiveness ... appears extremely significant. His attitude will be determined by his experience and training but also by those of his management team.'[22]

☐ *Management Recruitment*

Common sense dictates that as a firm grows it becomes more dependent on its management team. A CBI report revealed that there is a 'greater awareness of management weaknesses among growth firms ...', and that 'recruitment of outside managers also tends to increase with growth'. Table 8.3 taken from this

Table 8.3 Management weakness as a constraint on growth: internal barriers to growth (percentage of respondents citing factor as important)

Respondents were 667 private companies with turnovers between £2.5 and £25m

Management team too small/too stretched	65
Reluctance to dilute ownership	57
Reluctance to take on new debt	55
Lack of successful innovation	40
Preference for maintaining the manageability of small size	40

Source: Binder Hamlyn and London Business School (1994) 'The Quest for Growth', reprinted from *Managing to Grow* (London: CBI, 1995) p. 11

report, highlights the perceived importance of management.[23] There is much other research evidence to show that not acquiring the right management expertise and not building the appropriate structure is one of the main reasons why growth-orientated firms fail to achieve their objective of growth

□ *Other Factors*

Overall, one cannot deduce that other firm-specific factors are not important for growth: there is merely an absence of strong evidence to demonstrate the causal relationship. Indeed, even of the factors highlighted in this section, the evidence presented remains open to challenge. Controversially, neither workforce nor management training is shown to be a causal factor influencing the growth of the business. Their association is with larger but not necessarily growing firms, and they are as likely to be a consequence as a cause.

What research there is confirms the importance of management development in a growing business, and demonstrates individual examples of its impact on performance. It does not, however, isolate the impact of different approaches to management development (e.g. training, mentoring, counselling, non-executive director) across a group of small businesses.

This emphasis on rational business management approaches to growth has led to an increasing flow of literature that attempts to link with planning and so to performance not only the personal characteristics of the entrepreneur but also those of the management team.

As with many factors studied, definitional problems make comparability of findings difficult, not least in the area of planning. Despite this, few studies demonstrate a convincing link between formalised planning and improved performance of the small firm. Planning seems to be related to size, not growth.

Many familiar with micro and small firm behaviour will recognise that the 'informal and intuitive' dominates over formal planning procedures and is at least equally effective. Nor should the existence of a business plan be confused with planning! Overall however it might be foolish to deny the significance of product- and/or market-related decisions, cost/price decisions, and constraint decisions (including time and finance) taken by a strategically aware management team as critical to business growth, despite the absence of conclusive evidence.

■ External Environment

Yet another approach to understanding and explaining growth lies in examining the impact of factors or constraints external to the firm. These include macro-economic variables such as aggregate demand, taxation, regulations, labour market skills and labour relations, but also embrace sector- and regional-specific matters such as sector and/or market, competition, government assistance, location, and the availability (and use) of information.

■ Macro-Economic Variables

Looking first at macro-economic variables, it is clear that policies on demand, taxation, interest rates and public spending will affect the fortunes of small firms. Indeed government policies in these areas are intended to induce behavioural change by individuals and organizations. It is indisputable that these policies have a major impact on the trading performance of small firms.

Despite the continuing calls by small firm representative bodies for reduced regulations ('less red tape') it is not clear to what extent administrative and legislative burdens hinder business growth. It is reasonable to assume, however, that anything that absorbs time and resources that would otherwise be devoted to business development is likely to have a deleterious effect.

Studies in many OECD member countries, including the UK highlight the constraining effect of small business being unable to obtain good quality or skilled labour even in a relatively slack overall labour market. At any given time, how much the problem is on the supply side (recruitment processes, remuneration, employment rights and conditions), as opposed to the demand side, is not clear.

In general, governments' macro-economic policies are geared to all enterprises and not just smaller businesses. Moreover, while the impact of governments' macro policies can fall unevenly on different sectors and/or markets (and labour markets are partially differentiated), the specific effect on the growth of an individual business is likely to be much less than the effect on business in general and not least on international competitive comparisons. It is unlikely, therefore, that macro-economic and national policies will explain differential growth rates within different sectors, whatever are the effects across sectors.

■ Sector

A number of studies[24] in recent years indicate that the average growth rate of firms is higher in some sectors than in others. Particular attention has been paid in numerous studies to businesses in the high-tech sector where, for example, Westhead and Storey[25] conclude that high-technology small firms in the UK not only have higher growth rates but also have lower failure rates than small businesses in other sectors. Kirchhoff,[26] examining US data, only partially agrees: 'the chances of achieving high growth are almost twice as great for high tech firms as for low tech firms. Still, among high tech firms the terminations take a greater toll as low growth firms are unable to hang on for as long as low tech firms.' Kirchhoff attributes their superior growth performance to the high cost of innovation, which requires growth if the firm is to survive.

Sectoral studies serve the purpose of highlighting the particular constraints and opportunities of sectors (e.g. financing problems for the high-tech sector). They do not typically offer a basis for predicting the extent to which growth business will emerge or in what conditions, however. They also encourage analysis of the structure of an industry, and especially the role of large firms and their interaction with smaller ones. Large–small firm linkages may play an important role in influencing small firm growth. Growth can occur on the basis of servicing the needs of large firms; large firms can spin out numbers of small ones; strategic partnerships across a variety of functions can develop; large firms can provide management and technological support and advice. On the other hand, large firms through their power in the marketplace can hinder or eliminate small business growth through acquisition, control over intellectual property, slow payment and quasi-monopolistic practices.

It is misleading however to place too much reliance on sectoral performance from a policy perspective. As research[27] has indicated, performance within sectors varies much more greatly than across sectors.

■ Competition

It may appear, a priori, that for a given market size, the smaller the number of competitors the greater the likelihood of any given business capturing a large share of the market. However, many influences may be operating, such as (dis)economies of scale, product or market differentiation, the relative importance of large and small firms in the market, and transportation costs, which make it very difficult to define the 'competitiveness' of a market or sector. It is not surprising, therefore, that no correlation appears to exist between growth and competition. Porter does argue however that greater competitiveness in an industry's home market can lead to stronger export performance and growth. (See the section 'The Cluster Effect' later in this chapter.)

■ Location

The concept of location is more complex than it first seems. Locational differences such as urban, rural, peripheral or central can mean differences in many of the other factors such as competition, labour market, and government support. It then becomes difficult to determine which of the influences is at work.

However, it is safe to say, once again, that there is not yet enough evidence to suggest that size is location-determined. Possible exceptions to this conclusion would be businesses (usually service or service-related firms) serving local markets, because these are likely to be small, although the benefits of larger markets may well be offset by greater numbers of competitors. Findings by Vaessen and Keeble[28] in a recent analysis of small business by regional location do however suggest a link between growth and location. Peripheral regions are found to contain proportionately more growing small businesses than what they call the 'core' region (South-East England). A partial explanation is that greater R&D and training inputs are generated in the peripheral locations. These findings can however only be tentative. The counter-intuitive nature of their findings may suggest that differences in external environments are not sufficient to explain growth differentials. Indeed, to assume otherwise would be to suggest that the entrepreneur's and the business's behaviour are largely constrained by their location, an assumption that does not allow significant scope for variable responses. Either way, the policy implications are unclear.

■ Information and Advice

The provision of information and advice by government agencies is itself a growth sector in many countries seeking to support their small businesses. This form of support can also come from private sector sources (e.g. bankers, accountants, non-executive directors and consultants), and the use made of accountants and bankers, at least in developed economies, would appear to be much higher than that made of public information and advice services. Indeed the uptake of public sector provision seems generally to be very low (less than 10 per cent of potential users). However, satisfaction with information and advice, from both public and private sources, appears generally to be high. Importantly, despite the significant investment being made in these services in the UK, USA and European Union generally, there appears to be no convincing evidence that the uptake of these services improves business performance and growth, although growing businesses would appear to make greater use of information and advisory networks.

■ Government Support

Government support can take a wide variety of forms, but usually consists of grant aid, subsidised loans and/or the provision of subsidised services such as consultancy, training and the provision of information and advice.

The impact of direct financial support from government or its agencies is the issue most often studied. Such support normally comes from local or regional agencies. The small business community generally expresses dissatisfaction with the grants regime, or at least with its administration. A recent report[29] notes that it feels that grants go to large or foreign firms, that application procedures are too complicated and that not enough information is available on how to access them. Notwithstanding these views, significant sums across many regions have been provided to small business. Once again, research findings are inconclusive in determining whether financial support generates further growth, improved profitability or less-efficient performance.

One of the most thorough studies done on the impact of government financial assistance is by the Northern Ireland Economic Research Centre.[30] It finds that assisted businesses create more jobs than non-assisted ones. In Northern Ireland, for instance, in 1994–5 assisted businesses showed a net growth in employment of 11.9 per cent against a Northern Ireland overall rise of 3.6 per cent. However, much more research needs to be done before these results, which are contradicted by different studies, can be generalized. (See also Chapter 13.)

■ The Cluster Effect

There is however one theory that links issues such as location, competition and government support to the competitiveness, and hence to the potential growth, of businesses. This theory is propounded by Porter[31] (see also Chapter 5) who, following a four-year study of ten important trading nations, ultimately concluded that nations succeed in particular industries because their home environment is the most forward-looking, dynamic and challenging. These conclusions, he suggests, contradict the conventional wisdom that labour costs, interest rates, exchange rates and economies of scale are the most potent determinants of competitiveness. It is too easy, he says, for governments to adopt policies, such as joint projects for R&D, that operate on the belief that independent research by domestic rivals is wasteful and duplicative, that collaborative efforts achieve economies of scale, and that individual companies are likely to underinvest in R&D because they cannot reap all the benefits. That view, he claims, is flawed and fundamentally misperceives the true sources of competitive advantage.

Porter argues that, while successful businesses will each employ their own strategy, they achieve competitive advantage through acts of innovation. Further, he believes that it is demanding buyers in the domestic market who pressure companies to innovate faster. Why is it he asks, that certain companies based in certain nations are capable of consistent innovation? The answer is in four broad attributes of a nation. They are: *factor conditions* (labour force quality, infrastructure); *demand conditions* (the nature of home market demand); *related and supporting industries* (the presence of supplier industries and other related industries which are internationally competitive); and *firm strategy, structure and rivalry* (the conditions in the nation affecting how businesses are created, organised and managed and the nature of domestic competition). These four determinants form the points on Porter's 'diamond', and the diamond is itself a system. Together they affect the key elements that beget international competitiveness and, by implication, firm and industry growth.

How these determinants combine to produce a successful industry is complex, but Porter notes that internationally competitive businesses are usually found in geographically concentrated clusters of related businesses. 'Among all the points on the diamond, domestic rivalry is arguably the most important because of the powerfully stimulating effect it has on all the others,' asserts Porter, adding that 'Geographic concentration magnifies the power of domestic rivalry.'[32] One of the most commonly quoted such examples is that of 'The Third Italy': a proliferation of concentrations of various industrial sectors benefiting from a variety of effects that include pools of skilled workers and technicians; related input from maintenance, service and design businesses; supporting companies that offer materials, supplies and other services including subcontracting; and specialist businesses offering consultancy and advice on logistics, advertising, finance and general support. Support agency services develop that are geared to meet a cluster's needs in the form of education and training, research and development, fiscal and legal advice. In Italy these inter-relationships are reinforced by family connections and traditional links that significantly strengthen the power of the network. Such inbuilt cultural ties however complicate the situation for those who might otherwise think that they could merely 'import' the cluster effect.

■ General

This brief review covers only some of the factors that have been considered as possible influences on the growth performance of small businesses. This chapter has classified the range of factors into three broad categories – the entrepreneur, the firm and the external environment. Other classifications exist. The OECD,[33] for instance, categorises the key factors in the *competitiveness* of 'SMEs' as:

- *The owner's/manager's basic role* (drive)
- *Intangible investment* ('intelligence management'), including:

  - the ability to obtain information through environmental scanning and search
  - at least an intermittent R&D capability
  - the quality of the firm's organisation
  - the quality of its training

- *Tangible investment* (based on new management and production technologies)
- *The business's strategic capabilities* (innovation and flexibility).

However, as already noted, the research on these, and on other, classifications and their components has produced no conclusive results and no firm evidence to support interventions, either to increase the pace of growth or to increase the number of businesses growing.

Nevertheless, it would be foolish to set aside a pragmatic approach to this problem, such as to note what businesses themselves have been saying. One recent comprehensive study of business opinion is that carried out by the Cambridge Small Business Research Centre[34] across almost 2000 businesses. Their ranking of the constraints on their growth are shown in Table 8.4.

This shows that finance is seen as a major constraint followed by the level of demand and the firm's ability to deal with it (marketing and sales skills). It may be reasonable to accept these rather typical results (albeit no mention is made of administrative and regulatory burdens!) at face value, subject to two caveats: first, businesses may tend to blame external, and therefore uncontrollable, factors before internal, controllable, factors and second, there is a tendency to confuse causes and effects. In the latter case, financial constraints may become apparent because of a lack of demand or, in the case of a growing business, because of a reluctance to dilute ownership or control or because of poor financial management skills.

A second common-sense approach is to recognise that growth is likely to be dependent upon the interaction of a number of influences, and that these influences may be important in different combinations for different businesses. This makes generalisations very imprecise and of limited use as guides to action. Growth is likely to occur when a number of the key factors in each category combine, although it is most unlikely that there is only one or a few successful combinations, and the combinations for success could change as the business develops and market circumstances alter. The dynamic process implied in this interpretation of how growth is generated through the interaction of the

Table 8.4   Constraints on small business growth

Constraint	Ranking
Availability and cost of finance for expansion	1
Availability and cost of overdraft facilities	2
Marketing and sales skills	3
Management skills	4
Overall growth of market demand	5
Increasing competition	6
Skilled labour	7
Availability of appropriate premises or site	8
Acquisition of new technology	9
Difficulties in implementing new technology	10
Access to overseas markets	11

Source: ESRC Centre for Business Research, *The State of British Enterprise* (Cambridge Small Business Research Centre, 1992).

entrepreneur, the firm and its environment, local and regional as well as national and international, is at the heart of understanding the growth process itself. However, given the heterogeneity of entrepreneurs and of small businesses, and the complexity and diversity of markets in which they operate, any attempt to produce a comprehensive theory or any meaningful analysis of growth may be unrealistic, at least in the short term. One may also add that there is no single correct management for growth and that growth itself, as has been noted, is not a simple linear process: rather, businesses are growing, contracting and growing again several times and at different rates.

■ Targeting Growth

As has been explained earlier in this chapter, much of the interest in growth businesses arises because they represent employment potential and because there is therefore a wish to target them for support to enhance that employment potential. Such a policy of targeting growth has its proponents as well as its opponents. The arguments used by each are set out below.

■ Arguments for Targeting Growth Businesses

We can present four here:

It increases the effectiveness of support measures. As explained earlier, statistical evidence has been presented that a small number out of all businesses create a disproportionate proportion of new jobs. It is consequentially argued that targeted support for these 'growth' businesses should be more effective in promoting jobs than more generalised support, because it has a clear focus and concentrates resources where they are most needed and where they can produce the best results.

It minimises support requirements. By applying support only to growth businesses, the total support requirement, and its cost, is reduced.

It encourages a clearer strategic focus on the needs of such businesses. Targeting growth businesses forces small business support organisations to identify more clearly how to support such businesses and to develop appropriate strategies for such support. It also helps agencies to develop a better understanding of the processes of growth in the target market and how best to assist such processes. High levels of expertise are thus more likely to be developed.

More business starts are not needed. There are situations, such as that pertaining in the UK in the 1970s and 1980s, when it has been argued that the rate of business starts was higher than that in competitor economies. More business starts were not therefore needed and attention should instead have been focused on promoting business growth, which was needed.

■ Arguments Against Targeting Growth Businesses

We can present three here:

The economic inefficiency of targeting. While there are savings associated with not 'wasting' resources on the 'undeserving', targeting means that support cannot be automatic and there are costs associated with administering 'non-automatic' forms of assistance. It has also been argued that the growth firms seeking or using assistance are those that are less competitive and that, in consequence, the more competitive will lose trade as a result of subsequent unfair competition.

The inequity of targeting. This argument is based on the straightforward view that everyone is entitled to the same levels and forms of support – a sense of fairness – especially when the ability to target well is suspect.

A policy of targeting growth businesses is not workable and is misguided. There are two aspects to this argument: first, that it is not possible to identify in advance 'growth' firms and second, that, even if such identification is possible, a targeting policy is misguided. The reasons for this include the following:

- As this chapter has illustrated, there is little 'hard' evidence that it is in practice possible to identify any key distinguishing features of potential fast growth firms. Many have tried and, while encouraging developments have been reported, no one has yet found the 'Holy Grail' of a practical method of growth prediction. It may be politically desirable to pick (future) winners, but there is little evidence to show that it is feasible.

> *I haven't figured out a way (to anticipate which firms will be the gazelles and which will end up the mice). In fact, one of the fascinating things about the gazelles is that they sometimes appear to be mice for long periods of time.*
>
> **(David Birch[35])**

- The only sure way of telling which are the growth businesses, it has been said, is to wait and see which ones do grow. However, if the purpose of the targeting is to encourage and support growth then it is too late to target businesses after they have proved their growth potential by actually growing. Past growth is generally only evidence of past growth – it is not a predictor of future growth.

- The process of picking winners has been likened to selecting a potentially good wine. It is viewed as more of an art than a science and is the preserve of a tiny cognoscenti with exceptional 'noses' and 'palates'; it is a skill that takes years of training and experience to acquire, and not everyone can do it, even then. (Even the wine 'cognoscenti' generally only make predictions for wines with a good pedigree, with the result that most of them missed the potential of the 'New World' wines.) It is not therefore something that can be systemised into business agencies.
- The venture capital industry would pride itself on picking winners, and needs to do so to survive. However it only needs to select a few winners that would be enough for its own purposes, and it would acknowledge that it still selects a majority of 'dogs' that have to be compensated for by the occasional correctly chosen 'star'. Public support policy, in contrast, would seek to back all the winners and avoid any losers.
- 'Picking winners' is a misguided policy. It ignores the fact that most of the jobs in the small business sector still come from businesses with fewer than twenty employees, and that non-growth businesses and start-ups, as well as providing this employment now, are also the source of the growth businesses of the future. Not to support them therefore would reduce the pool of potential future growth businesses.
- Small businesses are not only relevant to job creation, but also contribute to the achievement of wider economic and social goals, including productivity, living standards, price stability, diversity, choice and personal opportunity.

☐ *In Conclusion*

The targeting debate is not over, however. The search for the Holy Grail, the formula for creating and/or picking winners, will no doubt continue. Growth businesses may still be desirable, even if they can't be spotted in advance. To quote Storey again, 'It is the failure of UK small enterprises to grow into large enterprises that may be at the heart of the country's long-term poor economic performance.'[36]

Key points

- When it was suggested that the major proportion of net new jobs was created by small businesses, governments and others saw that there could be economic benefit in supporting small businesses. More detailed analysis appears to have shown that it is a relatively small proportion of small businesses which grow. 'Over a decade, 4 per cent of those businesses which start would be expected to create 50 per cent of employment generated.'[37] However businesses with fewer than twenty employees still generate most employment.

- If small business support resources are limited, which is invariably the case, then it has been suggested that the way to maximise results is to apply those resources only to growth businesses and in the most appropriate way so that they can be most effective. Therefore there has been considerable interest in learning what makes businesses grow and how they can be spotted.

- It is important to realise that growth in a business context can have many meanings. For the investor it may be growth in shareholder value. For the business it may be growth in sales and in profits, and for government it may be growth in employment. These forms of growth may not all coincide.

- In the context of small businesses, three main areas of influences are examined. It is reasonable to deduce that the entrepreneur's (or leader's) ambition and desire to grow is critical and, in addition, the skills of the entrepreneur are particularly important in the early stages of growth. In addition it can said that many firm specific factors may be important for growth, but there is an absence of strong evidence to demonstrate the causal relationship. Yet another approach to understanding and explaining growth lies in examining the impact of factors or constraints external to the firm. These include macro-economic variables such as aggregate demand, taxation, regulations, labour market skills and labour relations, but also embrace sector and regional specific issues and factors such as sector/market, competition, government assistance, location, and the availability (and use) of information. All these are seen has having some impact but none are useful as predictors.

- In the context of the external environment, 'cluster' theory is of interest. It is based on research that shows that internationally successful businesses are often found in geographic clusters where the environment is most advantageous to them; that it is innovation that makes businesses competitive, and thus provides the potential for growth; and that it is demanding buyers in the domestic market that can pressure companies to innovate faster.

- As for the issue of whether to target growth businesses or not, the debate is not over. The search for the Holy Grail, the formula for creating and/or picking winners, will no doubt continue. Growth businesses may still be desirable even if they can't be spotted in advance.

CHAPTER 9
Intrapreneurship

The last chapter considered the growth of small businesses because much small business policy and support has been focused on them in particular, in order primarily to gain the employment benefits their growth brings. Growth in the early stages of a small business can be seen as a natural extension of its original formation, and at least to some extent it requires the same sense of venture, of initiative and of opportunity. However, once a business reaches a steady state then a different attitude can prevail. After a period of little significant change, management effort increasingly goes into maintaining the *status quo*, and change becomes something to be resisted or avoided. Yet in a dynamic business environment, where competition is severe and where market developments present new opportunities, to stand still is to court regression.[1]

Maintaining growth in a mature business is therefore still important, but it can require a different approach. Business formation and early growth, which frequently depend on the ideas, drive and personality of the founder, is seen as the essence of entrepreneurship. Growth in a mature business also requires enterprise ideas, drive and culture, but these must come at least in part from those working in the business as well as from an owner manager. Generating these factors inside the business, a process of internal enterprise, has been called 'intrapreneurship' and is the subject of this chapter.

> *Today's businesses, especially the large ones, simply will not survive in this period of rapid change and innovation unless they acquire entrepreneurial competence.*
>
> **(Peter Drucker[2])**

It was an American, Gifford Pinchot III, who invented the word 'intrapreneurship'[3] to describe the practice of entrepreneurship within large businesses, a necessary practice if those organisations are to continue to develop indefinitely.

Organisational development implies change and improvement; it means doing new and more productive things that can sustain or enhance profit. This development requires the application of enterprise in the mature organisation; the process which has been described as intrapreneurship, or corporate innovation.[4] But before proceeding to examine the nature of intrapreneurship it seems sensible to clarify its connection with the concepts of entrepreneurship, enterprise, and innovation.

Intrapreneurship and Related Concepts

Entrepreneurship

Entrepreneurship has been described in terms of 'the ability to create something from practically nothing. It is initiating...and building an enterprise rather than...watching one. It is the knack for sensing opportunities where others see chaos, contradiction and confusion. It is the ability to build a 'founding team' to complement your own skills and talents. It is the knowhow to find, marshal and control resources.... Finally it is a willingness to take calculated risks.'[5] This definition emphasises the range of activities that are needed to initiate and to launch the development of a new business venture, and it does not dwell on the nature of the business that is then created. A great deal of entrepreneurship, or enterprise, must still be exercised, even in a mundane small business, if that business is to survive. The interactions 'between smallness, exposure to the environment..., ownership and personal control...condition the culture of the business'.[6] The task environment is complex and changeable, and the continuing exercise of enterprise is essential for success. Problems have to be solved for which there is little or no precedent.

Learning and problem-solving are common activities in many working environments, nowadays, but some people consider that true entrepreneurship occurs when individuals 'ignore the established ways of thinking and action' and seek novel ideas and solutions that can meet customer needs. Entrepreneurship is therefore 'the innovatory process involved in the creation of an economic enterprise based on a new product or service which differs significantly from products or services offered by other suppliers in content or in the way its production is organised or in its marketing'.[7] In this approach entrepreneurship is therefore concerned with newness: new ideas, products, services or combinations of resources aimed at meeting the needs of consumers more efficiently.

Innovation

Innovation has been considered in Chapter 3, but it is also relevant to mention it again here. It has been described as the successful development of competitive advantage and, as such, it is the key to intrapreneurship. For example, Pinchot Gifford, in his classic book called Intrapreneuring, feels that intrapreneurs in businesses are 'the dreamers who do.... Those who take hands-on responsibility for creating innovation of any kind within an organisation. The intrapreneur may be the creator or inventor but it is always the dreamer who figures out how to turn an idea into a profitable reality.'[8] More recently Kuratko and Hodgetts argued that 'the major thrust of intrapreneuring is to develop the entrepreneurial spirit within organisational boundaries, thus allowing an atmosphere of innovation to prosper'[9] and the intrapreneur therefore is an individual who initiates innovative change in large firms.

Inventors are usually individuals, but intrapreneurship is frequently carried out by groups or teams. Caird points out that there are leading innovators who are frequently the driving force behind innovations. They are 'the project champions', and the project 'has no chance of being realised without their belief and commitment'.[10] However, while the lead innovator may have inventing or managerial skill or both, many of Caird's innovators lacked marketing and general management skills, and these were provided by members of the project team.

Innovation itself can take several forms, all relevant to intrapreneurship[11]:

- Innovation in processes, including changes and improvements to methods. These contribute to increases in productivity, which lower costs and thus increase demand.
- Innovation in products, or services. While progressive innovation is predominant, radical innovation opens up new markets. These lead to increases in effective demand, which encourage increases in investment and employment.

Innovation in management and work organisation, and the exploitation of human resources, together with the capacity to anticipate techniques.

It is important in this context to recognise that innovation is not confined to the manufacturing sector. Today the services sector plays an increasing role in enterprise and economic development.

9.1   The Ten Commandments of innovation

- Take risks – adopt a 'can do' philosophy
- Stimulate creativity and seek out new ideas
- Reward success and tolerate failure
- Set realistic targets and review
- Adopt an open management style

- Focus on the customer – cultivate partnerships
- Actively manage investors
- Know what your competition is up to
- Work with other companies and academics
- Patent/protect

(Presentation on behalf of the DTI)

■ Enterprise

If intrapreneurship is the continuing generation of innovation by applying entrepreneurship within established businesses then it is in turn, an example of the broader meaning of enterprise. As a result the terms entrepreneurship, enterprise, innovation, change and intrapreneurship are frequently used interchangeably and, while this is due sometimes to a looseness in writing style, it is clear that there are many similarities between the terms. It is therefore possible to summarise intrapreneurship as the display of enterprise by individuals or groups within established organisations in the pursuit of innovative changes to meet the future needs of the organisations.

■ The Barriers to Intrapreneurship

In a competitive business environment, it might seem obvious that organisations should seek out new business ideas and opportunities and make the necessary arrangements to bring them to a profitable conclusion, but research reveals that many large organisations face difficulties in doing this. Indeed, some writers on intrapreneurship have contended that these inherent difficulties are such that many large corporations will survive in practice only by restructuring their businesses as confederations of small businesses.[12] These difficulties inhibit the exercise of the entrepreneurial spirit and are barriers to intrapreneurship. A description of them is therefore relevant to this chapter:

■ Resistance to Change

Change implies an alteration in the *status quo*, and many people have pointed out that there are strong individual and organisational reasons for resistance to change.[13] Individuals frequently resist change because they have invested a great deal of energy in mastering an existing job, and fear that their investment will be wasted. If people have spent several years perfecting some professional skill then the last thing they want is a new machine or a competing profession that will render their skills obsolete.

Homeostasis is another issue and it seems that individuals, while resenting a complete lack of stimulation, do prefer any excitement to be limited. When they experience severe jolts, as they are likely to in periods of extensive change, their defence mechanisms will attempt to steer their 'systems' back to the status quo. They will therefore resist change unless they see and understand the need for it and, as a result, actually welcome it. Past experience plays a key role in determining how individuals perceive events and this may well mean that employees in a larger organisation do not perceive the problems, or experience the dissatisfaction with the *status quo*, that managers do. Their attitudes and behaviours have been moulded by existing conditions, and they simply do not 'see' the difficulty, and therefore see no reason to change.

Zaltman and Duncan[14] suggest that people with certain personality traits are quite resistant to change. Domineering individuals, or people with a low need for achievement, a low acceptance of ambiguity or a low locus of control, may well be resistant to change. In general, we could say that individuals will resist change if they perceive the change as increasing the difficulties they will face. Handy argues that individuals will bring about change only if they believe in themselves and have self-confidence. If people have serious doubts about their capacity to see a change though then they will play safe and stick to the status quo. Unfortunately many large organisations reduce self-confidence by requiring their employees to do as they are told unquestioningly. He also argues that many committed individuals fail to bring about successful organisational change because they don't take into account the needs of other individuals and groups. The latter may comply with the changes but have no commitment to them.[15]

■ Management Barriers

As businesses get bigger, managers proliferate and acquire a greater share of power, especially when the ownership of the business is dispersed among shareholders. It has always been recognised that one of the primary purposes of managers is to look to the future, but management is a multifaceted job and the stewardship and control functions often predominate. Managers can regard themselves as trustees, and this engenders caution. They are responsible for expensive human and material resources, and they feel duty-bound to use these resources wisely. They are concerned to earn an acceptable rate of return on their resources and to protect the lives and livelihoods of their employees.

Stephenson and Gumpert note also that managers have numerous constituents who must be partially satisfied. Consequently, decision making and change is a cautious process of negotiating with major players, and pursuing a less risky, middle-of-the-road strategy. Caution is also necessary, because large organisations typically commit large amounts of resource to important projects at one time. A lot of analysis is usually done before a project is supported, but once the decision is made then the organisation is committed. Entrepreneurs, on the other hand, evaluate many projects simultaneously and quickly drop those that do not look promising. Stephenson and Gumpert also point out that there is a connection between managerial power and the resources managers control. This being so they are reluctant to take risks and often therefore reinforce the *status quo*.[16]

■ Organisational Barriers

Research also reveals that as organisations get older and bigger they tend to install standard operating procedures and rules that constrain initiative. The first time a new job is tackled there is a time-consuming learning process, but after it has been repeated several times a satisfactory method will be identified, remembered and used again. If the task is done continuously then recommended methods will be written down and employees told to follow them as the correct procedures.[17] As the volume of output increases there is more division of labour and specialisation, which leads to the creation of functional departments. Behaviour of individuals must be predictable, and this is achieved by introducing standard work practices. To make sure that individual and group tasks coalesce, schedules, process plans and control mechanisms are introduced.

However, as the complexity of the task increases, people lose sight of the ends they are serving. 'Management must find the means to make behaviour lower down more predictable and so it turns to rules, procedures, job descriptions, and the like, all devices that formalise behaviour.'[18] Organisations, as they develop, introduce standard practices, but also develop less tangible but equally powerful cultures. They develop characteristic ways of doing things that are guided by a set of shared norms and values. Organisations are infused with values, and this culture transmits to people in the organisation what they should be doing, what they ought to believe in or what the organisation is really about. Standard procedures and culture are powerful controlling mechanisms, and can easily defeat initiatives for change.[19]

Intrapreneurship is about change, flexibility and innovation, and there are many types of change that can improve the competitiveness of organisations. There is an implication in some the strategic management literature that with sufficient will and skill organisations can become almost anything they want to be. However, in practice this rarely happens. Organisations specialise, which can mean that a huge investment in plant, machinery and manpower may have to be written off if the specialisation changes.[20]

Drucker recognises that many of these factors affect organisations but considers that size, *per se*, is not 'an impediment to entrepreneurship and innovation; [the main impediment] is the existing operation itself and especially the existing *successful* operation'. Total commitment to the existing is needed to ensure continued success and to manage 'the daily crises' that normally occur. The current activity requires priority attention 'and deserves it'. Drucker goes on to argue that most successful firms of today will derive a significant proportion of their income from a similar product range in ten years' time, but for long-term survival they must also look for a new range. This is not easy. 'The temptation in the existing business is always to feed yesterday and starve tomorrow.' The current business is not in trouble, and there does not seem to be any pressure to innovate.[21]

■ Facilitating Intrapreneurship

As has been mentioned in Chapter 8, Porter pointed out that continuous innovation is essential for organisational survival in competitive markets but, in view of the barriers, achieving it requires hard work, appropriate attitudes and proper structures. However, just as there is no single agreed route to developing enterprise, there are a number of suggestions of what constitutes intrapreneurship and how it can best be encouraged and supported. A number of suggestions about the nature and constituent parts of intrapreneurship are therefore presented here.

■ Roles

Lessem in particular highlighted the importance of managerial roles and behaviour in supporting intrapreneurship. He identified the key to intrapreneurship as the intrapreneurs themselves and the roles they perform.[22] For him, the intrapreneur combines many of the qualities of the entrepreneur and the manager. Having worked with numerous entrepreneurs over the years, he is convinced that the classic entrepreneur, or even a manager who creates a new small venture within an existing business, is not what is needed in large organisations today. The impatience of the entrepreneur with the constraints imposed by the organisation produces too much conflict with the desire of managers to control events. For Lessem, the concept of intrapreneur is important for two reasons. 'Firstly, it cuts across the division between management and enterprise. But secondly, it forms a bridge between enterprise and development.'[23]

For Lessem, there are several roles or archetypes that can elicit effective development in differing business contexts and personal situations. In some situations rugged *entrepreneurs* are needed. They have an instinctive approach to opportunities and an impatience when faced with obstacles. They seldom let a real or perceived lack of resources inhibit their search for new profitable opportunities. However, in a large venture their impatience and aggression can create conflict.

It is recognised that large companies may not be attractive to entrepreneurial types unless they find opportunities in sales and new product development. The organisation should however offer them the chance to take on risky projects where they may scale the heights or plumb the depths. Their success should be rewarded, but failure must not lead to censure. Mature organisational entrepreneurs can develop the capacity to focus on business renewal as a goal.

In some instances entrepreneurial activity is not enough for development; what is needed is an *adventurer*. The latter is a major risk-taker who enters uncharted waters in search of opportunity. There are difficulties in making huge changes in strategy, but in some instances this is required and the courage and forcefulness of the adventurer is indispensable. In an increasingly global economy, organisations need the drive and audaciousness of the adventurer to enter new and difficult markets.

Innovators are needed also. They are first or early users of new ideas and are the essential link between technology and business, between research and accomplishment. In the larger organisations they must create structures and a climate conducive to the generation, experimentation and realisation of new ideas. They encourage creativity, but they also have a strong commitment to the commercial exploitation of ideas. Innovators get their rewards from seeing the successful transformation of an idea into a successful good or service, but there can be a tendency to marginalise adventurers and innovators in successful businesses. Firms must find mechanisms to allow innovation to co-exist with current product efficiency.

Entrepreneurs, adventurers and innovators do not ignore management matters, but successful large firms also need a sense of direction and discipline. Exploring random innovative ideas may be exciting but there must be some pattern in a firm's strategy and *leaders* ensure that new projects are aligned with their vision for the business. Leaders stand back from the intensive competition in firms and act as somewhat impartial arbitrators, coordinators and conflict handlers. The leader is the wise owl who takes an overview, reconciles differing perspectives, and creates a climate of cooperation, but who also exercises authority when needed to keep the business on the rails. Like the leader of an orchestra, the business leader has concern for the final product and for the people, and uses a range of methods of influence to make sure that all play in tune.

In addition the role of effective *change agents* can be crucial. They effectively bring new products to market, implement new management systems and reorganise working arrangements. Change agents like freedom from controls and are not bound by convention, but they also possess the managerial and political skill to manage change programmes. They appreciate the importance of creating a general awareness that the *status quo* will not do in a turbulent era and in creating an image of the future and letting key players know what it will look like. Further, using change management theory, they can design and implement the practical first steps to bringing about change. They also recognise and can deal with resistance to change. Change agents are keen to do new things and get their motivation from the mental excitement that accompanies change. They are lifelong learners, and engender this spirit among those they meet.

Change agents are important, but they cannot achieve miracles on their own. Another key intrapreneurial type therefore is the *enabler*. Many authors point out the importance of creating a climate or culture for enterprise and innovation and the lack of appropriate cultures in many organisations. Therefore a facilitator or enabler aims to

> develop self renewing, self correcting systems of people who learn to organise themselves in a variety of ways according to the nature of their tasks, and who continue to expand the choice available to the organisation as it copes with the changing demands of a changing environment.[24]

Enablers use soft behavioural skills to encourage people to question ideas, challenge conventions and seek, through collaboration with insiders and outsiders, to come up with forward-looking ideas.

Lessem describes one more intrapreneurial type: the *animateur*. Organisations are technical and economic tools, but they are also living social systems, which need to be humanised and enlivened. An *esprit de corps* or sense of community is vital for a developing organisation, and this is where the animateur assists. The emphasis is on teams and on development through cooperation, problem-solving and concern for the organisational community. Enablers and animators develop the supportive atmosphere and trust that is essential for individual and group risk-taking in pursuit of better options.

This approach is useful in that it recognises the importance of numerous roles, from the aggressive and competitive adventurer and entrepreneur to the people-oriented enabler and animateur, in the continued development of mature organisations. Several of these intrapreneurial types can deliver innovation in appropriate situations, but others create the flexible structures and behaviours that must sustain it.

9.2   Who is the intrapreneur?

Primary motives.   Wants freedom and access to corporate resources. Self-motivated, but responds to corporate rewards.

Time orientation.   End goals of 3 to 15 years, depending on the nature of the project. Strives to meet self-imposed and corporate timetables.

Action.   Does whatever is needed to accomplish tasks. Is not interested in status.

Skills.   Knows business intimately, but recognises the importance of managerial and political skill.

Confidence.   Self-confident and courageous. If necessary will outwit the organisational system.

Focus.   Both inside and outside the business. Pays attention to customers and gets insiders to do the same.

Risk.   Likes moderate risk. Does own market research to understand risks.

Failure and mistakes. Regards mistakes as a learning experience, but is sensitive to the needs of the organisation for stability and hence may hide risky projects from view.

Decisions. Adept at communicating own private vision to others and willing to compromise to make progress with this vision.

Attitude towards the system. Dislikes the system, but learns to manipulate it.

Background. Often from entrepreneurial, small business, professional or farm background. Often middle-class and highly educated, particularly in technical fields.

Source: 'Who is the Intrapreneur?' adapted from G. Pinchot III, *Intrapreneuring* (New York: Harper & Row, 1985) pp. 54–6. Copyright © by Gifford Pinchot III. Reprinted by permission of HarperCollins Publishers, Inc.

■ Systems and Structures

Of those who have written about intrapreneurship Peter Drucker is among the foremost. Like Lessem, he highlights the importance of managerial behaviour but considers also that appropriate policies and structures are needed to sustain intrapreneurship. He considers that the essence of innovation and entrepreneurship is the development of new or different processes, products or services that utilise resources more productively than formerly. He contends that innovators must systematically review the changes taking place in society to identify and exploit business opportunities. Entrepreneurial managers must also scan the environment to become aware of changes in those management principles and practices, production processes, and market structures and requirements that can conceivably have an impact on their organisations. Intrapreneurs must also be aware of changes in knowledge, but are warned against an overemphasis on knowledge-based innovations. Some are spectacular and transform markets, but although the vast majority of innovations are more mundane they have a much greater cumulative impact on profits and employment.

It is important to emphasise the weight Drucker attaches to solid, systematic investigation in the process of modernisation. That is seldom the result of genius or high-technology discoveries; more often it is the application of systematic search and logic to a host of organisational procedures and practices. Installment credit or hire purchase, for instance, had a much greater impact on the business sector than more novel and spectacular changes. There are barriers to successful organisational innovation, but, if the right managerial policies and practices are put in place then innovation can become normal.

Many managers protect what they have currently, but if they are to change they must become aware that it is company policy to systematically give up those products and practices that are unproductive. They must therefore place all activities periodically 'on trial' for their lives. Managers should answer critical questions on the contribution products make to productivity and should be encouraged not to shore up the obsolete. Obsolete or declining products absorb scarce resources at the expense of the new. The best people tend to be charged with overcoming the problems associated with old products, whereas they should be encouraged to develop the new. Entrepreneurial business 'management must take the lead in making obsolete its own products and services rather than waiting for a competitor to do so.'[25]

Another approach is to use successful innovators as role models. They are asked to make presentations to their peers to explain their actions: to outline those factors that lead to success and those that cause difficulties. The fact that senior managers encourage this activity sends a clear message that innovative behaviour is appreciated. Then, if innovation is to become an important business function, mechanisms must be initiated to assess innovative performance. It is important to know what the expected outcomes of the innovation are likely to be, what resources are necessary and when results are to be achieved. Innovation concerns the new and largely unknown, but serious attempts must be made to gain feedback on progress to assess performance.

Policies, practices and appraisals assist innovation, but innovative ideas and their commercialisation are generated by people. Since behaviour is influenced by context, the organisational context must support innovative behaviour. Successful innovation emerges when organisations have appropriate personnel in post, when management systems support change and when a suitable climate obtains. The complexity of large organisations will stifle classic entrepreneurs, even if they are the company founders. Without appropriate policies the organisation is likely to become performance-oriented rather than innovation-oriented. 'Companies that have built entrepreneurial management into their structure...continue to be innovators...irrespective of changes in chief executives or economic conditions.'[26]

■ Adhocracies

The essence of this chapter is that enterprise is both possible and necessary in organisations that need to continue to develop by departing from existing product and process ranges while maintaining the efficiency of existing portfolios. There are, however, organisations that are habitual and sophisticated innovators. Organisations, for instance, in the computer, biomedical, film, or management consulting businesses are constant problem solvers and innovators. No sooner have they completed a project for a client, or developed a new prototype, than they are required to start again and create something else new.

Mintzberg indicates that flexibility is the key to this type of organisation.[27] This flexibility extends to the domain of strategy. Since these are innovative, problem-solving ventures, and individuals and teams are constantly working on new projects, no one can be sure how things will work out. So long as they fit in with the broad vision of the firm, successful projects that emerge from below will strongly influence strategy. Their structures are also highly flexible. There is no extensive division of labour or departmental specialisation, and little reliance on procedures, rules and plans. The reason is clear. As innovators they do not follow standard operating procedures and must use their brains to devise new ways of tackling new jobs.

Because they are refined and complex innovators, these firms rely heavily on the knowledge of their expert staff, and quite often senior managers do not fully understand the intricate details of the work done by these staff. The power of knowledge becomes important, and managers must delegate and have confidence in the ability of their experts. In addition, the experts will come together to work in project teams to work on client problems. Teamwork is not easy, but the managers of project teams must be skilled in group dynamics, facilitation and motivation. The intrapreneurial roles of enabling and animation are vitally important, and, because the work can only be done well in small groups, managerial spans of control are limited.

These structural arrangements are the antipathy of bureaucratic principles. Bureaucracies are control-oriented organisations, adhocracies are freedom-seekers, and if both are housed in the same location then the culture of one will adversely impact on the effectiveness of the other. Drucker argues for a physical separation of innovative from performance business.

■ Corporate Venturing

It has been suggested that some business strategies, such as downsizing, have actually caused organisations to reduce their capacity to innovate and to identify and build on new opportunities. To offset such tendencies, and in recognition of their need to continue to develop opportunities, businesses are adapting specific strategies to build entrepreneurial orientation into their organisations. This is often referred to as corporate venturing.

Corporate venturing strategies are often based on identifying an organisation's special competencies to provide the basis for creating new business and improving competitiveness, and they may include specific awareness measures to encourage employees to participate in the search for new ventures. Successful strategies are also characterised by intense internal communication and networking, and by a specific encouragement of risk-taking and a recognition that failure is an occupational hazard in successful innovation.[28]

■ Other Issues

However, while managers play a vital role in promoting innovation, they cannot order it. In a real sense they must empower their innovative personnel rather than exercise power over them. Hales notes that much of managerial endeavour is geared towards overcoming resistance to their authority, and in spite of a host of techniques – such as participative management, quality circles and incentive schemes – many managers still exercise power over others. However, he notes that many organisations are recognising that 'power in the sense of "transformative capacity" or "power to" now resides in the interdependence which is characteristic of work organisations.'[29] For innovation and enterprise, 'power to' is more important than 'power over'.

□ *The Mindset*

Many of the attitudes, behaviours and organisational arrangements which support innovation are presented by Sven Atterhed and his colleagues, from the ForeSight Group, in Figure 9.1. Flexibility, experimentation, empowerment and risk taking are crucial in engendering an innovative spirit and capacity in larger organisations.

Imported techniques can assist, but Atterhed argues that such mechanisms will achieve little if managers still try to reduce uncertainty and protect existing practices. He suggests that it is important to have a 'managerial mindset and

Source: Slightly modified from © The ForeSight Group Diagram, S Hamngatan 37, 41106 Göteborg, Sweden.

Figure 9.1   Manager mindset and behaviour for innovation

behaviour that encourages enterprise and innovation and equips people to be open to the new'.[30] The new mindset requests and requires that innovation is the responsibility of all. For Atterhed this will not happen, unless management develops a new mindset.

□ *Networks*

So far, intrapreneurship has been described as largely an intra-organisational process, as that is the original essence of the concept. However, there are situations where inter-firm contact and cooperation can help the process, especially innovation. Firms can search for opportunities, and try to realise them by developing products to meet market needs. If, however, having seen an opportunity, a business does not have the wherewithal to address it it may help to collaborate with one that can supply the missing component. This can also bring benefits of shared knowledge, reduced development and process costs, reduced risks of failure and knowledge of key benchmarks. In some markets it is also common for customers to initiate innovations.[31] Users are often the first to recognise a need and may then pass such information on to manufacturers, or use it in cooperation with them to develop an appropriate new product.

A level of collaboration has long characterised innovation, but it has been argued that inter-organisational cooperation is much more common in today's world. Why is this? Alter and Hage argue that, with the pace of change in technology and markets, the risks in carrying out innovation have increased considerably.[32] Innovators need time to recoup development costs, but in current conditions, product life-cycles may be too short to guarantee recovery. They also argue that the state plays an increasing role in much industrial innovation. Often it encourages lots of players to get involved and promotes collaborative practices to let many of the players share in the benefits. Porter (see Chapter 5) argues against encouraging joint ventures between domestic competitors, because this reduces the incentive to maintain a competitive advantage. However collaboration and the development of long-term relationships with customers and suppliers can help to reduce costs and enhance competitiveness.

Such inter-organisational relationships, however, will not develop overnight. Parties must be aware of one another and feel that the others have something of use for them. They must also communicate to explain their needs and examine possibilities for exchange. A degree of consensus is also important. They must have reasonably compatible values and be able to work problems through by means of 'adjustment and compromise – a process that entails negotiating and bargaining'.[33]

Market uncertainties, experience in developing long-term relationships, and the complexity of the innovation process have led many firms to form links with a number of outside organisations when generating ideas, developing prototypes and testing markets. As James notes, 'The significant change in the business environment...has changed the focus of alliance strategies (for innovation) to the point where they are now becoming the rule rather than the exception.'[34]

■ Postscript

Innovation is at the heart of the spirit of enterprise. Practically all firms are born from a development which is innovative, at least in comparison with their existing competitors in the marketplace. If they are subsequently to survive and develop, however, firms must constantly innovate – even if only gradually. In this respect, technical advances are not themselves sufficient to ensure success. Innovation also means anticipating the needs of the market, offering additional quality or services, organising efficiently, mastering details and keeping costs under control.[34]

(EU Green Paper on Innovation[34])

Small businesses are a reservoir, a source, both for the creation of jobs and for the development of diversity within economies. Capitalising on this reservoir, however, means growing those small businesses and maintaining the attitudes of enterprise in the business upon which that growth will depend. That internal enterprise, in larger businesses, requires some different approaches from the enterprise which typically starts a small business. It has been called intrapreneurship.

Key points

- Growth in the early stages of a small business can be seen as a natural extension of its original formation, but when a business reaches a steady state different attitudes can prevail and further change can be resisted. Maintaining growth in a more mature business can therefore require a different approach, a process of internal enterprise, which has been called 'intrapreneurship'.
- Intrapreneurship is therefore connected to the concepts of entrepreneurship, enterprise, and innovation. Entrepreneurship has typically described the drive that starts a business, and a similar drive is needed to maintain its advance. Innovation is the successful development of competitive advantage and, as such, can be said to be the key to intrapreneurship. That innovation can take several forms: innovation in processes and methods, innovation in products, or services, and innovation in work organisation. Entrepreneurship and innovation, applied to the continued development of business, are still enterprise even if the business is a larger one.
- There are however inherent difficulties in intrapreneurship. These are such that some writers on intrapreneurship have contended that many

large corporations will in practice survive only by restructuring their businesses as confederations of small businesses. They include the barriers of human resistance to change, the barriers of management roles and motivation, and the barriers of organisational structures and systems. Size, *per se*, is not an impediment to entrepreneurship and innovation, but the attitude and methods that size can bring are.

- The process of intrapreneurship itself has been analysed in terms of the roles an intrapreneur must play, including those of entrepreneur, adventurer, innovator, leader, change agent, enabler, and animateur, many of which do not fit in easily with a large-company ethos. The structures that best support the processes of intrapreneurship have also been considered, with recommendations for solid systematic investigations into the relevance of current products and procedures and into the process of modernisation.

- Some organisations, in industries such as computers, biomedical products, and management consulting, are constant problem-solvers and innovators. Flexibility is the key to their success. They are also frequently knowledge-based and have structural arrangements that are the antipathy of bureaucracy. Empowerment is important, as well as having the right mindset.

- Finally intrapreneurship need not always be entirely internal. Many businesses network with others to promote their own innovation and advancement.

PART III
Promoting Enterprise

Part I of this book looked at the concept of enterprise and showed that the word 'enterprise' has a range of meanings. This includes what has been described as a 'narrow' meaning, referring specifically to small business, which was the prime focus of Part II. Small business is important for reasons of diversity and social stability, and for supporting the competitiveness of other businesses. Particular attention has however been focused on it because of the indicated links between small business and job creation. Governments, especially in times of high unemployment, want more jobs. They are therefore prepared to intervene to secure the development of more enterprise.

Part III therefore looks at this intervention: intervention which cannot of itself create enterprise but, at least in theory, can promote it. It is people who can act in an enterprising way and who can start small businesses, and intervention can seek to encourage them to do it more and to make it easier or more rewarding for them. That is what is meant by promoting enterprise.

Chapter 10 therefore starts by considering the reasons for intervention. It looks at the benefits sought and the arguments that there are obstacles and barriers to enterprise that intervention could address in order to produce these benefits. It also considers the pressure that sometimes exists for intervention, if only to show that something is being done.

The forms of intervention to be used will however depend on theories and assumptions about the nature of the enterprise process and of the obstacles it faces. It is necessary to have some understanding of the process from culture through to growth business in order to see how intervention might work and what intervention might therefore be successful. These issues are examined in Chapter 11.

To succeed, intervention should be based on clear objectives, be delivered through appropriate structures and use relevant approaches. Chapter 12 looks at these issues and at the possible areas for intervention and the forms it might take.

The variety of intervention practised raises the question of how successful it is. Evaluating enterprise intervention is not easy. The requirements for it can be complex and there are many difficulties in doing it. These considerations are covered in Chapter 13, which also looks at the findings of some of the research to date.

ENTERPRISE ⟶ SMALL BUSINESSES ⟶ JOBS

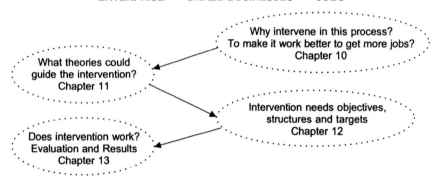

CHAPTER 10
Why Intervene?

Throughout the world governments and governmental organisations, whether national, regional or local, are intervening in the economies of the countries, regions or local areas they are trying to govern. Much of this intervention is intended to promote more enterprise, usually in the form of business and not least of small business. Before looking at the methods that might be employed in such interventions, however, it may be relevant to consider why intervention to promote enterprise may be required or justified.

■ An Obvious Argument?

> *Small firms were the source of the majority of net new jobs created between 1969 and 1976 in the USA.*
>
> **(David Birch[1])**
>
> *The UK results are broadly similar to those of the United States ... indicating that smaller firms provide a disproportionate share of new job creation.*
>
> **(Colin Gallagher[2])**
>
> Faced with a serious unemployment problem, such as that in the UK in the 1980s and 1990s, and persuasive evidence that small businesses are effective as job creators, and are particularly resilient in an economic recession, there would seem to be a strong prima facie case for government intervention in support of small businesses.

The usual, and apparently obvious, argument for intervention to promote enterprise, is jobs. To prevent or reduce unemployment, jobs are required, and if small businesses provide jobs then the assumption is that more small businesses will provide more jobs. Therefore, if intervention will mean that there will be more, and faster growing, small businesses then intervention will achieve the desired benefit of more jobs.

There are however other factors at work, which may affect this reasoning, and which are not always considered. For instance:

- Some jobs in small businesses may be the result of transfers of work from bigger businesses, which in turn may have resulted in efficiency gains but may not lead to net job creation. Productivity gains in bigger businesses can result in greater output but fewer jobs. Therefore figures showing net job creation in smaller businesses do not necessarily mean that they are better wealth creators.
- The creation and growth of new small businesses can result in considerable displacement of jobs from existing ones.
- A strong emphasis on jobs in economic interventions may result in a bias against improvements in productivity, because such improvements, which can benefit an economy, may actually result in net job losses.

This is not a criticism of small businesses, and does not mean that they are not important. It is just a caution that small business development does not inevitably result in net economic growth, and that increases in employment in some small businesses do not necessarily mean more jobs overall.

However, the 'more small businesses equals more jobs' approach would seem to be so obvious that it is often apparently followed without further exploration. Storey points out that in Europe there are a wide range of policy initiatives to assist small businesses, but that the governments concerned have yet to formulate a coherent policy towards the sector.

In no country, as far as we are aware, is there the equivalent of a 'White Paper' which articulates the range of public policies towards smaller firms which currently exist, which provides a justification for the existing configuration of policies, and which provides criteria for judging whether or not policies are successful.[3]

Are such policies successful, and is the obvious argument correct? For it to hold, small businesses must provide jobs, more and/or faster growing small businesses must provide more jobs, and intervention must promote more and/or faster growing small businesses. The evidence that small businesses create jobs has been considered earlier, in Chapter 7. Whether intervention is actually effective however is a different issue and depends on whether intervention can have a positive

Table 10.1 **The why and how of intervention**

Why intervene?	*To maximise economic, social and other welfare benefits.*	*Provided*:
		• The benefits are worth the costs.
	But the benefits sought can include both wealth creation and jobs, and the promotion of one does not necessarily mean the promotion of the other.	• Alternative approaches could not provide more benefit for the same cost or the same benefit for lower costs.
How to intervene?	*By addressing obstacles and barriers to development*	*Provided*:
	For instance by reducing 'market failure'.	• Addressing the obstacles does achieve the benefits sought.

effect on small businesses and whether the cost of that effect, in terms of both the cost of the intervention and the cost of any side effects, is less than the benefit gained and is less than the cost of alternative interventions to produce the same benefit. Intervention must not just make the recipient businesses better off, but it must overall make a positive net contribution to the economy, and a better contribution than might be achieved from any alternative interventions. (See Chapter 13 for a further discussion on this issue.)

There are arguments that intervention is not necessary because it will not achieve a net economic benefit. The overall economic argument is essentially that if intervention is to be justified then there must be a 'market failure' (see later in this chapter) to be addressed, and addressing it must increase the welfare of society as a whole. There are however reasons to think that intervention in some form is inevitable because it is politically desirable. This obviously introduces into the argument a political element based on the perceived attractiveness of the benefits to be gained. Consideration of the justification for intervention therefore requires a look at the range of benefits that might be gained from intervention (including political benefits), at the barriers or obstacles preventing, or hindering, those benefits which intervention may help to overcome, and at the overall balance between costs and benefits. Table 10.1 attempts to summarise the above discussion.

■ The Benefits Sought

Intervention has a cost and should be considered only if it is likely to result in a net benefit. Therefore if there is to be intervention to promote more enterprise then it should be because of the benefits more enterprise can provide.

■ The Economic Benefits of Small Business

Some of the economic benefits of enterprise have been considered in earlier chapters, in particular the employment benefits, the evidence for which was considered in some detail in Chapter 7. However, they are also relevant here, so let us summarise them:

- Enterprise, in its narrow definition of small business, can create wealth, but so also can larger businesses (see above).
- Small businesses can provide jobs (see Chapter 7).
- It has also been argued that small businesses have a greater proclivity to innovate than their larger counterparts and are therefore crucial in helping a country respond to the myriad of changes in the economic, technological and social environment.[4]
- Small businesses can make an important contribution to the infra-structure needed to support larger competitive businesses (see Chapter 5 for cluster theory). Particularly today, when 'downsizing' has been more common than vertical integration, it is almost impossible to find a business that does not in some way depend to a considerable extent on small business subcontractors.
- Other benefits provided by small businesses are increased competition, choice and diversity; regeneration and revitalisation of sectors and regions; and political stability and social cohesion.

Whether actual interventions are based on all these benefits is a different issue. In many cases the objectives of the interventions are not clearly stated, and have to be deduced from other information. Storey has inferred objectives from observing public policy in the UK. His list is presented in Table 10.2.

■ The Social and Wider Benefits of Enterprise

As noted above, small businesses can also provide a range of social benefits. They can provide jobs in areas where few big businesses can operate, such as very rural areas, and in this way they can distribute jobs more widely. Small businesses can supply a range of personal and community services, such as restaurants, window cleaning, household repairs, and local corner shops. Most artists are, in effect, small businesses, as also are legal and medical practices. Small businesses are therefore essential to the way of life many people enjoy.

Enterprise in its wider sense also provides many benefits. People who have been successfully encouraged to be more enterprising will be more confident and self-reliant. As a result, they may suffer less from social exclusion and from

Table 10.2   Objectives of small firm policy

Intermediate	Final
1. Increase employment	– Increase employment – Reduce unemployment
2. Increase number of start-ups	– Increase number of start-ups – Increase stock of firms
3. Promote use of consultants	– Promote use of consultants – Faster growth of firms
4. Increase competition	– Increase competition – Increase wealth
5. Promote 'efficient' markets	– Promote 'efficient' markets – Increase wealth
6. Promote technology diffusion	– Promote technology diffusion – Increase wealth
7. Increase wealth	– Votes

Source: D. J. Storey, *Understanding the Small Business Sector* (London: ITPB, 1994) p. 260.

deprivation. This is not to say that enterprise will solve all their problems, but that it can help them to start to overcome some of them. Many immigrant communities often seem to thrive because they are enterprising, even if that enterprise has been born of necessity; although it may be that it is the more enterprising who leave their original countries and become immigrants. Enterprise sustains change and encourages new approaches that allow individuals, organisations and societies to adjust effectively to changing environments. Whether it is in business, in politics, in the arts or in community work, enterprise in its wider sense is beneficial in responding to change, which, in all except the short term, is inevitable.

Obstacles and Barriers – Market Failures?

Indicated above are some of the benefits to be gained from enterprise in both its narrow and broad senses. If intervention is to be considered however then it must be because it will enhance the level of those benefits. The argument that it will do so is generally that there are obstacles and barriers preventing the desired outcomes and that these obstacles and barriers can be reduced or removed by intervention. Obstacles and barriers that discriminate more against some than others, that prevent a 'level playing field', can generally be classed as 'market failures'.

According to neo-classical economic theory there is a tendency towards perfect markets. Attempting to intervene in a perfect market would not result in any improvement in that market. The value of any apparent benefits in one area would be outweighed by the cost of displacement effects elsewhere, and there would be no net economic benefit. However, after a disruption in the market, there may be some factors that delay the return of the market to perfection. Intervening to address these inherently temporary factors could therefore produce benefits. Such factors are 'market failures' in that they represent a failure of the market to perform perfectly.

Others however point out that the neo-classical perfect market is a myth and that many of the assumptions about markets made by neo-classical economists do not hold true. There are always imperfections in markets. Many organisations have the power to dominate markets and use it. Large corporations dominate them, product differentiations by means of marketing manipulations are manifold, and predatory practices are commonplace. The result is many 'market failures', which place small businesses at a disadvantage and are likely to be permanent unless steps are taken to address them.[5]

The term 'market failure' can therefore mean different things to different people. To the neo-classical economist, if market failure exists, it is only a temporary phenomenon that will eventually go. If it is not temporary, it is not a market failure, and trying to address it will not result in a net benefit. To the avowed realist, however, a market failure is potentially a permanent feature, which will continue to disrupt unless addressed. The market failures that have been highlighted are therefore mainly ones which have been identified by the realists.

■ Market Barriers to Small Business Development

☐ *The Advantages of Big Business*

There are multinational firms with turnovers that exceed the gross national product of most nations. The sheer size and economic power of such firms allows them to dominate consumer and factor markets. They can use huge advertising and marketing expenditure to make it very difficult for new entrants to gain a foothold in their markets. They can benefit from economies of scale. In the procurement field, large firms can secure discounts and organise just-in-time contracts that shift the burden of stockholding to their suppliers. In the labour market they can attract the best staff with their competitive remunerative packages and career prospects for employees.

Some of the origins of their advantages are:

- The ability to spread fixed overhead costs over a larger output confers significant advantages on large businesses. Larger businesses may have higher fixed costs than small ones, but such costs tend to increase in discontinuous steps that are proportionally higher for small producers than for larger ones.[6]

- Large businesses use their size and power to advantage in other areas. When they need finance they can use the capital market with greater facility than small businesses, and they can benefit from considerable economies of scale. Indeed, it has long been argued that an equity gap exists for small businesses which cannot find market sources of the type and amount of capital they need.[7] (This is explored in more detail in Chapter 12.) This gap exists in part because of the inefficiency of the capital market with respect to small businesses. In an efficient market, buyers and sellers of finance act through intermediaries and legal remedies are available in cases of dispute. However, many small businesses are unquoted companies and the divestment and exchange of information between the parties is less than perfect. Firms are reluctant to divulge sensitive data, and investors are reluctant to lend in the absence of detailed information. In this situation, an effective working relationship must be built up between the principals before business can be done, but this is time-consuming and costly for both the small businesses and the venture capitalists involved.[8]
- Bannock and Peacock argue that small firms are also at a relative disadvantage in complying with a range of statutory and administrative regulations imposed by government. Compliance with VAT is a case in point. They indicate that the cost of compliance as a percentage of turnover falls sharply with increasing sales value.[9]

A counter to these arguments is that in many cases large firms have earned these cost advantages. Developing a business requires considerable skill, and cost advantages are their reward for this endeavour. In this sense these are not market failures. However, supporters of small firms argue that the perpetuation of this advantage will damage the potential of the small business sector to provide economic benefits and that intervention to reduce the advantage is therefore justified.

☐ *The Need for Support*

Businesses, if they are to develop, need access to a range of skills and abilities in areas such as organisation, management, production, marketing, selling, strategy, finance and law. Bigger businesses can have all of these in-house, but smaller businesses must inevitably go outside to find at least some of them. They need such support but are often reluctant to seek it. There are a number of reasons for this. Sometimes the need for support is not appreciated. Sometimes they may fear that exposing their efforts to others may lead to their ideas being stolen. Sometimes they may be reluctant to approach experts because they are afraid the experts might despise their efforts and because the traditional consultancy approach is itself offputting to many small businesses. They might also be discouraged by the price of the advice.

It has been argued that if the felt need of businesses is great enough then they will consume the consultancy services on offer and pay the market price for them. This economic argument, however, overlooks a number of realities about the nature of the demand for services by small businesses. It assumes that small business owners can analyse fully the complexity of their world and identify precisely their needs, that they possess the interpersonal and social skills to deal with sophisticated experts, that they have sufficient information about the availability and cost of services to make a rational choice, and that they have the money to pay for the services on offer. In reality none of these conditions may exist. Because there does not appear to be an overwhelming demand by small businesses for support and assistance in overcoming difficulties and seizing opportunities, this does not mean that there is not a considerable latent demand for assistance. A key role for experts is to clarify the problems clients face and to help them to overcome their difficulties. Proactive provision of services could assist small businesses to become more efficient than they are currently.[10]

Of course large firms have also gone through a learning phase and have survived, so why should emerging small businesses now be pampered? A view put forward by Bannock is that large firms are disproportionately represented in the British economy to the detriment of economic development. He argues that the percentage of small businesses should be increased, and feels that 'we cannot leave it to the market.'[11] If small businesses face temporary market or managerial problems then financial and other means of support could provide a vital breathing space until circumstances improve. If we want small firms to make the maximum contribution to the economy then it makes sense to assist businesses that are basically viable until their expertise and experience improve and allow them to reap the benefits which size and age confer on organisations. Of course such a policy will not add overall to the economy if the supported small businesses, by virtue of that support, force out of business existing businesses that are fundamentally no less competitive. The displacement effect must always be considered.

■ Barriers to Enterprise Development

The barriers considered above are those that affect small businesses once they are established. Market failure as a barrier to enterprise refers specifically to enterprise in this context of small business. However, there are other barriers that are more apparent when the development of enterprise in its wider sense of an enterprise culture is considered. Barriers of culture or of education exist that prevent people starting businesses, or even thinking of starting them, and intervention might be considered to address these also.

☐ *Cultural Barriers*

One way of identifying the presence of other barriers is to look at the variations between levels of enterprise in different regions and countries. In terms of economic success, the UK is being described by some as the enterprise centre of Europe, yet even within the UK there are variations in the level of enterprise, as has been pointed out in Chapter 4. It has been argued that some societies have economic and social structures that encourage and facilitate enterprise while others do not. For example, within the UK Northern Ireland's recent economic history is characterised by a reliance on a self-sufficient agriculture sector, large employing organisations in declining industries and a dominant public sector. Its social and political problems are severe and some suggest that it has a dependency culture. It therefore lacks a strong small business tradition and the culture that might support one. That is an obstacle to enterprise.

In this situation social conditions are such that the option of entrepreneurship as a form of employment is not commonly recognised. There are very successful entrepreneurial ventures in Northern Ireland, but most individuals lack the knowledge, skills and mind-set to pursue this career option successfully. They see two economic possibilities: if they are lucky they can have a job working for someone else, or if they are unlucky they will be unemployed and relying on unemployment benefit payments. In this, and in other situations of economic and social deprivation with second- and third-generation unemployment, the facilitation of the entrepreneurial process could be viewed as one means of overcoming social disadvantage. However it is not easy: the problems are long-term ones that are likely to require long-term solutions, and many government activities in this sphere are viewed with suspicion because they can have strong political overtones.

The typical Northern Ireland view of a market economy may not be very close to the American or liberal model of capitalism, but markets do exist there. In some areas of Eastern Europe, however, markets were poorly developed. Under the so-called communist system the state determined what was to be produced and how, and employees aimed to extract the greatest benefit from the state at minimum cost to themselves. This was a situation where the enterprise option, far from not being recognised, often simply did not exist, or was not developed. Under these conditions the removal of state controls has tended to lead not straight to a market economy but instead to chaos and opportunities for the criminal fraternity. These countries want a market economy, and enterprise is no longer actively discouraged. Possibly the classical economists might be proved correct and perfect markets might evolve, given enough time. However, the countries concerned want improvements now and are willing to consider intervention to get it.

It would therefore appear that certain countries and regions are more entrepreneurial than others. Economic price theory might suggest that a market-driven reduction in wage rates and other costs, plus the exit of firms from certain industries, would provide opportunities for profit in regions like Wales and Scotland. However, there are those who argue that such free markets in the second half of the twentieth century are a myth, and that it is unlikely that market forces alone will redress the balance between regions.[12] That implies that if the imbalance is to be redressed then intervention of some sort will be necessary.

□ Education

Intervention may be considered either to promote small businesses specifically or to promote enterprise in its broader sense, or both. Enterprise in its broader sense is about the development of attitudes of enterprise or entrepreneurialism in individuals. Gibb argues that enterprising people are adventurous go-getters who have a self-reliant approach to life.[13] He argues that enterprising persons exhibit behaviours ranging from persuasion and problem-solving to independent action, and that these are supported by a collection of skills and attributes. He contends further that some aspects of enterprise are learned, and as such are amenable to development by education and training. However, he questions whether some traditional approaches to education, with their reliance on teacher-led passivity, are what are required to promote the spread of enterprise. If his model of education is accepted then there could well be grounds for state-led interventions to redirect aspects of the educational system towards an enterprising mode of teaching.

Educational interventions may enhance the degree of enterprise within the population, but entrepreneurship requires more than the display of enterprising attributes. Entrepreneurs need appropriate attributes, but they also need relevant knowledge and skills, and they must be sensitised to the possibility of an entrepreneurial career. Individuals have a enormous range of potential career options, and if the number of small businesses is to be increased then sufficient individuals will have to be attracted to entrepreneurship. However, entrepreneurship is not a mainstream occupation. Indeed, earlier theories considered that marginal individuals were the most likely potential entrepreneurs, and there is a case for positive intervention aimed at the populace at large, or the labour market in general, which can secure a flow of individuals who will actively consider this career option.[14]

■ Why, and Why Not

Economic arguments justify intervention in a market economy when there is market failure. Some economists, however maintain that market failure, although a necessary condition, is not alone a sufficient condition for intervention. There must in addition be evidence that the overall welfare improvements resulting from the intervention will be sufficient to justify the cost of that intervention, and that there is no other better way of achieving the same improvements.

It might be expected that attempts to promote enterprise and entrepreneurship would find favour in most quarters. However, this is not the case. It is said that enterprise thrives in a free enterprise economy, and many advocates of this economic system caution against interference with market forces. These people argue that the laws of supply and demand, operating through the price system, send signals to interested parties, who respond to market opportunities and threats. Those persons who are able to interpret market forces accurately will reap economic rewards, and this pursuit of self-interest leads to the most efficient utilisation of economic resources. Enterprising individuals are inclined to be energetic, forward looking people who take bold steps to realise opportunities, and it can be seen that free enterprise economic systems are an attractive milieu for the enterprising individuals to display their skills. There is no point in promoting entrepreneurship and enterprise: the enterprising will avail of opportunities, and the aggregate outcome of their decisions will produce greater welfare than decisions made by central authorities.

That argument assumes perfectly competitive markets, and many maintain that markets are far from competitive. Nevertheless, it is still contended that there is no generalised market failure in the small business sector. Bennett points to the size and growth of the sector as evidence of advance. He argues that, when asked about those factors that inhibit development of small businesses, owners comment on general economic and regulatory factors such as the condition of the economy and the inhibiting impact of statutory regulations. Where specific needs are highlighted they arise in areas such as venture capital, marketing advice, training and cash flow problems: 'areas where well developed markets already exist'.[15]

Two comments in particular can be made in response to these views. First, many small businesses may be unaware of the immense power of large corporations and their subtle ability to inhibit competition. Those small businesses may occupy niche markets where, unless they threaten industrial giants directly, they may be tolerated. Second, the methods used by those who seek to identify the problems experienced by small firms rarely delve, in a detailed way, into the problems small firms experience. Researchers commonly present entrepreneurs with a long list of problems and ask them to say whether this or that problem applies to them. Just as Bennett argues that it is only by means of in-depth discussion with small business owners that the effectiveness of policy initiatives can be judged, so it can be argued that quantitative studies of the problems faced by small businesses will merely elicit pre-programmed responses. There may also be a tendency for small business owners to project their problems away from themselves towards more distant perceived impediments such as the government or the European Union.

On the issue of the provision of needed services, such as information, advice and training, Bennett argues that if the felt need of businesses is great enough then they will pay the market price for consultancy services on offer. As mentioned above, however, economic reasoning ignores many of the personal and interpersonal aspects of seeking external advice, whether it is from consultants, counsellors or mentors. Many owners have a real need for such assistance, but lack the information and confidence needed to identify, approach, and if necessary negotiate terms for suitable help.

10.1 An analogy?

In some respects classical economic theory is like the theory of natural selection in nature. According to that theory, in the long term the fittest will survive and nature itself is an effective way of ensuring that this happens. However in a system in which natural selection rules, what then is the role of selective breeding and intensive farming, both of which are much practiced in agriculture? The answer may be that the question is to some extent itself misleading. Left to itself nature has produced a very wide variety of life forms, all of which thrive in their own niches. However, for our own purposes we want to encourage the growth of some of these life forms and to make them better suited to our requirements. That is what agriculture does: it intervenes to create circumstances in which those that survive are those that we want.

May it not be that markets, left to themselves, will also produce a variety of businesses? However, if we specifically seek the benefits that some of those businesses bring, may we not also have to intervene to create the conditions that specifically encourage their development?

■ Intervention Exists

A pragmatic view of intervention is to recognise that it exists, and will in some form or another continue to exist. One form of existing intervention is laws and regulations to control business, laws that require businesses to be registered, laws that seek to control monopolies and laws that stipulate permitted labour practices are all interventions.

In addition to this precedent there is an almost irresistible temptation on governments to intervene. If it is understood that small businesses create jobs, and if significant numbers of people are unemployed and want jobs, then government will find that intervention to promote small business will be a popular option. Electorates may not be familiar with the subtleties of arguments to the contrary.

There are many advocates of a *laissez-faire* economic policy, but no government, even among those that purport to champion liberal capitalist economics, appears to have adhered strictly to such a policy. Governments intervene in numerous ways to manage their economies and redistribute wealth. As the editors of *business week* note, the most successful economies, in spite of huge differences among them, all have 'broad support throughout their societies for basic national economic goals and for measures of industrial policy to achieve them'.[16] In many respects the debate about intervention is not therefore about the principle of intervention but about the means that are to be used.

10.2 Four main objectives in SME policy pursued by EU Member States[17]

- Creation of employment
- Competition
- Strengthening the production chain
- Diversification

However, these objectives have had to be inferred from observing policies in operation. Only a few countries overtly select employment creation as an objective. None of them emphasise competition, strengthening or diversification of the production chain explicitly as an objective.

There is debate about the wisdom and efficacy of state intervention in support of enterprise and entrepreneurship, but the sheer size of the small business sector makes it very difficult for governments to ignore the real or perceived needs of the sector. In addition the variety of the goals pursued by small business policymakers and their susceptibility to measurement, or lack of it creates ideal conditions for the political manipulation of policy. There are many people in the 'small business support industry', and any apparent willingness to promote small businesses, especially when combined with any uncertainty surrounding policy objectives, provides them with ample opportunity to use their creativity in providing and developing small business support services. The great difficulty in conducting scientific evaluations of policy measures only adds to this confusion.

Part of the debate should be about the effectiveness of those means, yet, as a number of writers have pointed out, there have been no sophisticated, systematic evaluations of specific interventions to enhance the achievements of small businesses in creating new jobs. The result is that many uncertainties arise in connection with the usefulness of various policies. These uncertainties permit, or even encourage, a political dimension of policy to develop. If actions appear to look good and there is no clear evidence for what they achieve, or fail to achieve, then the actions may be pursued, not for the results they bring, but for the credit that applying them will earn for those responsible.[18]

This is politically motivated behaviour, and it is particularly prevalent when an objective is desired but its achievement cannot easily be measured. These conditions apply in small business support. There is a considerable willingness to support small businesses, combined with a lack of information on what actually works. In these circumstances, intervention, if at least superficially justified, may actually be engaged in for political reasons, connected with the desire for recognition or advancement by the people involved, rather than because of any real desire to promote enterprise.

This support is frequently justified on the grounds that it promotes employment, but there are additional arguments for supporting embryo small businesses. Economists extol the virtues of small businesses in facilitating structural changes in industries. As old and inefficient firms expire, new, more productive small businesses fill the gap. But numerous studies have pointed to the vulnerability of small businesses, especially in their formative years. If individuals are to be encouraged to set up in business then they might warrant assistance in their dangerous early years. Many small business people are in need of help as they struggle with the manifold and complex tasks of business formation, launch and early development, and it seems sensible to offer them assistance.

■ Requirements

If interventions are to happen then they should be evaluated to see if they produce useful benefits in terms of their intended purpose. Evaluating interventions is not however always straightforward (a subject developed further in Chapter 13), and there are also problems in establishing what intervention is required in the first place. This arises because it is difficult to find out what help businesses do need. Established firms may not request specific assistance from government in overcoming their difficulties, because they are more concerned with aggregate demand and general labour market issues. However, this does not mean that they do not have problems that could be overcome with help.

Key points

- Small businesses are the source of many new jobs. The usual argument for intervention in support of small businesses is therefore that it can promote more small businesses and thus more jobs. There are, however, other factors relevant to this argument, such as the difference between creating wealth and creating employment, which mean that the rationale for small business intervention is not as clear as it might at first seem.
- If small business intervention is to be justified then there must be benefits, which are worth the costs involved and which cannot be supplied as well by alternative interventions. The purpose of small business intervention is not often made clear, but it would appear to be to promote economic and/or social welfare benefits of which the most obvious is employment. Small businesses can create jobs, but in addition they can also provide more innovation, which is needed for future competitiveness, and they can provide essential support for other businesses. Enterprise in its wider manifestation can also provide social benefits.

- To be justified, intervention must also be effective. It must be based on a valid way of achieving the outcomes sought. Usually that way is by addressing obstacles and barriers to enterprise, of which there are many. Some of these are classified as market failures, and there are economic welfare arguments about the value of intervening to address these. Classical theory may suggest that the market will make its own adjustments, but others maintain that there are real and lasting imperfections that will only be corrected by outside intervention. These problems include the power of big businesses, the imperfections of the capital market and the impossibility of small businesses employing directly all the skills and expertise they need.

- There can also be barriers of culture and education to the development of enterprise. In the former communist countries of Eastern Europe and the Soviet Union, for instance, there had for many years been no tradition of enterprise or role models for it.

- To be justified, intervention must make a positive change worth more than the cost of the intervention. Classical theory suggests that, while the direct results of intervention may be positive, the indirect results, such as displacement, can negate the direct benefits. Others argue that imperfections exist, and that if more enterprise is required, and there are barriers to its development, then intervening to reduce the barriers will be beneficial.

- However, whatever the arguments, intervention is practised. Governments are subject to political pressures as well as economic ones, and the political pressures for supporting enterprise seem irresistible. Governments do therefore intervene to promote enterprise, even if the objectives of their interventions, and their results, are often unclear.

CHAPTER 11

Theories and Assumptions (that might guide intervention)

Chapter 10 considered some of the arguments for and against intervening to try to promote more enterprise. If however, for whatever reason, the decision has been made to intervene, then on what basis might it be done? What theories and models are there to guide that intervention?

This chapter looks at some of the assumptions that have been made about enterprise, and the theories about it that have been advanced, that might indicate where intervention could be effective and what form it might take. Examples of specific types and areas of intervention are given in the next chapter (Chapter 12), but before they are discussed it may be helpful to have some ideas of how enterprise might be influenced. This approach not only might indicate the theory which underlies some of the intervention methods practiced but also might provide the basis for new approaches.

Some of these ideas have been described in previous chapters but have been referred to again here, in order to show a comparative selection of these ideas without the need to refer back frequently. There is however no absolute guarantee that the theories are correct. Like any theory in science, they are useful only in so far as they help to predict behaviour in a way which conforms to what actually happens in practice. The theories do not have to conform to some absolute level of truth to be helpful, nor do they all have to be consistent one with another. Newton's proposals for laws of gravity may have been proved to be less accurate than Einstein's ideas on the behaviour of space, but they are still good enough for many predictions about the movement of objects in space. The wave theory of light may help to explain light interference, although it is apparently inconsistent with particle theory, which can better explain other observable phenomena.

■ Categories

There are a variety of theories and models, and they need to be presented in some order. The order chosen here is that of the stages of development of a

222

business, as described in Chapter 6 because it seems to be a particularly useful way of categorising them. The different stages of development are distinguished by the different needs appropriate to each one, and, as it is these needs which may be susceptible to intervention, such a categorisation may be particularly appropriate to this chapter. For the purposes of this book, which has looked at both the broad and narrow views of enterprise, the assumptions and theories can be divided into two sorts: there are those that are relevant to the readiness of people to display enterprise, and then there are those ideas about the formation and subsequent development of businesses that may be started as a result of that enterprise.

The development of that readiness to display enterprise, or of enterprise culture, may be a particularly appropriate starting point because of the belief, which conforms to many observations, that enterprise is 'made not born'. The exercise of enterprising behaviour is not, it is suggested, something that depends solely, or largely, on inherited characteristics, but instead can to a very considerable extent be developed by learning and experience. If that is so then intervention to promote more of it may be both possible and practical. Promoting the culture may be the start.

■ Enterprise Culture

■ Awareness

The pursuit of entrepreneurship can be liken to choosing an occupation. To be successful it requires an initial awareness of it, an interest in it, a desire to try it and the decision and action to try it followed by a sufficient degree of attainment in it. That process must start with an awareness of the possibility of doing it.

It would be wrong to assume that everyone is aware of the possibility that he or she might be enterprising, or that it might have potential for him or her. Research by Curran and Blackburn indicates that sixth-form pupils in Britain, unless either or both of their parents or close relatives are in their own businesses, are unlikely to be interested in this as a career.[1] People may not want to try entrepreneurship, either because it is not, for them, desirable, or because the possibility has never occurred to them. The first intervention step may therefore be to raise awareness of entrepreneurship and its potential benefits: a process of encouraging people to want to be entrepreneurs.

Before individuals can conceive of themselves as entrepreneurs, they must be aware that this is a possible career option. A time when this might most appropriately be raised by or with young people is during the time they are in school. Interventions at this stage are generally based on communicating enterprise awareness through the consideration of entrepreneurship. There are programmes that try to introduce young people to the notion of small business and the possibility of setting up a new business. However, Gibb suggests that many of these programmes are not themselves delivered in an enterprising manner.[2] They focus on the technical aspects of managing a small firm, and fail to provide participants with insights into the dynamic and ulti-mately enterprising nature of small business management. Instead it is important to incorporate the 'essence of small enterprise' into the learning method. If this is done then participants will acquire useful technical knowledge but will also learn how to cope with the complex, variable and ambiguous world of the small business.

Gibb argues that the small scale of operation in an SME renders the owner vulnerable to environmental uncertainties and a reliance on outside stake-holders. In addition, owners and their staff must complete numerous tasks and develop a holistic view of their work. The ensuing task environment is complex and changeable, and the fact that owners are in charge means that they cannot walk away from problems – they must see tasks through to completion. As a result, owners experience a strange mixture of freedom and flexibility coupled with customer-led demands to meet their needs. Myriad demands create a need to develop problem-solving skills and a capacity to obtain requisite information and resources through networks of personal contacts. To survive in this environment, owners and managers in small businesses must be adaptable and able to learn from experience. They learn by doing, by taking risks, by problem-solving, by interacting with others and by tolerating ambiguity. They also initiate more than they react to situations. If the essence of entrepreneurship is to be inculcated in potential entrepreneurs then the essential elements of a small business environment must be created in the learning situation. It is important to create an uncertain task environment and to encourage learning by 'self-discovery'. Teachers must be facilitators rather than fonts of knowledge, and must create an effective learning environment that uses a project of suitable complexity as a learning vehicle. Table 2.4 in Chapter 2 summarises some key differences between an educational and an entrepreneurial focus.

As well as school-based programmes, other means can be employed to raise enterprise awareness. Again, Gibb has indicated some of them in his illustration of the components of an enterprise culture shown in Figure 2.1 in Chapter 2.

However, there may be dangers in being too positive in promoting enterprise. Creating a rosy picture of the entrepreneurial world and ignoring the difficulties that can arise may not help; and neither may talking about 'the enterprise culture' for apparently political reasons without any attempt to explain what it means and what might be the emotional, psychological, social and financial costs of unsuccessful participation.

■ Developing a Preference for Enterprise

Raising the level of awareness may stimulate interest in enterprise, but if entrepreneurial behaviour is to be increased then more individuals must actually develop a preference for it.

As was indicated in Chapter 3 Krueger believes 'perceptions of the entrepreneurial climate are critical... To encourage new business founders, communities must cultivate an environment that they will perceive as being favourable.'[3] To do this it is helpful to understand the process underlying the intention to become an entrepreneur. Krueger notes that intentions have antecedents that are derived from a person's experiences and the meaning an individual ascribes to them. Krueger's intentions model (summarised in Chapter 3) suggests that the act of creating a venture must be considered to be desirable and feasible by would-be entrepreneurs. Interventions should therefore aim to reinforce these perceptions.

□ *Perceived Desirability*

Potential entrepreneurs should perceive that a new venture can deliver what they want. Research on the motivation of the entrepreneurs reveals that they have multiple motives and that economic ones rarely predominate. Highlighting the potential autonomy and sense of achievement that can be gained may therefore be more important than the potential financial rewards. Research has also revealed that many people consider entrepreneurship when they are experiencing dissatisfaction with jobs or careers. That may indicate when it might be most appropriate to reinforce an entrepreneurial message and those at whom it might most effectively be targeted.

The personal desirability of entrepreneurship is important, but if the entrepreneurial act is also perceived as socially desirable then this is likely to encourage prospective entrepreneurs. A positive community attitude to enterprise is important, because essentially the capacity for enterprise is embedded in a community. Markets, resources, information and support, both practical and psychological, all originate there and, if that community is perceived as hostile, many potential entrepreneurs may be deterred. Enterprise must be seen as attractive in relative as well as in absolute terms. Excessive taxation of small business compared with other sources of income and wealth has been suggested as an example of an intervention that is counter to enterprise.[4]

□ *Perceived Competence*

In developing a preference for an occupation, as well as evaluating the attractiveness of the potential outcomes, individuals generally assess their chances of attaining those outcomes. To do this they consider whether they can obtain:

- The necessary knowledge and skill
- The resources required
- The means to overcome any shortfall.

If individuals have the opportunity to develop and manage enterprising projects in their existing employment, or to practice entrepreneurship on a part-time or temporary basis, they will have an appreciation of what is involved and can assess their attributes against the perceived requirements. Entrepreneurial counselling can also help people to assess their competence in this area. Krueger believes that if the process of review is carried out sensitively, and if the emphasis is on positive steps to develop skills and overcome environmental obstacles, then this can be effective in building confidence.[5]

■ Preparation

Success = Idea + Know-How + Know-Who

(Rein Peterson and Robert Rondstadt[6])

Building an appropriate culture does not itself create more enterprise. It does however provide an important precondition, like preparing a seedbed before sowing seeds. The formula above can also be interpreted to indicate that entrepreneurial success starts with the idea: both the idea of starting a business in the first place and then the idea of what business to start. Technical know-how appropriate to that business idea will be needed as well as business know-how to guide the establishment and running of the venture as a business. Know-who is also highlighted to indicate the importance of developing and using a network of contacts to obtain resources, advice, guidance and other forms of assistance.

The early stages of preparation can be seen as preparation for the possibility of a business at some time, before a decision may have been made to start up or not. The later stages can be preparation for a venture that has already been decided upon. Chapter 3 included a view of enterprise based on attributes and resources which an individual may possess (see Table 3.2). If these attributes and resources are appropriate for an entrepreneurial venture then it makes it more likely that the individual will engage in such a venture, given the right opportunity or 'trigger'. Therefore if the individual thinks that entrepreneurship is something that he or she might like to try at some time then he or she might endeavour to acquire the appropriate attributes and resources.

Acquiring and developing such attributes and resources in preparation for the possibility of enterprise can be seen as necessary foundation work. Preparing to start an enterprise, once the decision has been made to do it is to prepare to build a structure on those foundations. Actually the distinction is not hard and fast. If the necessary foundations are not in place when the decision is made to build, that means that it will be necessary to address them then. Nevertheless, the analogy does help to separate the general preparation from the specific.

■ Start-up and Growth

At this stage in the development of a business the focus for intervention starts to shift from the person to the business. It become less about helping a person to develop than about helping an idea or a business to overcome specific barriers.

The barrier analogy may be a helpful one. Realising an idea or starting a business inevitably means encountering a number of difficulties and obstacles. To get to the desired destination it will be necessary to reduce them, cross them, avoid them or find ways through and around them as appropriate. Intervention can help by signposting pitfalls, by removing obstacles, by lowering barriers, and also by improving jumping capability, by raising the takeoff point for jumping fences, and by raising confidence showing that in general it is possible to complete the course.

■ Start-Up

There are numerous barriers which can impede the launch of new businesses or other enterprising projects. Interventions in support of them can try to remove or reduce the tangible restrictions or to enhance the capacity of the actors to overcome the constraints. This can be addressed in both the short and the long term (see Table 11.1).

In the short term, intervention to remove barriers is usually one-off help to overcome problems, and intervention to improve competence is mainly simple instruction in issues such as business plans, cash flow management and simple selling. Sometimes the instruction may be tied to grants to ensure that it is consumed with them. This is the equivalent of providing fish to feed the hungry, and possibly combining pills with it to provide some medication.

Table 11.1   Schema of small business intervention strategies

Time-frame	Type of problem	
	Barriers to overcome	*Capability to be acquired*
Shorter	The direct provision of help to entrepreneurs to overcome obstacles, e.g. by offering grants, loans, advice, consultancy, etc.	Provide basic knowledge and skills training and lay the foundations for future development.
Longer	Reduce or remove obstacles by addressing market failures, by improving the infrastructure, by changing regulations, etc.	Develop owner-manager and in-company capacity for learning, for analysis and for accessing appropriate assistance.

In the longer term, barriers can be addressed by effective management of the economy to increase aggregate demand, increase financial stability, meet changing labour market and educational needs and improve the context within which business development takes place. In the longer term, competence can be enhanced by increasing the organisation's capacity itself to learn through skills in accessing information, in analysis, in planning, and in using appropriate outside sources of advice without the need for 'hand-holding'. In essence, owners and businesses are assisted to develop the attributes, knowledge and skills that are needed for sustainable development.

The latter is the equivalent of teaching the hungry to fish, but can have its problems when free fish are readily available without the need to learn how to catch them. Grant regimes have resulted in an attitude of dependency, including examples of refusals to contemplate action without a grant, even when the action concerned would clearly be profitable without one.

■ Growth

The difference between interventions for start up and for growing businesses is more one of emphasis than of the issues targeted. At start-up the securing of markets and the marshalling of resources is critical, but once the business is underway lack of know-how may be a less severe handicap than other barriers because it can to some extent be acquired 'by doing'. However, business and management knowledge and skill become crucial for growth, and it is important to consider how small businesses are to acquire them. Individual owner-managers are responsible for their own self-development. However, as their ventures move from owner-managed to owner-directed status they will have to develop a management structure and delegate key roles. The changing roles for self and others will bring a requirement to master new skills. Some of these skills can be learned on the job, but a lack of previous relative experience is likely to be a handicap. Help in this area would therefore seem to be particularly beneficial.

Like start-up businesses, growing businesses also face external barriers, especially in connection with finance and employment. For instance, an important source of finance for growth is the venture capital sector. However, only a small proportion of formal venture capital usually finds its way to small businesses. In contrast to the formal venture capital industry, private 'business angels' do seem to make a significant contribution to the development of small businesses. Nevertheless, generally there are still considered to be funding gaps in the private financial market that intervention might try to address.[7]

Another popular target for intervention is the promotion of innovative and high technology businesses. Innovation is widely regarded as a key factor in business survival, development, growth and competitiveness, and high-technology businesses are thought to offer the potential for greater growth, higher returns or longer life than 'low' technology, which is easier for others to copy. The apparent link between innovation and economic prowess in Japan is often cited as an example in making this point.

For small businesses to become innovative, or to remain so, they will need to have access to new ideas developed by others and/or to develop and protect their own ideas. In addition they will need financial resources to tide them over the non-productive phases of research and development. Other suggestions for intervention in this field include addressing the system for registering and protecting intellectual property, either by making it easier for small businesses to take out patents and other protection or alternatively, by making it more difficult for large firms to defend their patent rights. This would encourage small businesses to adapt and develop technological ideas developed by others.

Attempts have also been made to intervene to replicate the highly productive clusters of high technology firms found in California and Massachusetts. In these networks the proximity of other innovative firms, universities and support services produces an innovative community with a significant output of patents and innovations. The mechanism often tried is the science park, sometimes linked with a university. However, there appears yet to be little evidence that a science park necessarily has a significant impact on the innovative performance of its tenant firms.[8]

■ Decline and Termination

One stage of business development not often considered for intervention is that of decline and ultimately termination. Nevertheless, there could be economic benefits to intervention here also. The benefits of reversing a decline may seem more obvious, but there may be benefits to be gained even in termination. If a business is going to terminate then it is better for its owners, its staff, its customers and its creditors if it does so in an orderly and controlled way, rather than trading beyond the point of insolvency and then collapsing in debt. Adverse knock-on effects on creditor businesses will be avoided or reduced, and the business proprietors may even be prepared to learn from their experience and try again, instead of being discouraged, perhaps permanently, from developing further business ventures. The medical profession acknowledges that, while a terminally ill patient is by definition past the stage when medicine can effect a cure, there are still three things that can be offered to help at such times: support, information and choices. Similarly, there may be forms of intervention that provide benefits even in the termination stage of business.

■ In Conclusion

In occupational choice, individuals are continuously conducting evaluations and appraisals. Macro-economic considerations such as the general health of the economy will be appraised, along with a review of personal attributes deemed necessary for occupational success. If the potential outcomes of endeavours are valued, and if individuals consider that their endeavour will lead to requisite performance and associated rewards, then they will expend energy in pursuit of them.[9] That applies both to enterprise in a business context and to enterprise applied in other situations.

At an early stage, perceptions are all-important, and there are possibilities of misconceptions because evaluations and appraisals are conducted on the bases of suppositions. While entrepreneurial choice has quite a lot in common with occupational choice in general, it has some unique features that should be borne in mind when considering intervention. As individuals move through life, their career choices are moulded by 'the opportunity structures to which individuals are exposed, first in education, and subsequently in employment. Individuals' ambitions in turn, can be treated as reflecting the influence of the structures through which they pass.'[10] However, education and work opportunities do not normally expose people to the realities of entrepreneurship. Few educational courses delve into the nature of enterprise/entrepreneurship, and most individuals experience employment through the eyes of the employee. They learn the skills of successful employment. People generally choose occupations that they know something about, and in the absence of a conception of entrepreneurship this may not be a realistic option for many.

Furthermore, enterprise is a somewhat heterogeneous occupation. Entrepreneurs run manufacturing firms and service organisations. Similarly enterprising individuals may display their talents in health care, education or the church. These individuals are responsible for the technological aspects of their ventures, and the socioeconomic tasks of administration, coordination and leadership. A range of technical and managerial ability is needed, and previous education and work will rarely prepare individuals fully for these tasks.

In addition, entrepreneurs must develop a viable business idea and marshall appropriate resources to create a business venture. The manifold technical and management skills, coupled with the need for ideas and resources contributes to the complexity of entrepreneurship as an occupation and the need to consider many leverage points for intervention. Enterprise also differs from normal employment, in that potential entrepreneurs are not screened in the way that potential employees are. There are no formal entry qualifications, there is no formal selection and interview process, and there is no appointment and review procedure.[11] Business counsellors, bankers and other advisers may proffer advice, but no one can prevent a person starting a business if he or she decides so to do whatever his or her abilities. Further, when it is done, there is no compulsory process for identifying and rectifying any deficiencies in relevant skills and knowledge.

The absence of selectors and the complexities of entrepreneurial choice should indicate the need for wariness about prescribing simple solutions to the problem of attracting and developing entrepreneurs. This complexity is confirmed by the fact that many business founders tend to choose entrepreneurship later in life than others choose a job or career path. By their mid-thirties, potential entrepreneurs will tend to have been exposed to a selection of jobs or roles, and while they may not have had direct experience of entrepreneurship, they may have had an opportunity to assess interests, values, abilities and opportunities. This being so, intervention in this area may need to address a number of issues experienced by people at different stages of entrepreneurial development. Since each individual is unique, a very wide range of interventions would be needed to reach all of them in an appropriate way.

It is also relevant to remember that intervention can be direct or indirect. It can seek to target the individual or business directly, or it may seek to change the context or conditions in which they operate, which will in turn influence the individuals or businesses concerned. Gibb's diagram (Figure 7.1) helps to make this point by showing that the purposive support network, through which much of the intervention might come, is the least directly influential layer in the network. It may be more effective to try to work through some of the other layers than to try to go directly to the business owners concerned.

Key points

- As entrepreneurs and businesses go through different stages of their development their influences and needs change, and so therefore do the opportunities for intervention.
- The first stage is the development of the enterprise culture, which can both provide an awareness of the possibility of enterprise and develop of a preference for it. The society in which individuals live, the education they receive, and the environment in which they work can all be very influential in this and are therefore possible targets for intervention.
- Preparation for enterprise involves the identification of an idea or opportunity to pursue, the building of experience, skills and other attributes, and the acquisition of finances, networks and other resources. Intervention may help there.
- Start-up is a common focus for intervention, in particular to help those wishing to start businesses to overcome the barriers they face. Such intervention may attempt to reduce the barriers or to raise ability to overcome them. It can use measures with short-term or immediate effects, such as grants to overcome financial difficulties, or it may seek longer lasting effects by seeking to address market failures or by developing a capacity to learn. However entrepreneurship is a heterogeneous occupation and the requisite resources, knowledge and skills will be diverse.
- Intervention, both for start-up and for growth businesses, may attempt to address market problems, fiscal and monetary issues, or legislative

and regulatory barriers. Intervention to promote better business skills and confidence, and to provide advice and information, are also possibilities.

- Intervention to assist declining, or even terminating, businesses may also produce benefits, and should not therefore be discounted automatically.
- Simple, direct solutions to intervention should however be suspect. There are no formal selectors for entrepreneurship that can prevent occupational entry to those who are unsuited to it. The variety of people trying it is therefore considerable, and so are the influences on them. Direct intervention may be considered, but it may also be effective to seek to influence people through others.

CHAPTER 12

Intervention Methods (objectives, structures and approaches)

■ Introduction

Because of the growth in the perceived importance of smaller firms for economic development, virtually every country in the developed and developing world is now intervening in some way to promote enterprise skills, and more entrepreneurs, to encourage the development of more self-employment and to grow more indigenous businesses.

Some of the rationales for these interventions have been described in Chapter 10 and some of the theories and assumptions behind them in Chapter 11. This chapter describes the array of objectives, structures and approaches used for intervention. These are the methods, not the strategies, used for the promotion of entrepreneurship and small business, and indeed often the strategies appear to be missing. In the UK despite apparently hundreds of initiatives since the end of the 1970s, an overall strategy, in the sense of a coherent set of objectives and associated means of achieving them, has been lacking. The last real attempt in the UK to articulate a coherent SME policy in a single document, some claim, was the Bolton *Report on Small Firms* in 1971. At least part of the reason for this gap lies in the fact that the small business sector is characterised by very considerable diversity with competing interests, making the prioritisation of needs very difficult for politicians and policy-makers. This has led Bennett among others, to suggest that 'fragmentation of government programmes for SMEs appears to reflect the fragmentation and variety of the problems that SMEs confront.'[1]

In this the UK is not alone. An OECD paper[2] reviews the experience of its member countries in encouraging entrepreneurship and their contribution to job creation. Amongst its observations are:

- Member governments lack the presence of a comprehensive strategy towards entrepreneurship and job creation

- The explicit promotion of entrepreneurship as a source of job creation is scarce in policy formulation
- Better policy coordination is needed to exploit more fully the potential of entrepreneurship and new business in order to help start-ups and existing firms in the creation of new jobs.

■ Objectives

Having a strategy implies having objectives and targets, and therein lies a problem for policy-makers. The objectives of small business strategy are often not explicit. European Union publications (e.g. the White Paper 'Growth, Competitiveness, Employment – The Challenge and Ways Forward in the 21st Century', 1993) have emphasised the objectives of employment growth, economic growth and competitiveness of enterprises, and these appear to have had some impact on member states' policies. Nevertheless, to be able to understand and evaluate strategies, the objectives must be explicit. Often they are not.

Storey claims that the objectives of public policies to assist small firms are rarely specified directly.[3] Instead, it is necessary for analysers to infer objectives by observing the policies in operation, rather than by finding them being clearly stated as a coherent response to an agreed role that government plays. According to de Koning, Snijders and Vianen[4] this is true of most European countries. Inferring objectives is made harder by the frequent failure of policy-makers to distinguish between means and ends. However, the following objectives appear to be generally agreed:

- increased wealth through economic growth
- job creation
- increased competition
- promotion of and spread of innovation and technology
- greater diversification and choice
- revitalisation of traditional sectors/international competitiveness
- expanding and strengthening the production chain
- more efficient markets
- greater social cohesion (including removal of discrimination).

■ Structures for Intervention

In the UK the inability to formulate a coherent policy agenda is undoubtedly compounded by the fact that policies affecting small business and enterprise directly and/or indirectly are dispersed over several ministries. The UK has a special small business department: the Small Firms Division within the Department of Trade and Industry (DTI) and a Junior Minister with, *inter alia*, a small business responsibility. The division has a role in the formulation of small business policy and a coordination role on small business issues that are the responsibility of other ministers. Small business is however also influenced and affected by the actions of the Department for Education and Employment and the Department of the Environment, not to mention the Treasury (finance and taxation). Guaranteeing consistent and coherent treatment of the sector is made difficult by this dispersion of policies across ministries; as a result, support schemes have tended to grow piecemeal.

An important distinction also has to be made between the formulation of small business policy and its implementation. In the UK, as in many EU countries, the formulation of small business policy is very largely determined at the level of central government, while the implementation of measures is achieved through a network of regional agencies. Within the overall framework of policy, these agencies can, and indeed are often expected to, alter the emphasis and priorities of implementation according to local needs and circumstances. In the UK such agencies include the Training and Enterprise Councils (TECs) in England and Wales, the Local Enterprise Councils (LECs) in Scotland, the Local Enterprise Development Unit (LEDU) and the Industrial Development Board (IDB) in Northern Ireland. In addition, regional and local authorities contribute a network of support services.

The TECs and LECs have been complemented in Great Britain by the establishment of the DTI-initiated Business Links in England, by Business Connect in Wales and by Business Shops in Scotland. Business Links are funded by the DTI, but this funding comes through the TEC network, which is the responsibility of the Department for Education and Employment. TECs and Business Links therefore find themselves under direction of two different government departments.

The role of Business Links, and their counterparts, is to create partnerships of providers of small business services in their region. Such providers include TECs, chambers of commerce, local authorities and enterprises agencies. The aim is to ensure that the small business consumer is presented with a seamless collection of services accessed through 'one-stop shops', or through 'first-stop shops'.

Although greater efficiency, professionalism, and quality of impact is believed to be possible where services are concentrated, bringing together the location of individuals and organisations offering support services into close physical proximity is difficult to achieve and very unusual. Mostly, what is achieved or sought is in fact a 'first-stop shop' where users can receive advice and information from a range of services immediately available and can be signposted to those others believed to be most useful to them.

Ideally, of course, the aim of Business Links and similar organisations should be to create a service based upon effective networking among them. Ultimately what is envisaged by some is technologically linked service providers that can 'link clients with overseas trade partners, help them find full or part-time staff, introduce them to business 'angels' offering equity investments or furnish them with whatever else the company of 2001 might require'.[5] However, they have some way to go before such an ideal can be realistically tackled and for the moment the expected benefits of Business Links and their equivalents would appear to focus on:

- Bringing the main suppliers of enterprise support together in partnership arrangements so as to bring about their meaningful integration and coherence and for the client, a single point of contact
- Upgrading the quality of services and support
- Having a strong and visible network across Britain with a high degree of physical concentration of supply partners in each location.

Two different strategies have been evolved for such networking. Business Links in England aim to be 'one-stop shops', while Business Shops in Scotland are based on a 'first-stop shop' strategy. The distinction between the concept of a 'one-stop shop' and a 'first-stop shop' is however often missed. Both derive, it would appear, from a desire to reduce proliferation and dispersion of support services and to make accessing them easier and less confusing for the potential user. To do this the 'one-stop shop' strategy aims to concentrate them, or at least their representatives, into one location: the 'one stop shop'. On the other hand the 'first stop shop' concept assumes that it will often not be feasible to concentrate all the relevant sources of support in this way. Instead it is suggested that there should be initial contact points, the 'first stop shops', which will either offer assistance directly if they can, or will be able to signpost the inquirer to the right place for specific assistance. The aim is that the knowledge throughout the network about the other organisations in it should be such that an inquirer to one, if he or she doesn't get the right place initially, will be so directed that his or her second stop will be correct. (The right place might therefore be the second place to be contacted which is why this approach is also sometimes referred to as the 'second stop shop' concept.) This is a different approach from a 'one stop shop' and indeed it has been further observed that one does not get a 'second stop shop' by aiming at a one stop shop' and missing.

Part of the problem for the 'one stop shop' is that, while government-organised or controlled organisations can be instructed by government to behave in a particular way, others cannot. Because of the potential social and other benefits of enterprise and small business, many other organisations have sought to offer support or assistance. They are more likely to want to maintain their independence and sense of identity and are therefore more likely to resist conforming to the mould of a 'one stop shop'. Indeed there would seem to be an element of incongruity in requiring oganisations, whose aim is essentially to support enterprise and its associated varieties, themselves to conform to an externally determined strategy or mode of operation.

■ Postscript to Structures for Intervention

This description of organisational arrangements has focused specifically on aspects of small business support in the UK rather than elsewhere. It has however served to highlight the relevant problems and principles that have a wider relevance.

■ Approaches

There are essentially two broad approaches to achieving small business policy objectives, however ambiguously those objectives are stated:

1. The first approach is the one that concentrates on the creation of a favourable environment for business creation and growth. This policy approach results in measures to liberalise trade, to deregulate, to privatise, and to reform legal and taxation regimes as well as to create a positive climate to reinforce a culture of enterprise. Not all these measures are designed with only, or even mainly, small businesses in mind, but a number are aimed at addressing distortions or areas of market failure that are believed to harm smaller businesses specifically.
2. The second approach is that of supporting the actual start-up and growth of individual businesses by providing direct assistance to the individuals or businesses concerned.

These two approaches are not mutually exclusive, and in nearly all countries they are adopted simultaneously. This was for instance specifically acknowledged in the UK by the former Department of Employment, which stated that

There are three strands in the Government's approach to small firms. First, and of most importance, the role of the government is to ensure that small firms can flourish in conditions of fair competition and to create space and incentives for enterprise by minimizing taxation regulations and red tape. Second, the Government strongly supports and re-enforces the change to more positive social attitudes towards the small business sector. Third, the Government helps to fill gaps in the supply side by providing commercial services for small firms, largely to improve their access to finance, information, professional advice and training. Wherever possible the Government's approach is provided in partnership with the private sector.[6]

A multi-strand approach is not however universally accepted. It has for instance been argued by many, on the basis of numerous surveys, that the main factors which restrict the growth of businesses relate to the macro-economy. Accordingly the CBI SME Council recently claimed that 'it is through the creation of a healthy economy and conditions for growth that employment will be generated ... the CBI therefore believes that Governments should focus on creating the right conditions for SMEs to start and grow rather than introducing individual policy objectives aimed at market distortions'.[7]

■ Policies and Instruments

To achieve the objective of intervention, policies and instruments are adopted. The main UK government small business policies have for instance been categorised as shown in Table 12.1.[8]

Table 12.1   UK government SME policies

1. *Macro policies*
   - Interest rates
   - Taxation
   - Public spending
   - Inflation

2. *Deregulation and simplification*
   - Cutting 'red tape'
   - Legislative exemptions
   - Legal form

3. *Sectoral and problem-specific policies*
   - High-tech firms
   - Rural enterprises
   - Community enterprises
   - Cooperatives
   - Ethnic businesses

4. *Finance assistance*
   - Business Expansion Scheme/Enterprise Investment Scheme
   - Small Firms Loan Guarantee Scheme
   - Enterprise Allowance Scheme/Business Start-Up Scheme
   - Grants   →

$\longrightarrow$

5. *Indirect assistance*
   - Information and advice
   - Business Growth Training/other training
   - Consultancy Initiative

6. *Relationships*
   - Small firm division
   - Lobbyist/policy formulation

Source: D. J. Storey, *Understanding the Small Business Sector*. (London: ITBP, 1994) p. 269.

The annual reports of the European Observatory for SMEs distinguish between policy *fields* and *instruments*. To quote the 1994 annual report,

Although the instrumental design of schemes aiming at the same target can differ by Member State, the fields SME policy measures focus on tend to converge towards a set of 9 fields of activity. These are:

Start-ups and Growth	Research and Development	Capital and Finance
Investment	Exports	Cooperation
Sub-contracting	Education	Job Creation[9]

The instruments of intervention identified, each of which can be applied to one or more fields, are:

- direct subsidies or grants
- subsidised loans
- loan guarantee/participation
- tax relief
- service
- export guarantees
- subsidised start-up for unemployed
- subsidised personnel
- subsidised buildings, power, communication networks, sites.

All the instruments of intervention identified above are geared towards the second of the two approaches described earlier: intervention at the level of specific businesses or individuals. The Observatory report also indicates that, of these instruments, financial inducements are the most popular form of intervention in support of many policy fields. Inducements commonly take the form of direct subsidies, grants or loan guarantees, and subsidies are used to reduce the cost of loans, employees, premises and various services.

Table 12.2   Policy fields and instruments

Fields	Instruments
General tax facilities	
Regional development	Financial means (guarantees on loans,
Technology and R&D	venture capital, insurance)
Export	
Enployment	Fiscal regulations (tariffs, exemptions)
Start-ups	
Information and counselling	Information and counselling
Finance	
Education	Training
Business licensing	Others (programmes and legislation).
Administrative simplification	
Environment/energy	

Source: adapted from K. de Lind Van Wijngaarden and R. Van der Horst, 'A Comparison of SME Policy in the EU Member States', *Business Growth and Profitability*, vol. 2, no. 1 (March 1996) p. 40.

Van Wijngaarden and Van der Horst offer a similar framework. They identify the most important 'fields' and 'instruments' (measures taken in the different policy fields to achieve the objectives)[10] as shown in Table 12.2.

Again, the fields are a mix of more general and specific areas, and combine market segments and functions with processes. Indeed, information and counselling appear both as a policy field and as an instrument!

The above frameworks make no real attempt to relate intervention measures to the stages in the growth of a business, as described in Chapter 7, or to the pre-start-up stage, which influences the number of new businesses created. Therefore the framework shown in Table 12.3 is offered in an attempt to categorise fields and instruments according to a stages of development model of business formation and growth. It suffers from the limitations associated with such modelling, described in Chapter 6 but is intended to assist by providing greater coherence across target markets, ends and means.

While instruments (support measures) are general in description, the table outlines a representative range of the very many variations that apply. It is apparent that certain measures, such as information and counselling, finance and training, are available throughout most or all of the development stages of a business. However, both the nature and extent of delivery mechanisms can change at each stage.

■ A Comprehensive Framework

To provide a more comprehensive framework, elements of these various illustrations have been combined into the model shown in Figure 12.1 to illustrate the

Table 12.3 A taxonomy of small firm initiatives

Stage of business	Policy field or need	Instrument
Culture	A positive, encouraging and supportive environment	Community programmes Capacity-building Role models Enterprise in education
Pre-start	Ideas	Spin-off ideas Technology transfer Ideas generation workshops and publications
	Small business know-how (accounts, finance, selling, marketing etc.).	Small business skills training Training trainers
	'Know-who' networks	Networking advice Network access points – for both business and technical assistance
	Counselling	Pre-start counselling
Start-up – external	Customers	Purchasing initiatives
	Suppliers	Local sourcing initiatives Trade directories
	Advice/consultancy – business	Business expertise available Coordinating of third-party provision (Business Links) Training and counselling
	Advice/consultancy – technical	Technical advice, research etc.
	Networks	Business Clubs Export Clubs
	Information	Data bases
	Producing the 'business plan'	Business Plan services
	Premises	Incubation centres Managed workspaces Business/science parks
Start-up – internal	Finance	Grants, loans, loan guarantees schemes 'Business angel' networks
	Market expertise	
	Administratration expertise	Training services
	Financial management	Advice/counselling
	Employment expertise	Mentors
	Company formation	
Established	Ideas	Ideas generation workshops Spin-off ideas Technology transfer programmes
	Encouragement	Guidance services, including
	Specialist guidance	banks, accountants,
	Investment	solicitors

$\longrightarrow$

$\longrightarrow$

Stage of business	Policy field or need	Instrument
Growth	Market opportunities including exports	Trade missions Market visits Export development advisers Export credit insurance Market information – trends, contacts etc.
	Product development	Technical advice/support for product development
	Strategic approach	Development courses
	Management skills	Salary support Subsidised staff attachment programmes
	Finance	Grants, loans, etc.
Decline	Confidence Customers Money	Mentors
	Strategic review and planning	Advice and guidance
Termination	Legal and other advice	Provision of advice and counselling
Other dimensions	Business sector	Sectoral initiatives, including sector-based training
	Business support environment	Information and education
All	Information on small business needs and behaviour	Research coordination Research databases Research centres

fields of intervention for small business policy. Such a model provides a categorisation mechanism with which to analyse and describe small business policy fields, and on which to plot intervention measures. In so doing, no attempt is made at this stage to be prescriptive but merely to describe. Indeed, prescription would require, as already noted, some agreed objectives based on what sort of economy is wanted and the desired role of small business therein (see Chapter 13).

■ Areas of Intervention

This analysis framework is an attempt to highlight the main fields of public policy in small business support, and it includes the broad elements indicated below, which are considered in more detail on the following pages.

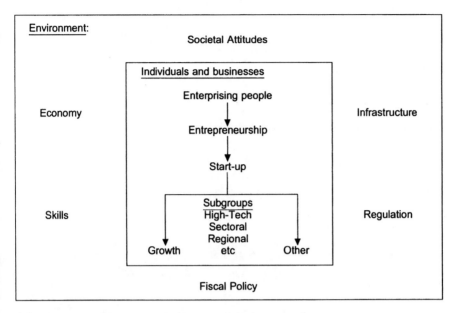

Figure 12.1   Small business policy analysis framework

1. The business environment is included. It affects the performance of all firms, not just small businesses, but it is nevertheless crucial to a healthy small business sector, regardless of firm size, motivation or stage of development. Improvement of the business en-vironment, the first of the two broad approaches to small business support, as described above, is defined as comprising six broad cate-gories: the economy, skills, infrastructure, regulations, fiscal policy and societal attitudes.

2. Individuals and their businesses are also included. This field embraces:

    (a) The development of enterprising people (in the broad sense) and the supply of entrepreneurs to start-up businesses is another area of intervention.

    (b) Assisting the start-up business in its birth stages and subsequent aftercare can be viewed as critical not only to survival rates but also to quality and quantity of the subsequent growers.

    (c) Removing the barriers and giving incentives to established businesses wishing to grow and the growing businesses is often perceived as central to policy and is now quite common. Less common is support for the other, non-growing, businesses although sometimes they are considered still as potential growth businesses and therefore worthy of some attention. Intervention often takes the form of support of specific subgroups such as high-tech or exporting businesses and there can also be a focus on selected sectors or geograpahic regions.

■ The Business/Enterprise Environment

□ *The Economy*

Most governments strive for stable growth, low inflation, low interest rates, and a steady exchange rate as the economic backcloth against which it is felt that businesses can plan effectively in the context of reasonable certainty of future trading circumstances. It is thus obvious that the impacts of taxation and public spending are self-evidently critically important policy intervention measures. The effects of the trade cycle upon the birth, death and growth rates of all businesses are well known, and the effects can be particularly severe on the more vulnerable small firms sector.

□ *Fiscal Policy*

There are various fiscal measures aimed at helping the growth and survival of small businesses. These range from a reduced rate of corporation tax to inheritance tax concessions and extended value added tax (VAT) exemption thresholds, as well as tax incentives for business angels and investors.

Although, when asked, small business owners will say that they want lower taxes to allow them to keep more of the rewards for enterprise, the relationship between lower taxes (more disposable income) and economic activity does not however appear to be straightforward. For example, Rees and Shah investigated the hours worked by self-employed persons and found that personal and family factors like age and number of children were key determinants.[11] However, when these variables were controlled, they found that the number of hours worked fell when personal taxation rates fell.

□ *Skills*

The business need for labour market skills is apparent at all levels from management to operative. The ability to access appropriate skills at affordable prices is an essential ingredient in any supportive economic environment. Small businesses, especially growing ones, would appear to have more acute difficulties in accessing skills. Indeed, small firms would appear to experience genuine problems in dealing with the formalities and legalities of recruitment in an increasingly sophisticated environment. In particular, there is evidence that the small business sector both is reluctant to recruit graduate labour and has difficulty in doing so.

□ *Infrastructure*

An efficient and effective infrastructure is needed, including appropriate transportation systems and networks, communication networks and an adequate supply of business premises, appropriately located.

□ *(De)Regulation and Administrative Simplification*

It is noticeable that regulation or, more colloquially, 'red tape and bureaucracy', tends to come at or near the top of any list when surveys are made either of the problems of small businesses, or of the constraints on their growth. Clearly, a certain level of regulation is needed to create a healthy business environment; adequate standards are needed in the areas of health and safety, employment rights, environmental protection and reducing anti-competitive practices, and, as is often claimed, one man's right is another man's burden. Nevertheless, it has been argued that statutory regulations in the above areas and in taxation, statistical reporting and company registration are disproportionally burdensome for small businesses. It is asserted that employment legislation prevents small businesses from employing more labour, and that requirements such as the statutory audit for incorporated business discourages them from availing of this legal form of business. VAT compliance, data protection registration and other statutory requirements have also been listed as barriers. However, it has been suggested that, while these and other burdens have been identified by lobby groups as barriers to small business development, they are not necessarily perceived as such by all small businesses.

Governments across the world at least pay lip-service to reducing the burdens on small business. In the UK there has been increasing emphasis on deregulation since the publication of the White Paper *Lifting the Burden* in 1985. The OECD and the EU also have task forces or equivalents examining the issue. The UK established the Deregulation Unit within the DTI in 1985, and in 1994 the Deregulation Task Force was set up. (The Labour Government elected in 1997 is replacing 'Deregulation' as a title by 'Better Regulation'!) The results of these and other initiatives suggest that increasing attention will be paid to:

• Measuring the impact of new regulations on small businesses
• Critically examining existing legislative measures affecting business with a view to eliminating many of them
• Increasing emphasis on making regulations 'goal-based' and not over-prescriptive (i.e. emphasising outcomes, not processes, in enforcement procedures).

It is not the purpose of this chapter to argue for or against regulation; however, it is worth noting the opinion that 'there needs to be a more coherent and systematic investigation of the precise nature of the disadvantages facing small firms in this domain as the basis for a policy thrust'[12], the aim of which is to remove the disadvantages of small businesses compared with large ones.

☐ *Societal Attitudes*

A government's position is usually that it supports and encourages more positive attitudes in society to enterprise, entrepreneurship and the small business sector. The phrase most commonly used to describe the approach is 'creating an enterprise culture'. Certainly, the language of enterprise has never been more popular in politics, economics and business. Critics, however, say it has simply become a synonym for success or a political slogan or is a searching for a heffalump – a creature of supposed vast importance that no one has ever actually seen!

2.1   Pathfinder initiatives – 2

In Northern Ireland, the Department of Economic Development (DED) 'Pathfinder' initiative (launched in 1986) led to the creation of an Enterprise Task Force which generated an extensive series of initiatives aimed at increasing business start-up rates and improving attitudes towards business creation and success. The starting point for the enterprise taskforce was a recognition that, among the economic weaknesses to be addressed, was the lack of an enterprise tradition.

Initially in this context, enterprise was defined as the propensity of people to create jobs, for themselves and for others, by engaging in a legitimate activity which will earn them a living, or by developing their existing jobs. This was a relatively 'narrow' view of enterprise but, as the initiative progressed, a progressively wider view was taken. Eventually some of the spin-off programmes were being specifically targeted at enterprise promotion in its wider meaning.

The different interpretations of the word 'enterprise' and aspects of its development have already been described in earlier chapters. It is true to say, nevertheless, that governmental efforts in this area have concentrated generally on the 'narrow' approach of business entrepreneurialism. The broader 'educational' interpretations have not been ignored, but little of significance has been done. A notable exception was the 'Enterprise in Higher Education' initiative of 1990–5 in the UK universities.

The lack of an enterprise culture has been variously identified through, for example, low business start-up and growth rates, significant external ownership of businesses, an over-large public sector and high unemployment rates. Specifically, policy in this area would seek to create a climate that enhances perceptions of the feasibility and desirability of entrepreneurship. Overall, it is accepted that the image of enterprise in a community will impact on the perception of enterprise by potentially enterprising people within it. The instruments used in fostering such a policy include publicity campaigns, highlighting successful role models, business start-up and awareness programmes, and seminars, information and advice.

12.2 Enterprise education

It is often articulated that the supply of entrepreneurs will ultimately be increased more if awareness of the feasibility and desirability of starting a business is established at a young age.

Thus the education system is assisted to foster, support and encourage those interested in knowing what it is like to run a business. Young Enterprise, a mostly privately funded charity, is the leading UK organisation engaged in this process. Its aim is to develop 'enterprise skills' and currently its major programme involves setting up and running mini-businesses.

Similarly, government and others have assisted entrepreneurship programmes for final-year undergraduates. Other programmes have targeted youth, the unemployed, corporate employees, women and the disabled.

Encouragement of community enterprises and businesses is a further manifestation of enterprise support. Local areas suffering not only from a lack of employment but often a lack of confidence, resources, and skills are facilitated to build upon the enterprising capacities of their people.

There have also been examples of programmes that have attempted to improve a community's or society's self-image and self-confidence, and to change it from a can't-do to a can-do attitude. This has been done on the grounds that such an improvment will in turn make it easier for other enterprise ideas to take root. In terms of the horticultural analogy drawn towards the end of Chapter 4, such schemes aim to prepare the soil so that it is better able to germinate seeds and to support and sustain any seedlings that may then appear.

■ Individuals and Businesses – The Enterprise Process

The second broad approach to policy described earlier in this chapter is that of promoting the enterprise process by interventions targeted at the level of the individual business or at the person preparing to start a business. This is in contrast to the interventions just considered which were at the macro-economic level – albeit there is no clear division between where one approach ends and the other begins.

These interventions are aimed either at individual people or at individual businesses. However, rather than target all people or businesses, such interventions generally target segments or subgroups of this population categorised by age, by stage of development, by business sector, by geographic region, by market area, or by type of ownership: categories where unique sets of problems and/or opportunities are perceived to exist. Some of these categories are described further below.

□ *Pre-Start-Up*

There are interventions to help people thinking about, or preparing for, business start-up. The most common form of intervention in this area is probably business skills training in its various forms, but there are also interventions to assist and guide market research, and schemes to help with early product/service development. Included in the latter are initiatives that try to assist inventors to meet business people capable of understanding the potential of new ideas. In the field of ideas, however, a phenomenon encountered by many who offer assistance is the 'mad inventor', someone who believes that his or her invention is wonderful and the basis for certain commercial success. He or she believes that they have done the 'hard' bit, so all that is needed is help with the 'easy' bit of turning the invention into a thriving business. In this situation the appropriate intervention can be to disillusion the inventor and to reduce his or her unrealistic expectations.

There are also variations of intervention that help with the sourcing, identification and development of business ideas, and with the formation of enterprise teams to combine the different strengths of individuals in order to promote one successful venture.

□ *Start-Ups*

It has been noted that, while a healthy level of start-ups is essential for new ideas, innovation, competitiveness and the overall vibrancy of the economy, policy emphasis is increasingly placed on the perceived quality of start-ups, such as their potential for growth or for exporting. It has been argued that non-discriminating support to start-ups is counter-productive, because many will fail, and that this implies that a more selective approach to business support should be adopted. (The arguments for and against this were described in Chapter 8.) Thus in Britain the role of the Business Links and the TECs and LECs appears to be to offer most support to firms with the motivation to grow (and to target companies with between ten and two hundred employees). Under the Business Start-up Scheme (formerly the Enterprise Allowance Scheme), support for start-ups was delivered uniformly across all areas. But under the Single Regeneration Budget (and more recently with the Government's proposals for 'Challenge Budgets') support for start-ups is not guaranteed.

Interventions in the field of start-up have included financial assistance, training, networking, information, advice and counselling. It has also included the provision of workspace geared specifically to meet the needs of small businesses. These have taken the form of managed workspace ('MWS' – premises with easy leasing terms and, typically, with the availability of central services such as secretarial support and business advice), often on attractive leasing terms. In addition, there have been variations on the business incubator concept. Special attention has also been paid to enabling the small business sector to take advantage of the information technology and communications revolution.

☐ *High-Tech Businesses*

Businesses in the high-tech category are believed to have particular problems needing tailored solutions. Specific support for them is often considered because of their contribution to innovation and their potential for growth, and because they are likely to be the seeds for the new industry sectors of the future. Their particular needs are seen to arise from the relatively high cost of research and development and its associated risks, which makes them unattractive to conservative or risk-averse lending institutions. High-tech businesses can also have the potential for fast growth, which means that the need for finance will be even greater. Such problems are frequently compounded by (1) the funders' lack of understanding of the potential of the products or processes, which is due very often to their specialist nature; (2) the need for significant 'up-front' investment before there will be any clear evidence of the ability of such businesses to trade; and (3) their owners' frequent failure to pay enough attention to communicating meaningfully in a non-technical way.

Since the 1980s, therefore, a range of schemes have been introduced to help high-tech businesses. Examples of such help include the following:

- Grant aid towards research and development costs. In the UK the Small Firm Merit Awards for Research and Technology (SMART) and Small Firms Award for Projects Under Research (SPUR) are typical of such schemes.
- EU assistance for the establishment of Business Innovation Centres (BICs). (These, though, are not restricted only to high-tech firms.)
- In Northern Ireland, a number of innovation programmes aimed at technology entrepreneurs, supported by specially dedicated seedcorn funding.
- An increase in the number of science parks often linked to universities. These attempt to provide a suitable environment for high-tech businesses to grow in the company of their peers and with close links to academic research and support.

□ *Geographical Areas of Disadvantage*

Policies have been adopted to assist in the regeneration, through enterprise and small business development, of areas of special disadvantage. Run-down inner cities and depressed rural areas have benefited from initiatives designed to promote 'community enterprises' and cooperatives. In addition, managed workspace has been publicly funded in whole or in part in an attempt to provide localised support that is relevant and real (and visible).

This provision often takes the form of local enterprise agencies, which can become the centrepiece of policies to create a focus for urban or rural regeneration involving local people in their management and activities. Such local roots can greatly strengthen the ability of local agencies to be true centres and role models for stimulating a local enterprise culture. As well as premises, they can offer various other forms of business support – particularly training, advice and information – and can be vehicles for moulding regional programmes to meet local needs.

□ *Population Subgroups*

Efforts to encourage the population in general, and certain subgroups in particular, to become more aware of and receptive to the possibilities of enterprise have already been referred to earlier in this chapter, under 'Societal Attitudes'.

Many such interventions begin with young people when they are in school. Schools do have cross-curricular themes to pursue such as 'economic awareness', which creates an opportunity to develop a positive culture, attitude and motivation towards enterprise and business. In most instances it is used to give an introduction to what is loosely referred to as the 'world of work'. In the UK, Young Enterprise's Company Programme (an initiative, described in Chapter 2, for teams of students in secondary and tertiary education to run their own businesses) applies from the age of sixteen. Other Young Enterprise programmes are aimed at younger age groups. The Livewire Scheme and the Prince's Youth Business Trust are also both aimed specifically at young people who wish to start a business.

Special programmes, usually awareness raising or start-up seminars and training, have been targeted at groups that are believed to be under-represented in entrepreneurship or that may share common problems or disadvantages. Barriers to the potential for women, for example, to run their own business has led to special funding from the European Union and a range of national and transnational programmes to enable that potential to be realised. In Northern Ireland a portfolio of training programmes has been developed ('target programmes') aimed at subgroups of the population that have particular disadvantages or potential. They have covered women, youth, unemployed, employed, disabled and graduates. In Great Britain the danger of ethnic minorities being economically and socially marginalised by a vicious cycle of dependency is well recognised. It derives from the lack of business tradition, the shortage of entrepreneurs, the death of enterprise and the absence of role models, all of which reinforce lack of confidence. As a result, special funds and initiatives to break that cycle have been created.

□ *Exporters*

There is a danger that support for specific small businesses will result in displacement of other local small business activity, and will not therefore result in net local benefits. However, if the businesses assisted are exporting then this danger will be largely avoided. Because of this there have been a variety of incentives to encourage greater export performance by the small firm sector, mainly through financial subsidies and information-based assistance (such as travel and trade show subsidies, export credit guarantees, subsidised market research, free access to data bases, and information on trends, market requirements and potential contacts). Growth has become associated, in the minds of many, with the need to export, and such businesses are finding an increasing amount of support from the private sector (particularly the banks), as well as from the public sector.

■ Forms of Assistance

Where assistance is directed at filling perceived gaps on the supply side, it usually takes the form of providing various services to small businesses. Such services are not necessarily available to all small firms, but, as indicated above, may often be targeted at specific groupings that apparently share a number of common needs. Some examples of such assistance are described below.

■ Financial Assistance

Since 1931, when the Macmillan Committee reported and identified what has since been known as the 'Macmillan Gap', shortage of finance has been one of the central issues in discussions on the support needs of small firms. This need was reiterated in the Bolton Report (1971) and in a number of other reports and papers since. While other sources of finance are now available, the issue continues to be central to many intervention strategies. There is, at least in some economies, a strongly held view that the major problem now for the funding of small businesses lies not in an overall shortage of finance, but in the appropriate means of focusing that finance, and, for instance, avoiding an over-reliance on overdrafts and security-based lending. As a result, in the UK, the relationship between banks and small businesses has been under strain and scrutiny for some time, and the subject has probably been the single most prominent issue in small business literature over many years.

To help in the area of small business finance a number of initiatives have been developed. Descriptions of some of the different types of such initiatives are now given in the following paragraphs.

☐ *Reducing Late Payment of Debts*

Late payment by customers can be a severe handicap to small businesses, and the consequent adverse effect on cash flow and viability has been a constant complaint by small firms and their representative organisations. Various initiatives have been identified to address this. In the UK the legal procedures for recovery of debts through the courts have been simplified, and the present government has indicated an intention to introduce a statutory right to claim interest on overdue payments. In addition, the CBI has promoted a Prompt Payment Code, which encourages organisations to adhere to agreed payment terms and to publish details of their payment performance, and a British Standard for payment performance (*Achieving Good Payment and Performance in Commercial Transactions*, BS 7890) has been launched.

☐ *Small Firms Loan Guarantee Scheme (SFLGS)*

A Small Firms Loan Guarantee Scheme was introduced in the UK as a pilot. It was based on the commonly held belief that the ability of small firms to borrow for expansion was limited by the lack of security they could offer lenders, in particular the banks. Under the scheme, the government therefore provides a guarantee to the banks for a percentage (variously between 70 per cent and 85 per cent) of specified loans. The lending however must still be justified on normal commercial criteria, and the borrowers must pay an interest rate premium on the loans provided.

☐ *Enterprise Investment Scheme (EIS) and Venture Capital Trusts (VCT)*

The Enterprise Investment Scheme and its precursors, the Business Start-Up Scheme (BSUS) and Business Expansion Scheme (BES), were introduced in the UK to increase the supply of relatively small amounts (up to £100 000) of equity capital to mainly manufacturing and tradeable service businesses. EIS, introduced in 1993, provides tax relief to individuals (business angels) investing in qualifying unquoted companies. Unlike its predecessors, EIS allows the investor to be a manager or director in the businesses concerned. The Venture Capital Trusts (VCT) are a pooled investment mechanism to enable private investors to spread the risk of investing in private companies. They aim to increase the supply of risk capital for businesses with growth potential. As with EIS, tax relief is a prime incentive, but the investors are also expected to benefit from the greater marketability of their shares.

□ *Alternative Investment Market (AIM)*

Replacing the Unlisted Securities Market (USM) in the UK, the Alternative Investment Market has been created by the Stock Exchange as a new market for smaller companies. The AIM has lower entry costs than a full Stock Exchange listing.

□ *Business Angel Networks*

'Business angels' is the term often used for informal investors in small businesses, who tend to operate on the basis of personal knowledge and contacts rather than through formal equity markets. In the UK pools of potential business angels are being developed by Business Links, banks and others through a variety of local and regional networks.

□ *Grants and Loans*

As well as schemes of the kinds considered above, there is a wide variety that offer direct grant aid to encourage business development. Often such support is targeted at increases in competitiveness through improvements in key areas of the business such as management, marketing, design, production, research and development, quality systems and training. Grants may also be available to assist with the cost of capital acquisitions such as premises, machines and equipment.

Instead of grants, assistance may sometimes be provided in the form of subsidised low-interest loans ('seedcorn' loans). The costs of administering such funds may be subsidised, but usually interest and repayments are expected to provide a continuing source of revolving support without the need for additional capital injections.

Grants have been suspected of developing further dependence on them. There is an impression that in many cases grants were introduced because government wanted to assist small businesses, and a financial budget was the facility they could most easily make available to the relevant agencies. However, the agencies often in effect took that money as the tool they were to use, especially because money was what small businesses frequently said they wanted. Agencies therefore gave out money in the form of grants, instead of asking what tool would be most effective for achieving their purpose and then considering how to convert the money into it.

□ *Community and Group Self-help Schemes*

An alternative to externally supplied grants or loans for small businesses may, in various parts of Europe, be found in community or group self-help financing schemes such as credit unions and mutual credit guarantee schemes. The theory behind such schemes is that each individual in a community may be able to save a small amount, and if these are pooled they are together much more effective than they would be separately. Alternatively, shared resources can be used together to guarantee a bigger loan than any one person could manage alone. Mutual credit guarantee schemes apply the same principle to small businesses, which combine into self-help groups to pool their financial resources in order to fund, or secure credit for, significant projects for the member businesses as appropriate. Thus, one or two at a time, the members can afford to undertake a project they could not have afforded on their own. Such schemes apply ideas similar to those on which the early building societies were based. Intervention may help to get them started by providing encouragement and by making available information on how to set up and run them.

☐ *LETS (Local Exchange Trading Systems)*

A further form of self-help scheme is one that uses no money at all. Strictly it is not a small business funding system, but a means of facilitating micro-business trading in a local area. A LETS scheme will provide a local currency based on credits and debits that permit and facilitate trading within a local area without the need for money to pay for transactions.

LETS schemes generally need a central body to administer the recording of credits and debits. When a newcomer joins the scheme then he or she will be given an initial credit of local exchange units, which are often given a particular name. As a member supplies products or service to other members, or consumes products of services provided by others, his or her account will be credited or debited, accordingly. It thus helps those with low incomes, or who are otherwise short of money, to engage in local economic activity and it ensures that the credits for products or services supplied will be retained and re-used in that local area.

■ Other Assistance

Although financial assistance may be the most obvious, there are many other types of assistance measures. Subsidised provision of a variety of forms of information, advice, training, and counselling is a growing part of attempts to improve the internal efficiency of small businesses. Some such forms of assistance are described below.

☐ *Information and Advice*

Small businesses are believed to be at a disadvantage relative to larger ones because of their limited ability to scan the environment and filter for information relevant to their progress. It is argued that this example of market failure in access to information needs to be addressed if small businesses are to realise their growth potential. Consequently, part of the remit of the network of business support agencies is to remedy this information gap.

One method of doing this is to use personal business advisers. Subsidised consultancy also can enable businesses to engage professional specialists to help them to analyse their situations and prescribe improvement actions. Another type of special initiative relies on experienced business people acting as 'mentors' to selected local businesses. Working typically only for expenses, the mentors assist owners and managers with information, advice and counselling, usually over a six to twelve month period.

☐ *Management Development and Training*

Support for management development in small businesses has developed significantly over recent years, as both the private and the public sectors have identified a gap in the market. It is well known that the right mix of management skills is important for any business, and is critical if a business is to grow successfully. Yet usually the smaller the business, the less the extent of its training activity. In the UK Small Firms Training Loans were introduced in 1994 to help pay for training. The scheme is administrated by TECs in England, which consider applications before they are sent to the lending bank, and offer help and advice where necessary. An initiative also exists to develop key workers in 24 000 small firms as trainers and assessors, known in England as Skills for Small Business and in Wales as the Small Firms Training Initiative'.[13] It has been launched by all TECs, and targets businesses with fewer than fifty employees.

12.3   Graduates and small businesses

Both business and graduates perceive the other as a high risk, though they have much to offer each other. Small businesses can benefit from the abilities of graduates, yet many small businesses have a resistance to the perceived cost of employing them, requiring immediate added value from the extra cost of a graduate's salary. Graduates, in particular those who might want a business of their own eventually, have much to gain from working for small businesses, but do not want to find that they are working for employers who will not value their skills. Moreover, graduates tend to perceive that larger employers offer more formalised development programmes, greater opportunities for advancement and greater security of employment.

Specific schemes have therefore been devised aimed at encouraging the recruitment of graduates by small businesses. They include measures such as match-making between individual graduates and businesses, training for the graduates in small business issues, and subsidies for graduate salaries for an initial settling-in period.

□ *Marketing*

Small businesses may have difficulty finding and researching new markets, especially export markets. Various programmes of support to help them have been devised. They include export marketing grants, trade missions, 'meet the buyer' programmes, trade shows, market intelligence reports, export credit guarantee schemes and export development counsellors, as well as assistance with the development and production of sales literature and advertising materials.

□ *Networking*

If 'Success = Idea + Know-how + Know-who' (see Chapter 11) then intervention to help networking to provide the 'know-who' is clearly appropriate. Generally however it appears not to be addressed nearly as often as 'idea' and 'know-how'. Networking can be promoted by highlighting its usefulness, and thus legitimising it by giving pointers in how to do it best, and by providing opportunities for it. The latter can for instance be achieved through enterprise and business clubs, and through trade fairs. One example of an intervention to promote networking is the EU's Europartenariat Programme to stimulate the development of less favoured European regions through international fairs to promote the development of business relationships.

12.4 Leverage

It is also noticeable that a positive trend is developing whereby interventions are designed to maximise the 'leverage' of associated services and support. An example is the Emerging Business Trust Ltd in Northern Ireland, which was established to offer loan finance to businesses located in areas with particular social and economic problems. In lending money, the Trust not only meets a direct need of the business for finance but also:

- Gives banks greater confidence to lend themselves.
- Encourages other financial institutions to extend credit.
- Demonstrates to financiers, such as leasing companies, that they can earn a return in this market sector.

As the loans can be conditional upon the review of a business plan and on accepting counselling or training, it may also lead to:

- Knowledge and skills enhancement.
- Advice on other contacts that might be of assistance.

■ UK and European Small Business Support – A Summary

☐ *UK*

Overall the characteristics of the UK approach to small business support may be summarized as:

- Creating a healthy business environment, with increasing emphasis on deregulation and reduced and simplified administrative burdens.
- Selective intervention where market failure can be demonstrated.
- Developing forms of support geared to improving the competitiveness and export performance of small firms, emphasising marketing, quality, productivity, benchmarking, product development, management and workforce skills.
- Encouraging greater private sector involvement in the delivery of services through 'partnership' arrangements.
- Decentralised delivery combined with variations in the priorities and scope of support services to cater for differences in local and/or regional needs.

☐ *European Union*

Within the EU as a whole, policy towards small businesses may be summarised as focusing on two approaches (as in the UK): first, addressing the economic environment with the emphasis on fiscal measures and increasing labour market flexibility; and second, developing additional enterprise support schemes, with the emphasis on R&D and the supply of finance (Table 12.4).

In fact, the majority of measures in the EU countries are concentrated on three instruments:

- Grants and tax reliefs
- Counselling and information services
- Subsidised loans.

There is little evidence of tension between support for new enterprises as opposed to established and growing ones. In the EU both approaches are considered to be complementary.

Small business policy in most countries of the EU is closely linked to regional policy. The UK is an exception, most policies being national in coverage.

Table 12.4   Overview of SME start-up support policy in the EU

Country	Financing	Fiscal	Information councelling	Training	Other
Austria	×		×	×	×
Belgium	×	×	×	×	×
Denmark	×		×	×	
Finland	×		×	×	
France	×	×	×		×
Germany	×		×		
Greece	×	×			
Ireland	×		×	×	
Italy	×				
Luxembourg	×				
Netherlands	×		×	×	
Portugal	×	×		×	
Spain	×	×	×		×
Sweden	×		×	×	×
UK	×		×	×	

Source: K. de Lind Van Wijngaarden and R. Van der Horst 'A Comparison of SME Policy in the EU Member States', *Business Growth and Profitability*, vol. 2, No. 1 (March 1996) p. 43.

Recent research indicates that, while policy fields and instruments may be similar from country to country, their implementation and delivery mechanisms can vary considerably, resulting in significant differences in the perception of their effectiveness.

■ Making a Choice

This chapter has indicated that there is a wide range of possibilities for intervention and therefore some choice will inevitably have to be made between them. That choice will depend on many factors, including local policies and priorities, but a key influence would be the perceived effectiveness of the different options. Evaluation of the results of intervention is therefore the subject of the next chapter.

However, comparing methods is not easy. Not only, as the next chapter indicates, is the evidence of effectiveness not clear, but different methods can act at different stages of the process. It is not therefore usually a choice between alternatives where the decision is for one or the other, but between approaches which can work together which means that the choice is between a whole range of possible combinations. Box 12.5 illustrates this dilemma using a horticultural analogy.

12.5   What is the best thing to do if you want to harvest more?

Do you?

Improve the growing
environment?

Sow seeds?

Support the growing plants?

If you want to pick more fruit?

The problem of where to apply limited resources in order to maximize the benefits to be obtained

Key points

- Because of the perceived importance of smaller firms for economic development, virtually every country in the developed and developing world is now intervening in some way to promote more enterprise. However, such interventions often lack an overall strategy in the sense of a coherent set of objectives and the coordinated means of achieving them. Aspects of small business policy and intervention are often dispersed across different departments and, as a result, support schemes have tended to grow piecemeal. Their objectives appear to include increased wealth and economic growth, job creation, and other benefits including greater social cohesion.
- Agencies are often established to deliver much of the direct intervention, but the dispersion of policy and the involvement of different organisations can often result in a confusing variety of apparent

sources of help. Attempts to coordinate this and give it some form of structure can follow the 'one-stop-shop' strategy of trying to concentrate services into one location, or the 'first-stop-shop' strategy of ensuring that different sources of support are well signposted from single access points.

- The means of achieving small business policy objectives take two broad approaches, which are not mutually exclusive: They are:

  - *Creating a favourable environment for enterprise*, which can involve actions in the areas of the economy, skills, societal attitudes, infrastructure, regulation, and fiscal policy.
  - *Intervening to support the enterprise process*, by direct and indirect support to individuals and businesses. This is often tailored to specific stages of development and to subgroups such as pre-start and start-up, high-tech businesses, geographic areas of disadvantage, population subgroups and exporters. The forms of assistance used include financial assistance (such as grants, loan guarantees, and venture finance), information and advice, management development and training, marketing and networking.

CHAPTER 13

Intervention Evaluation and Results

■ Introduction

It would be expected that intervention would be justified, or not justified as the case may be by the results it achieves. While there may be some circumstances where being seen to intervene is itself thought to be important, most people would expect that, if intervention is to continue, then there would be clear evidence that it achieves its purpose. If that is so then the fact that many governments across the world, including that of the UK devote substantial resources to assist enterprise and small business development suggests that the results are indeed positive.

The evidence for positive results is not however as clear as might be expected. Relevant results are frequently hard to measure or to ascribe to any particular intervention. Unambiguous evidence of direct positive outcomes appears to be sparse. It is also recognised that there is ambiguity, inconsistency and even confusion in the thoughts and words of those who influence policy-makers, as well as in the actions of those policy-makers themselves. This has produced a spreading belief that there may be too many policies and/or programmes of uncertain effectiveness.

As a result, it is not surprising that increasing attention is being paid to the efficacy of policies in the small business area. Measuring the results of the substantial resource investments in promoting and pursuing enterprise development is climbing up the agenda, not just for the public sector, but also for private sector investors in this process. Issues of efficiency, economy and effectiveness are becoming an integral part of the formulas that determine priorities, and monitoring and evaluation are being called for and are becoming a required component to be built into new initiatives at the planning stage.

Consequently, the requirements for the measurement and assessment of results, the development of rigorous and comprehensive evaluation criteria, the methods available, and the problems that these entail, all need to be considered. The results already obtained need to be examined, along with any conclusions that can be drawn from them. These issues form the subject of this chapter.

■ Requirements

Many people would like to know the results of intervention programmes, not least those responsible for their design and implementation. Providing meaningful information about results is not however just a simple matter of measurement. Before that can be done a number of issues have to be considered.

Who are interested in the results, and what do they want, or need, to know? The stakeholders in intervention include the clients, or recipients of the intervention, who are often considered to be the customers of intervention but who rarely pay more than a small portion of its costs. If the customer is the one who pays, then government is frequently the customer as it often pays the major share of the cost and therefore has a legitimate interest in knowing what it is getting for its money. Then there are other stakeholders, including the deliverers of the intervention, and the voters and taxpayers in whose name it is done.

What do these stakeholders want to know? For government, at least in the UK there is a desire for evaluations to provide answers to major policy questions some of which are listed in Table 13.1. For other stakeholders the position is less clear, although they will generally share the same concerns.

Answering the questions in the table requires rigorous and comprehensive evaluation criteria and methods: the 'what' and the 'how' of measurement. The question of what to measure however itself raises a number of other questions:

Table 13.1   Major UK small business policy questions

- To what extent is there a case for a selective targeting of small business support, and if so, then on what basis should this be undertaken?
- To what extent can more firms be encouraged to grow beyond the twenty-employee threshold?
- Will the Business Link delivery system prove effective in generating effective demand for and supply of services to small business?
- Is the current analysis of the financial needs of new and growing firms correct?
- How critical is the role of management training and development in the small firm sector?
- How can the sector be facilitated to expand its exports and keep abreast of technological development?
- Which interventions 'work' (however defined) and which don't?
- Who should pay, the client or the provider/government?

- What is the link between enterprise, jobs and other benefits?
- With what should the results be compared? What results might be expected (benchmarks) and how does this compare with the results required?
- Over what time-scale it is reasonable to expect and measure results?
- What value could or should be attached to results which cannot easily be measured (due to their intangibility or difficulties in isolating cause and effect relationships)?
- To whom do the benefits, or the drawbacks, accrue (the 'stakeholders') and who bears the costs?

13.1   Monitoring and evaluation

In his work in this area, R. Scott[1] emphasises the distinction between *monitoring* and *evaluation*, because these concepts are often confused with each other.

Monitoring has narrower objectives than evaluation. It is limited to observing and recording partial indicators of inputs and outputs. Typical inputs would be that conditions of assistance have been met, a description of the programme of assistance and the scope, level and types of activity undertaken. These findings would usually be rounded off with some partial indicators of outputs such as jobs created or qualifications gained.

Evaluation is broader and usually has two primary aims:

- An *improving* and *learning* aim to provide information that will help those involved to learn and so improve the design, operation and outcomes of policy initiatives
- A *proving* aim to examine what difference the policy initiative has made to the individuals or firms or to the wider economic and social parameters it seeks to influence.

Evaluation studies will have additional benefits if they also indicate how and why initiatives have their effects. Such learning enables initiatives to be enhanced in an informed way. This can be particularly valuable when more than one initiative is aimed at a particular objective. In this case, it may be important to analyse not only individual impacts but also whether the combined effects are greater than the sum of those individual impacts.

Of the two main aims of evaluation it is that of 'proving', or examining the difference made by an intervention, that is often the trickier. Seeking to examine the impact of a policy requires knowing what would have happened in the absence of the specific initiative in question and then determining what has changed as a result of the initiative. The changes considered should not be restricted to the direct recipients of assistance only (for instance a small business being assisted), but should also embrace the effects on the wider economy, community and society (for instance on the other businesses that did not receive assistance). This implies clearly identifying the stakeholders interested in changes or more importantly, affected by them.

Different individuals, groups or organisations in society may well seek different outputs or combinations of outputs from policy interventions These outputs can range broadly across economic, social and political aspirations, with the different stakeholder interests often being incompatible or in conflict.

In short, society comprises many and varied customer groupings with different requirements. Thus a conclusion, such as 'The policy worked,' often begs the question, 'In whose terms?'. The need to take a wide view of the effects is reinforced by current emphasis on the concept of *social accounting* and the *social audit*. Traditionally recorded effects have tended to be limited to the direct and easily measurable effects, especially those that could be expressed in money terms. Now, with increasing concern for the environmental and social impact of policies and the functioning of organisations generally, wider measures, new measures and new measuring techniques are becoming imperative. Traditional accounting systems are too narrow in scope to deal with many of the complexities and interest groups in the modern world. Even if financial assessments of some effects were possible, such an assessment might be too costly, too uncertain or could take too long. Projects which target social need, for example, will have a number of objectives, achievement of which will be evidenced not only in some economic measurements but also in other qualities or values that cannot be added together and then scientifically compared. If a project produces apples and pears they cannot all be considered to be apples. Assuming that they could, or alternatively ignoring the pears, does not help!

13.2   The Macnamara fallacy

The first step is to measure whatever can be easily measured. That is OK as far as it goes. The second step is to disregard that which can't easily be measured or give it an arbitrary quantitative value. This is artificial and misleading. The third step is to presume that what can't be measured really isn't important. This is blindness. The fourth step is to say that what can't be easily measured really doesn't exist. This is suicide.

(Daniel Yankelovich, 1972[2])

■ Methods

Some general principles of evaluation studies can now be enunciated:

---

1. Clearly understand the objectives of the initiative, so that evaluation can be related as closely as possible to them. (But, as noted in Chapter 12, determining the objectives of policy initiatives is often very difficult, because they may not be made explicit.)
2. Look for and record not just intended effects but other effects as well, both direct and indirect. This may mean broadening the scope of the evaluation study. Policy initiatives can have effects beyond those intended, both positive and negative. For instance will an increase in business start-ups reduce the growth prospects of some existing businesses? Moreover, as already noted, the scope of an evaluation may need to embrace social and environmental as well as economic effects.
3. Record the effects as they impact on the various stakeholders.
4. Have common measures of the effect, so that comparisons can be made across different initiatives
5. Decide on the basis on which the effect of any initiative is to be judged. Is it to be compared with the situation in the absence of that initiative, or against the effect of a previous initiative, or a (future) alternative initiative, or of the effects of the best parallel initiative elsewhere (a benchmark)? In short, it is necessary to determine whether there are better ways to achieve similar results.
6. Determine what the effects of more, or less, expenditure on the initiative might be not just the effect of all or nothing.
7. Determine whether the policy initiative would be more effective if it were implemented within a different institutional framework and delivery mechanism.

Implicit in the foregoing are two concepts that are often ignored in evaluation studies of small business policies: the *deadweight* and *displacement* effects. They have the effect of reducing the net benefit of interventions. *Multiplie* effects have the opposite effect. They enhance the benefits and should also be considered. *Effectiveness*, *efficiency* and *economy* are measures of different aspects of the process:

- *Deadweight*. This is a measure of 'what would have happened anyway' without the measure. Because of deadweight, even the direct effects alone of intervention are often not easy to ascertain. It may be possible to show that a business has received assistance and has subsequently improved, but to what extent is that improvement due to other factors and would therefore have happened anyway, even had there been no intervention?

- *Displacement*. This is a measure of 'how much of the gain in one area is offset by losses elsewhere'. It may be that a business directly benefits from intervention and increases its employment as a result. However if the employment in a rival business reduces because the first business takes its market, the total employment between the two may not increase and overall therefore there may be no benefit. The increase in activity in one business merely displaces activity in another, albeit the quality of the jobs may change. While, superficially, improved small business creation and growth may appear to be beneficial, this is so only if there is net growth and wealth creation as opposed to redistributing existing wealth, and no adverse effects on non-economic benefits. (In addition the benefits of a measure should exceed the cost of the measure.)
- *Multiplier effects*. There can however be additional benefits from the indirect or side effects of intervention. If an increase of activity in a business directly affected results in an increase in activity in an other business, for instance because it is a subcontractor, that is a beneficial *multiplier* effect.
- *Effectiveness, efficiency and economy*. There are a trio of measures concerned with value for money. *Effectiveness* is the extent to which an intervention achieved its aims, *efficiency* measures the amount of direct output that the inputs achieved, and *economy* is concerned with the cost of those inputs.

Observance of the principles described above, coupled with a practical and useful evaluation method, would provide a sound basis for determining the value for money of an economy's (or region's) support programmes. It strongly suggests that the implications of small business polices has to be examined in a wider framework than has traditionally been the case.

13.3 Economic appraisals

Although a prior appraisal of a project is not an evaluation of its eventual results, there is a connection in that the issues raised in the appraisal are likely to influence the agenda for a subsequent evaluation.

At least in the UK the established government system for the prior appraisal of projects is essentially an economic one. The 'Green Book'[3] produced by HM Treasury to guide government departments in project appraisal describes a method of economic appraisal based on a comparison of net present values. Those values can only include items to which a monetary value can be assigned. The book does acknowledges that, in making a choice among options, there will frequently be a need to consider factors that cannot usefully be valued in money terms. However, by concentrating primarily, and in some detail, on the more easily appraised economic aspects, it can have the result of encouraging appraisers to ignore the other factors, or at least to treat them as if they were less important. This is particularly serious when the other factors are the main point of the project, or where they could be the deciding factor in prioritising projects.

It is only to be expected that the issues raised by the appraisal are then likely to feature in the requirements set for monitoring during the project, which will in turn influence the subsequent appraisal. A limited, and biased, agenda will have been set, even if only subconsciously.

■ Problems

It is unusual to find evaluation studies that observe the principles of evaluation fully. There are a number of possible reasons for this:

- The cost of a rigorous study may be viewed as too expensive. To fully establish all the results might cost more than the original initiative.
- Studies may be deliberately circumscribed so as to 'prove' a desired outcome.
- In some situations it is argued that there are so many variables at work that it is not possible in practice to isolate the effects of one or two.
- Even if a correlation can be demonstrated between inputs and outputs, it does not necessarily imply causation, or clarify its direction. Research is often supposed to be better if done impartially, but someone who is impartial is often not involved, and without involvement it is hard to get the insight needed to understand cause and effect.
- It is argued that many of the effects of an initiative can be intangible and therefore difficult or impossible to measure.
- It is not easy to determine over what period results should be measured.

Some of these notions have been brought into focus by *inter alia*, R. Bennett,[4] who argues that ' "scientific" evaluation methods as normally applied will be unlikely to offer much useful assessment of SME policy effectiveness'. He suggests that evaluation of intervention measures can only effectively be made by the business owners and managers affected.

Notwithstanding the genuine nature of some of the above problems and issues, they do not explain the poor record of evaluation work, not only in the UK but internationally also.

> *It ain't what you don't know that is the problem. It's what you know that ain't so.*

■ Strategic Implications

It has already been pointed out that, in the UK as elsewhere, there is an absence of explicit statements of objectives and targets to guide the development of policies to encourage and support small business. This situation, *inter alia*, has led to a piecemeal development of policies. Moreover, the review and evaluation of existing support measures has often been narrow in scope, lacking in rigour, and superficial.

The combination of these two strands – lack of objectives and inadequate review – has lead to a situation where policy is formulated, and support maintained, too often on the basis of 'pressure from small business lobby groups, short-term fluctuations in macro-economic conditions and political expediency'.[5]

This same problem is further highlighted by Stevenson in explaining the difficulties of formulating and implementing an Entrepreneurship Development Strategy in the Atlantic Region of Canada.[6] She listed the following obstacles:

- **Lack of existing comprehensive models**. It is argued, in essence, that few if any models of entrepreneurship development exist that are based on a comprehensive, integrated and well-researched strategy. Because of this, 'there was a great deal of risk in the initiative'.
- **Lack of clarity about what entrepreneurship development is**. It is claimed that 'there is confusion in the minds of policy-makers and practitioners alike' about the meaning of entrepreneurship development, about its relationship with small business, about how to stimulate new ventures and growth of existing ones, and about how to determine priorities.
- **Prevailing myths**. Attention is drawn to the 'born not made' ('nature v. nurture') argument about entrepreneurs. 'There are still a number of government officials, policy-makers and business leaders who do not accept that the supply of entrepreneurs can be increased...'

- **Adapting to the paradigm shift in regional development policy.** It is argued that entrepreneurship development requires a different approach to economic development – that the emphasis needs to be on 'community animation' rather than on the traditional 'industrial development' approaches of developing economic infrastructure, undertaking macro-economic planning or evaluating investment projects.

The above themes are reinforced by an OECD study,[7] which concluded that member governments lacked a comprehensive strategy towards entrepreneurship and job creation, that there was scope for more to be done in promoting the entrepreneurial culture and business start-up, that organisational arrangements and delivery systems could be improved and also noted that few of the programmes which presently exist in member countries have been rigorously evaluated.

■ Key Policy Questions

In summary, the key questions for governments seeking to support an enterprise development policy may be posed as follows:

1. Why do enterprise and small business development warrant policies of support?
2. If support is justified, what outcomes are sought and how will they be measured? This requires setting objectives and targets.
3. What are the policies and programmes for achieving the objectives set? Subsidiary questions might include:

   - What can be done to stimulate a stronger enterprise culture and entrepreneurial vitality?
   - What can be done to influence and support the process by which people decide to start their own business so as to know how to vary the number and quality of such businesses?
   - What is needed to improve the survival and growth rates of new and existing businesses and their international competitiveness?

4. What are the most effective delivery mechanisms for chosen forms of support? Subsidiary questions might include:

   - What is the appropriate balance between private and public sector delivery?
   - What is the appropriate balance between national as opposed to local initiatives?
   - To what extent is targeting relevant or necessary?
   - How can delivery be made more effective?

5.   What forms of evaluation frameworks/methods are needed to evaluate the impacts of policies and programmes?
6.   What works and what doesn't? Why does it work and how?

▌ Results – the Current State of Knowledge

Despite the difficulties described there has nevertheless been much research into the effectiveness of the various methods of enterprise intervention. As a result some indications are available of the results they have achieved.

In the UK a significant research programme took place largely over the period 1989–92. It was commissioned by the Economic and Social Research Council (ESRC) and coordinated by Storey. Some of the published results[8] of the programme have already been widely referred to in this book. There have also been many other assessments which have sometimes produced contrary evidence. The following summary of some of these has therefore to be selective, but it seeks to give a flavour of the results reported in a variety of areas. Unless otherwise indicated, its source is the ESRC work.

■ High-tech Firms

It appears that high-tech businesses have benefited from government grants in their ability to survive and grow. Not only did the grant amount matter, but the credibility associated with its receipt eased the problem of levering up additional external monies. Science parks also appear to meet at least some of the needs for those wishing to start high-tech businesses.

■ Rural/Urban Businesses

Some evidence exists that small manufacturing businesses in rural environments (not 'remote' rural ones) outperform similar firms in urban locations. However, there is no suggestion that such a differential is attributable to government intervention, but rather to issues of owner motivation.

'Enterprise policies' in inner urban areas of main cities do reveal some interesting results in the context of managed workspace and community enterprises. Managed workspace was found, in terms of job creation, to be a more efficient use of public funds than community enterprises. Jobs in the community enterprises however were more likely to be taken by persons from the locality and thus more likely to give the long-term unemployed a 'taste of enterprise'. As Storey points out, such results beg questions about the objectives of public policy.

■ Financial Assistance

☐ *Enterprise Allowance Scheme/Business Start-up Scheme*

The Enterprise Allowance Scheme (EAS) was introduced as a pilot initiative in 1982 and later became the Business Start-up Scheme (BSUS). It is arguably one of the better researched public policy initiatives. Almost 700 000 people started the scheme in the ten-year period 1982/3 to 1992/3.

The scheme could be evaluated against three criteria: job creation for the recipients (i.e. the recipients leaving the unemployment register), creation of employment (for others), and net reduction in the numbers of unemployed (e.g. after allowing for persons being employed who were not registered unemployed or reduced outward migration).

The results indicated that the scheme was cost-effective. It is estimated that the scheme cost £2000 for each individual removed from the unemployment register. However, the scheme has been subject to some criticisms. For instance, a study in Cleveland in the North-East of England found that the net effect in terms of job creation was negligible, with, it is argued, many of the new businesses in areas such (as hairdressing) merely displacing existing ones. Others have argued that instead of creating a 'culture of enterprise' it has merely created a culture of 'survival', with too many self-employed, low-income businesses operating at the margin.

☐ *Grants*

Grants are, at least in the eyes of many recipients, a popular way of intervening to promote small business development and the resultant job creation. The job creation aspect is frequently seen, by those awarding the grants, to be crucial to the extent that the amount of grant awarded in total was often reported in terms of grant-cost per job. Frequently this is specified as the cost-per-job promoted, because what is known at the time the grant is awarded is the number of jobs planned, or at least indicated in the business plan on which the grant award is based. If the plan works, which it does not always, the jobs will be created later. The number of jobs promoted can therefore be recorded at the time the grant award is made. The number of jobs actually created will not be known until some time later.

As well as the cost per job, evaluations have therefore also considered the difference between the jobs planned (promoted) and the number of jobs eventually created, as well as issues concerned with the 'quality' of the jobs. Summarising the results is not very helpful, because the range of answers is so large. Costs per job can range from 0 (a job which was created with no grants) to many tens of thousands of pounds. Job creation rates, for programmes in Northern Ireland, appear to have varied from only 40 per cent of jobs promised being realised to a success rate of between 70 per cent and 80 per cent. Job quality is particularly problematic. One measure of it is taken to be job duration, but this cannot actually be measured until the job ends, which may take many years.

13.4   A negative effect of grants

One way in which grants can lead directly to a reduction in productivity concerns capital grants. If a business can get a 50 per cent capital grant for the purchase of a new machine then it may be tempted to buy a better (faster, higher-quality, greater-capacity) machine than was originally envisaged. If however the business did not need the extra speed, quality or throughput, then it would not make full use of the machine and output would not therefore increase above that which a cheaper machine might have produced. The more expensive machine would, however, probably be more complex and have higher maintenance costs, which would not be grant-assisted. Thus the business would as a direct result of the grant, have higher production costs for no increase in output.

The evidence for the success of grants is mixed. Owen, who examined state aid to small businesses in three areas of Europe[9] (in South Yorkshire in England, Nord-Pas-de-Calais in France and the Hainaut region of Belgium), found that in all three areas the provision of grants led to additional economic activity. A report however by Hitchens, Wagner and Birnie on Northern Ireland's industrial productivity compared with West Germany's[10] found that Northern Ireland firms, despite lower productivity, were at least as profitable as their German counterparts. This was attributed in a large part to lower wages and to the level of government financial assistance. It was suggested that the level and nature of such assistance (which in the 1980s amounted to about 20 per cent of manufacturing GDP) impeded the efficient operation of some local businesses by reducing their incentive to carry out essential research and development, training and product innovation and design.

This work was instrumental in triggering a change in emphasis of Northern Ireland's grant strategy away from capital grants towards assistance with planning, product development marketing, strengthening management, applying quality standards as well as training and development of staff.

A subsequent study in Northern Ireland appeared to be much more positive about the effectiveness of grants. Scott's work[11] has used control groups in Leicestershire in England and in the Republic of Ireland to demonstrate the effect of the work of the government-funded Northern Ireland small business agency (LEDU). He found that LEDU-assisted businesses had higher employment growth rates than comparable but non-assisted businesses and that the cost per job year was estimated at between 5 per cent and 3 per cent below the estimate for the Regional Investment Grant in Great Britain.

It is worth noting, however, that the additional employment creation by grant-assisted small firms was due more to a higher survival rate 'than to variations in subsequent employment growth'. It may also be relevant that LEDU engages in a variety of interventions in addition to grants, including work to promote a more positive enterprise culture. The employment growth benefits may not therefore be due solely to grants. They may be more likely to be an indication of the overall effectiveness of LEDU than the measure of a single intervention.

☐ Small Firms' Loan Guarantee Scheme

A rigorous assessment of the impact of the Small Firms Loan Guarantee Scheme (SFLGS) was carried out by National Economic Research Associates in 1990. Overall, it concluded that the impact of the scheme on the small business sector was negligible, although it may have had some initial effect 'in providing a demonstration to the clearing banks that there were opportunities for profitable lending in the small business sector'.[12]

☐ Business Expansion Scheme

A 1986 review by Peat Marwick judged that the Business Expansion Scheme (BES) was 'effective in terms of generating additional jobs, at a cost to the Exchequer of between £8000 and £10 000'.[13]

However, as investments moved into non-productive areas and as the amounts invested became larger, the scheme failed to add value by assisting businesses needing small amounts of equity, which was the original purpose of BES. Again, while the scheme probably had some clear demonstration or 'symbolic' benefits, those benefits were that it 'encouraged financial institutions to take an interest in ... small firms, encouraged private investment in small firms ... and educated some small business owners in the benefits of external equity'.[14] For both investors and small business owners, its measurable impact appeared to be minimal. It was replaced in 1993 by the Enterprise Investment Scheme, which allows investors to play a role in their investee companies.

☐ Counselling and Advisory Services

Counselling has been one of the fastest-growing areas of small business support. Evaluation of these services does tend to typify the superficial nature of studies in this area. Such studies concentrate on head-counts (how many use the service) and satisfaction indicators (how many clients say they find it useful). The critical question, however, is how the service affects the performance of the business in terms of turnover, profitability or other measures.

On the issue of satisfaction indicators it would appear that reaction is largely positive from clients of these services. However, some studies reveal that small businesses found greater satisfaction with their banks and accountants than with public support services.[15]

The evaluation of improved business performance appears to be inconclusive. Relatively little research has been done in this area, and most of what has been done does not stand up to rigorous critical analysis. The conclusion of Storey is that 'we are not aware of any studies which demonstrate that the provision of information and advice is a significant factor influencing the survival of the business.'[16] It must be remembered, however, that the absence of proof does not mean that the influence of this form of support is not positive in terms of business performance; it has merely yet to be demonstrated!

☐ *Management Training and Development*

The conclusion reached in relation to advice and information applies equally to another area of considerable investment by the public sector: management training. Improving the quality of management is self-evidently the *sine qua non* of improved business performance. The question posed is 'To what extent does management training lead to improved management and therefore to improved business performance?'

While a great deal of research has been carried out in the field of management training (and to a lesser extent of consultancy), its value is limited. What research there is confirms the importance of developing management, especially in the growing firm, but it does not isolate the benefits either of management development in general or of different types of management development appropriate to the particular circumstances of groups of businesses.

This is clearly a cause for concern, which applies also to the role of consultancy in the small business. The DTI's 'Consultancy Initiative' was designed to encourage small business to use commercial management consultants. However, little is known of what benefit was achieved and under what circumstances. Official evaluations concentrated mainly on take-up and subsequent use of consultants and were inconclusive as regards the impact on the businesses.

The reasons for the lack of useful research evidence in the areas of advice, information, training and consultancy, and indeed other areas, are essentially two-fold:

- A lack of rigour exists in much of the research, and the methodology adopted is inappropriate to the objectives of the research (in so far as the objectives are genuinely to assess impact). There are various reasons for this, including a failure to distinguish between the training of managers and that of other employees, the time-scales not being adequate, the sample sizes being too small, the impact of multiple variables not being allowed for, and the absence of control groups for comparisons.
- The area of training and advice is a very complex one. It can be difficult even for rigorous research to clearly demonstrate the benefits of management development. Distinguishing between correlation, and causality, and knowing the direction of causality, is particularly problematical. Moreover, the effectiveness of management development activity in any business is subject to many influences not least the size and

structure of the management team itself, the nature of its products or services, its stage of development and, of course, the quality of the management development input provided.

☐ *Indirect Intervention*

The main impression surrounding many of the indirect forms of assistance is that the case for them is 'not proven'. Clearly the government, TECs and Business Links will need to make greater efforts to determine the value added from these schemes. Also, the research community will need to adopt a more rigorous approach to the 'proving' element of evaluation studies (as opposed to the 'learning' and 'improving' elements).

13.5   Training and Employment Councils

Training and Employment Councils (TECs) were introduced in England and Wales in 1990, with the aim of fostering economic growth and contributing to regeneration by strengthening the skill base and assisting local enterprise to expand and compete effectively.

A evaluation of TEC services in 1995 on behalf of the DTI concluded that 'information, advice and business skills training services provided by TECs to existing SMEs generate benefits to those firms that take them up, to the local economies in which they are situated, and to the national economy as a whole'.[17] According to this report, there are likely to be supply side gains for the national economy as a result of these activities.

However, TECs have been frequently criticised. Smallbone[18] lists some of the main objections:

- Their funding is inadequate for them to be really effective.
- They lack democratic accountability.
- They are run by representatives of large businesses for SMEs.
- They are failing to reach the majority of small businesses

For such reasons TECs have been seen by some people as at least partial failures.

Ultimately, the recipients of these services should engage in a more systematic approach to gauging the benefits for their investment of time and money and/or clearly articulate their own specific requirements. The recipient businesses could and should have an important role in shaping provision. It is regularly argued and generally agreed that small businesses lack management skills and information and advice, as noted above. However, the recognition of need does not define intervention to meet it. This dilemma derives from the unique nature of each business: while they have many generic and common features, each has its own internal characteristics and relationship to various stakeholders (customers, suppliers, funders, etc.)

To identify an appropriate management training, counselling or information supply response means determining, for each business, what its deficiency in the area is, what form of assistance is required, who needs it and how best to meet the need. Even when such questions are answered for a business, the opportunity cost of meeting the need has to be assessed. As the circumstances of each business are often so unique, generalised solutions, such as offering more management training or information and counselling, will ignore the specifics of each business's market, trading situation and internal characteristics. Hence, it is often argued that there is a need to put more onus on the individual business to identify and seek out provision appropriate to its own circumstances.

■ In Conclusion

It would therefore appear that some interventions are having, or have had, a positive effect. The evidence is, however, generally inconclusive. While some of the research into interventions has been criticised for its methodology, the lack of clear findings is probably due more to the complexity of the subject area than to avoidable shortcomings in the evaluations.

Policy makers would like to know how effective the possible forms of intervention are in order to select the ones that will be most cost-effectively achieve their purposes. The evidence available to them however is often imperfect, ambiguous and even contradictory. There appears to be no strong body of evidence to say that intervention works, but also there is no clear evidence that it doesn't.

13.6   The evidence of businesses

Most surveys of business opinion in the UK point to a number of simple conclusions, similar to those already articulated by a number of other commentators. Based on what businesses say their needs are, these surveys have suggested that:

- A key role for government should be to create a stable and positive economic environment, and encourage an enterprise culture.
- The needs of small businesses for government support do not differ significantly from those of bigger firms (except in special cases of the impact of regulations and diseconomies of scale).

- There is no strong case for a large array of firm or sector specific policies.
- Where services are required and supplied, the most common need is not for more but for better. Moreover, the case for public, as opposed to private, provision is often highly questionable.

Evaluating enterprise policy interventions is not easy. In commenting on this Bennett notes,

> Thus for small businesses we have the general conclusion that age, size and sector and location are crucial distinctions of small business characteristics (e.g. Storey 1994) but beyond that we know that a multiplicity of other variables is also important *in different combinations* for each business.

Thus, he argues, in researching small businesses to assess policy interventions, there are two possible courses of action:

The first, typified by 'matched pairs' research, involves so subdividing the population by careful sampling that any conclusions relate only to very constrained circumstances from which generalisations are difficult or impossible. The second involves taking large samples that include businesses from a wide range of different ages, sectors, locations and other distinguishing factors. The problem with such approaches is that 'it is usually impossible to obtain the sample size necessary to say anything useful about specific business problems: generalisation to the population is emphasised at the expense of detailed or specific assessments.' The range of different business circumstances is however such that even surveys with samples of up to two thousand can focus only 'on a restricted range of issues that does not allow each business to be put in a proper context'.[19] Bennett contends that it is in 'the area of evaluation of SME programmes that there is also one of the greatest methodological challenges'.[20]

Key points

- There are a number of stakeholders in the process of intervention to promote more enterprise. They include the initiator(s) of the intervention, which is often government, those who deliver it and those who receive it. They all have an interest in knowing how effective it is or what its impact was on unintended recipients.
- To answer their questions, rigorous and comprehensive evaluation criteria and methods are needed. Evaluation can have a number of aims including both an 'improving' and 'learning' aim to provide information which will help to improve policy initiatives, and a 'proving'

aim to examine what difference the policy initiative has made to the individuals or firms or to the wider economic and social parameters it seeks to influence. Evaluations also have to contend with issues such as 'In whose terms is success to be measured?' and 'How can both economic and social benefits be assessed?'

- The methods employed should be carefully considered and should address issues such as *deadweight, displacement,* and *multiplier effects* as well as *effectiveness, efficiency* and *economy*.
- The problems of doing this are considerable. For instance, they include a lack of clear objectives, a lack of existing comprehensive models, a lack of clarity about what entrepreneurship development is, prevailing myths, and adapting to paradigm shifts in regional development policy.
- There are some indications that interventions can work, but overall the evidence for positive results is not as clear as might be expected. There appears to be ambiguity, inconsistency and even confusion in the thoughts and words of policy-makers, as well as in their actions. Relevant results are frequently hard to measure or to ascribe to any particular intervention, and clear evidence of direct positive outcomes appears to be sparse.
- There appears therefore to be no strong body of evidence to say that intervention works, but equally there is no clear evidence that it doesn't.

Afterword

CHAPTER 14

Science, Art or Magic?

> *It is time for change. Time to realise that Governments on their own cannot provide us with permanent secure jobs and a growing standard of living... Time to accept that the solutions to our problems lie in our own hands. We need to foster a spirit of self reliance and determination to take charge of our future. The next decade will provide greater opportunities for enterprise and initiative than we have ever seen before. The extent to which our community will accept this challenge will determine our future levels of employment and national wealth.*
>
> **(The Culliton Report, Ireland, 1992[1])**

Who should provide opportunities in our lives, and particularly in our economic lives? Is a job something which is a right and which should therefore be provided for us? If there is a problem is it someone else's task to sort it out, and is that someone usually the government? Many people alive today were brought up in a culture where lifetime employment was seen as being both available and the norm, and therefore as the desired and natural state for individual economic activity, even though in reality it had not been the norm for very long, if at all.

The large businesses, which earlier this century seemed to provide the core employment in most economies, are dying, or are at least in decline. Like human beings, businesses are born, live and then die, and generally they die at an earlier age than humans. Lifetime employment is hard to find in those circumstances. Should we instead view employment rather as Buddhists view life? Should we expect that after our present life ends we will be reborn into a different existence; that when one form of employment ends there will be another? If so, who will provide those other forms of employment?

We have, in recent years, seen the re-emergence of the small business. That is not to say that it ever went away. There have always been small businesses in the form of farms, shops and many personal services such as those provided by hairdressers, restaurateurs, plumbers and window-cleaners. What has re-emerged is the small business in the mainstream of industrial manufacturing and services. Some of the reasons for this are presented in Table 14.1.

Small businesses are providing many of the new jobs, but it takes enterprising people to start small businesses. Even for those being employed in them, the new small businesses do not offer the same employment prospects as the declining big businesses. For both employers and employees economic security will increasingly depend on skills, ideas, and the ability to learn and to adapt to meet changing requirements. That means people who are enterprising. We have an interest in building an enterprise culture in which people feel that they can and should use their own initiative to secure their economic future.

This represents a challenge that is social as well as economic. It has been observed that in the USA, 'the nature of work has changed, but the nature of education hasn't... Global competition and new technology are overthrowing the assumptions behind mass production and, simultaneously, the lessons taught in American classrooms.'[2] People need a different approach: an enterprising approach.

Enterprising behaviour, however, is not something just limited to, or reserved for, a business context. Being enterprising and seeking to contribute in that way can impact on many of aspects of our lives. Enterprise is a mode of behaviour that can have a wide application, and the results of that application can themselves have a range of consequences, including both social and economic impacts. 'A close-knit social fabric can be good for democracy and the economy. A study of Italian regions... suggested that membership of choral societies is one of the three best predictors of a robust and effective local democracy and economy.'[3]

Table 14.1   Reasons for the re-emergence of small businesses

Supply	Demand
Technical changes	Market changes
● New products	● Demand for service
● New industries	● Demand for variety
Fragmentation	Uncertainty of demand
● Sub-contracting	● Individual customer requirements
● Buy-outs	● Stronger competition
Opportunity	Macro economic conditions
● Redundancy	● Unemployment
Government	Economic developments
● Privatisation	● Services
● Deregulation	● Just-in-time
● Tax benefit	● Niches

If private sector small business enterprise is growing, so too is community enterprise. Examples of community economic actions include the following:

- Community enterprises:
  - Community business
  - Community co-operatives
  - Development trusts
- Telecottages
- Community shops/cafes
- Community trusts
- Local Exchange Trading Schemes (LETS)
- Credit unions
- Community loan funds
- Subscription farming
- Food co-operatives
- Country Markets
- Community recycling schemes
- Community self-build
- Managed workspace
- City farms
- Community gardens
- Car sharing
- Community transport.

It is one thing, however, to see the potential for such initiatives and another thing to achieve them. There are many obstacles between potential and achievement, including habits, attitudes, beliefs and expectations. If we are used to seeing the economic cake as essentially fixed in size, where every gain by one person means a corresponding loss by another, we are likely to be concerned primarily with the distribution of that cake. If, however, we can see that a bigger cake is possible then we might look for creative ways of enlarging it.

If European politics in the nineteenth century was about dividing up the cake, Marxism was supposed to make the reallocation permanent. To the astonished Virginian in his buckskins, the idea must have seemed absurd. Everything you could possibly want or need was there, waiting for you, only provided you were prepared to cut it down, dig it out or plough it. That was the deal God had offered: you could have it, but only if you did the work.

(Simon Hoggart[4])

Getting more enterprise involves addressing obstacles: obstacles to enterprising behaviour such as belief and acceptability, and obstacles to its application to (small) business such as a shortage of ideas, finance and advice.

If we want more enterprise then it helps to have some idea of what it is. Is enterprise a science? Are there theories about enterprise that can be used to predict accurately how it will behave in specific circumstances? Is enterprise an art? Is it something that is hard to define, but that can be recognised when it is seen, that can only be demonstrated by a few, and that, while it has rules, often appears to succeed by breaking the rules? Or is enterprise a magic, because it is a mystery to us, because it is unpredictable and because we have no control over it?

In this book some of the issues relevant to such a debate have been presented. There is no one single accepted view on enterprise, on what it means, what gives rise to it, what is implications are, or how it can be promoted. However, 'one of the commonplace yet probably essential characteristics in the development of any new body of knowledge is the competing values of those who generate and use that knowledge.'[5] The authors hope that this book helps to present the emerging body of knowledge on enterprise.

Notes and References

1 Why Talk About Enterprise?

1. C. Handy, *The Future of Work* (Oxford: Basil Blackwell, 1984) pp. 16–17.
2. Ibid.
3. A. Toffler, *The Third Wave* (London: William Collins, 1980).
4. C. Handy, *The Age of Unreason* (London: Arrow, 1990).
5. From J. Walters, 'Turbulence Ahead for City's Airline' and S. Caulkin, 'Dismembering the Body Corporate' (both in *Observer* ©, 15 September 1996).
6. C. Handy, *The Age of Unreason*, pp. 34–5.
7. H. Mintzberg, *The Structuring of Organisations* (Englewood Cliffs, New Jersey: Prentice-Hall, 1979) p. 131.
8. D. Clawson, *Bureaucracy and the Labour Process: The Transformation of US Industry, 1860–1920* (New York: Monthly Review Press, 1980).
9. C. Handy, *The Age of Unreason*, p. 98.
10. Quoted in T. Peters, 'Travel the Independent Road' (*Independent on Sunday*, 2 January 1994).

2 What Does Enterprise Mean?

1. From the trailer to a twelve part series, 'Mastering Enterprise', *Financial Times*, 18 November 1996).
2. In answer to questions during a celebrity lecture in Northern Ireland, May 1993.
3. *DTI – The Department for Enterprise*, White Paper presented to Parliament, Cm 278 (January 1988) p. 41.
4. Ibid., p. ii.
5. Ibid., pp. 1 and 5.
6. Department of Economic Development, *Building a Stronger Economy – The Pathfinder Process* (Belfast: Department of Economic Development, 1987).
7. 'Towards 2000', the government's strategic guidance paper to TECs (May 1994) p. 6.

8. H. Eastwood, 'Step Towards Winning', *Enterprise* (September–October 1995).
9. Birmingham TEC, information leaflet.
10. Greater Nottingham TEC, information folder.
11. Leicestershire TEC, *Guide to Services* (1993) p. 1.
12. Sheffield TEC, information booklet.
13. Employment Department Group, *Small Firms Big Future – Enterprise Workshop* (Sheffield: Employment Department, 1991) p. 3 and 10.
14. London Enterprise Agency, *Annual Review* (1992) p. 1.
15. *Business in the Community*, 'A Review of the Enterprise Agency Network', June 1989, p. 5.
16. Training Agency (1990).
17. University of Ulster, 'Enterprise in Higher Education', leaflet.
18. P. Morgan (Director General, Institute of Directors), speech to Institute of Directors' Convention reported in *Director*, March 1990.
19. J. Ritchie, 'Explaining Enterprise Cultures', paper presented at the Tenth National Small Firms Policy and Research Conference, Cranfield Institute (1987).
20. Nottingham Polytechnic, *Enterprising Nottinghamshire Final Evaluation Report* (1991) and personal communication.
21. F. Coffield and R. MacDonald, *Risky Business? Youth and the Enterprise Culture* (Falmer Press 1991) p. 29.
22. 'Enterprise and Education' – *The Primary Enterprise Package* sponsored by Marks & Spencer.
23. From the crossword, *Independent*, 8 January 1996.
24. 'Towards an "Enterprising" Culture – A Challenge for Education and Training', *OECD/CERI Educational Monograph*, No. 4 (1989) pp. 6–7.
25. 'What Do We Mean by Enterprise?', *Employment Initiatives*, February 1990, pp. 3–4.
26. A. Smith, *An Inquiry into the Nature and Causes of the Wealth of Nations* (New York: Modern Library, 1937) (first published in 1776).
27. J. A. Schumpeter, *The Theory of Economic Development* (Cambridge, Mass.: Harvard University Press, 1951) (first published in 1934).
28. W. H. Whyte, *The Organization Man* (Garden City Doubleday Anchor Books, 1957).
29. J. K. Galbraith, *The New Industrial State* (Boston, Massachusetts: Houghton Mufflin, 1967).
30. B. A. Kirchhoff, personal communication (1993).
31. D. L. Birch, *The Job Generation Process* (Boston, Massachusetts: MIT study on neighbourhood and regional change, 1982).
32. 'Towards an "Enterprising" Culture', quoted in C. Ball, B. Knight and S. Plant, 'New Goals for a Enterprise Culture', *Training for Enterprise* (1990) p. 21.
33. D. C. McClelland and D. G. Winter, '*Motivating Economic Achievement*' (New York: Free Press, 1969).
34. A. A. Gibb, 'Enterprise Culture – Its Meaning and Implications for Education and Training', *Journal of European Industrial Training* (1987) p. 10.
35. C. Alter, and J. Hage, *Organisations Working Together* (Newbury Park, California: Sage, 1993).
36. G. Salaman, *Managing* (Buckingham: Open University Press, 1995) p. 60.
37. MCI Personal Competence Project: Summary Report (London, Management Charter Initiative, 1990).
38. Ball, Knight and Plant, op. cit., pp. 19 and 21.
39. A. A. Gibb and J. Ritchie, 'Understanding the Process of Starting a Small Business', *European Small Business Journal*, 1.1 (1982) p. 7.
40. F. Coffield, 'Hunting a Heffalump in the World of the Enterprise Industry', *Independent*, 29 August 1990.

■ 3 Enterprise in Individuals

1. M. Scott, A. Fadahunsi and S. Kodithuwakku, *Mastering Enterprise*, no. 7, *Financial Times*, 13 January 1997, p. 6.
2. *New Collins Dictionary* (Glasgow: HarperCollins, 1992).
3. A. A. Gibb, 'The Enterprise Culture and Education', *International Small Business Journal*, vol. 11 (1993) pp. 11–34.
4. W. G. Biemans, *Managing Innovation Within Networks* (London: Routledge, 1992).
5. G. A. Forehand, 'Assessment of Innovative Behaviour': Partial Criteria for the Assessment of Executive Performance', *Journal of Applied Psychology*, vol. 47 (1963) pp. 206–13.
6. R. M. Kanter, 'Change Master Skills', in J. Henry and D. Walker, *Managing Innovation* (London: Sage 1991) pp. 54–61.
7. Lord Young of Graffan cited in A. Tate, 'A Strategy for Enterprise in the University of Ulster', *Journal of Irish Business and Administrative Research*, vol. 14 (1993) pp. 1–11, p. 1
8. E. F. M. McKenna, *Psychology in Business* (London: Lawrence Erlbaum, 1987).
9. See D. McClelland, *The Achieving Society* (Princeton, New Jersey: Van Nostrand, 1961), and J. Rotter, 'Generalised Expectancies for Internal Versus External Control of Reinforcement', *Psychological Monographs*, vol. 80 (1966) pp. 1–27; see McKenna also for a discussion on psychoanalytical approaches to personality.
10. H. H. Stevenson and D. E. Gumpert 'The Heart of Entrepreneurship', in W. A. Sahlman and H. H. Stevenson, *The Entrepreneurial Venture* (Boston, Massachusetts: Harvard Business School, 1992)
11. J. A. Timmons, *The Entrepreneurial Mind* (Andover: Brick House, 1989).
12. S. Caird, *A. Review of Methods of Measuring Enterprising Attributes* (Durham University Business School, 1988)
13. Timmons, op. cit.
14. D. C. McClelland, 'Achievement Motivation Can be Developed, *Harvard Business Review*, November–December 1965, pp. 6–24.
15. Ibid., p. 7.
16. See this comment by an interviewee in S. Cromie, 'Motivation of Aspiring Male and Female Entrepreneurs', *Journal of Organisational Behaviour*, vol. 8 (1987) pp. 251–61.
17. P. F. Drucker, *Innovation and Entrepreneurship* (London: Heinemann, 1985) p. 128.
18. One of the statements used in a questionnaire designed by Rotter, op. cit.
19. C. R. Anderson, 'Locus of Control, Coping Behaviours and Performance in Stress Settings, a Longitudinal Study' *Journal of Applied Psychology*, vol. 62 (1977) pp. 446–51.
20. G. Salaman, *Work Organisations*, (London: Longman, 1979).
21. See evidence in S. Cromie and S. Johns, Irish Entrepreneurs – Some Personal Characteristics', *Journal of Occupational Behaviour*, vol. 4 (1984) pp. 317–324.
22. See comments by respondents in Cromie, op. cit.
23. I. L. Janis, *Victims of Group Think: A. Psychological Study of Foreign Policy Decisions and Fiascos* (Boston, Massachusetts: Houghton Mifflin, 1972).
24. S. Caird, 'The Enterprising Tendency of Occupational Groups', *International Small Business Journal*, vol. 9 (1991) pp. 75–81, p. 77.
25. Cromie, op. cit.
26. D. Miller, 'Strategy Making and Structure: Analysis and Implications for Performance', *Academy of Management Journal*, vol. 30 (1987) pp. 7–32, p. 10.
27. See J. A. F. Stoner and C. Wankel, *Management*, 3rd edn (Englewood Cliffs, New Jersey: Prentice-Hall, 1986) p. 397 for a discussion on the nature of innovators
28. See V. Thompson, *Bureaucracy and Innovation*, Alabama: Alabama University Press, 1969) for a discussion on creativity. Thompson's quotation is from page 11.

29. J. B. Cunningham and H. Lischerom, 'Defining Entrepreneurship', *Journal of Small Business Management*, vol. 29 (1991) pp. 45–60, p. 47.
30. E. Chell, 'The Entrepreneurial Personality: A Few Ghosts Laid to Rest?', *International Small Business Journal*, vol. 3 (1985), pp. 43–54.
31. M. Kets de Vries, 'The Entrepreneurial Personality: A Person at the Crossroads', *Journal of Management Studies*, vol. 14 (1977) pp. 34–57.
32. A. MacNabb, *Entrepreneurial Profiling* (Belfast: Institute for Enterprise Strategies, 1993).
33. E. Chell, J. Haworth and S. Brearley, *The Entrepreneurial Personality: Concepts, Cases, and Categories* (London: Routledge, 1991).
34. R. W. Hornaday, 'Dropping the E-words from small business research', *Journal of Small Business Management*, vol. 28 (1990) pp. 22–33.
35. See R. Boyatzis, *The Competent Manager* (New York: Wiley, 1982) and Management Charter Initiative, Management Standards Implementation Pack (London: MCI, 1991).
36. S. Caird, 'Problems With the Identification of Enterprise Competencies and the Implications for Assessment and Development', *Management Education and Development*, vol. 23 (1992) pp. 6–17.
37. Ibid., p. 14.
38. Ibid., p. 16.
39. D. Buchanan and D. Boddy, *The Expertise of the Change Agent* (Hemel Hempstead: Prentice-Hall, 1992) p. 92.
40. M. Casson, *The Entrepreneurs* (Oxford: Martin Robertson, 1982).
41. A. K Roberts, 'The Social Conditions, Consequences and Limitations of Careers Guidance', *British Journal of Guidance and Counselling*, vol. 5 (1977) pp. 1–9, p. 7.
42. A. MacNabb, op. cit.
43. J. Curran and R. A. Blackburn, 'Introduction', in J. Curran and R. A. Blackburn, *Paths of Enterprise* (London: Routledge, 1991).
44. A. A. Gibb, 'Enterprise Culture – Its Meaning and Implications for Education and Training', *Journal of European Industrial Training*, vol. 11 (1987) p. 11.
45. N. F. Krueger, *Prescription for Opportunity: How Communities Can Create Potential for Entrepreneurs* (Washington, DC: Small Business Foundation of America, Working Paper 93–03, 1995).

■ 4   The Culture of Enterprise

1. R. Burrows, *Deciphering the Enterprise Culture (Entrepreneurship, Petty Capitalism and the Restructuring of Britain)* (London: Routledge, 1991) p. 5.
2. Ibid., p. 9.
3. H. Pompe, M. Bruyn and J. Koek, 'Entrepreneurs in Small Business in International Comparative Perspective' – Sociological Institute, University of Groningen, The Netherlands. Papers presented at *The 13th International Small Business Congress*, London (1986).
4. G. Hofstede, *Cultures and Organizations* (HarperCollins Publishers 1994).
5. Ibid., p. 169.
6. Ibid., p. 169.
7. Ibid., p. 63.
8. Ibid., p. 10.
9. D. McClelland, 'That Urge to Achieve', *THINK* (IBM, 1966) p. 111.
10. Ibid., p. 111.
11. Ibid., p. 117.
12. Ibid., p. 114.

13. G. Redding, 'Three Styles of Asian Capitalism', in 'Mastering Enterprise', no. 7, *Financial Times*, January 1997 p. 10.
14. Hofstede, op. cit., p. 73 and p. 74.
15. Redding, op. cit., p. 10.
16. P. Dodd, '*The Influence of Culture on Enterprise*', Theme Pamphlet (London: Industrial Christian Fellowship, 1990) pp. 2–5.
17. Excerpts from L. Dane, *Contrasting Models of Policy Governing Small Business: Does Heavy Regulation Really Hinder the Small Business Sector?*
18. Burrows, op. cit., p. 4.
19. P. O. Reynolds, B. Miller and W. R. Maki, 'Explaining Regional Variations in Business Births and Deaths – US 1976–88', *Small Business Economics*, October 1995.

■ 5 Other Aspects of Enterprise

1. A. Smith, *An Enquiry into the Nature and Causes of the Wealth of Nations* (Edinburgh: Adam and Charles Black, 1882) first published in 1776.
2. For a discussion on Smith's and Hayek's contribution to economic theory, see D. King, *The New Right* (Basingstoke: Macmillan, 1987) pp. 70–90.
3. W. Hutton, *The State We're In* (London: Vintage, 1996) p. 237.
4. M. Friedman, *Capitalism and Freedom* (University of Chicago Press, 1962) p. 200.
5. W. Keegan, *The Spectre of Capitalism* (London: Random House, 1992) p. 106, cited in M. Thomas, 'Marketing – In Chaos or Transition', *European Journal of Marketing*, vol. 28 (1994) pp. 55–62.
6. Hutton, op. cit., p. xxviii.
7. M. Porter, 'The Competitive Advantage of Nations', *Harvard Business Review*, March/April 1990, p. 82.
8. Ibid., p. 74.
9. G. Redding, 'Three Styles of Asian Capitalism', in *Mastering Enterprise*, no. 7, *Financial Times*, 13 January 1997, p. 11.
10. N. F. Krueger, Jr, *Prescription for Opportunity: How Communities can Create Potential for Entrepeneurs* (Washington, DC: Small Business Foundation of America, Working Paper 93–03, 1995) p. 16.
11. Ibid., 'Executive Summary'.
12. W. Hutton, 'Ethics Man Finds No Place in the New Enterprise Era', *Guardian* ©, 21 March 1994.
13. K. Gold, 'Must We Buy Schooling from Marks and Spencer?', *Observer* ©, 21 January 1990.
14. C. Handy, *The Age of Unreason* (London: Arrow, 1990).
15. C. Alter and J. Hage, *Organisations Working Together* (Newbury Park, Claifornia: Sage, 1993) p. 14.
16. E. H. Schein and W. G. Bennis, *Personal and Organisation Change Through Group Methods* (New York: Wiley, 1965) p. 7.

▌ 6 Small Business Categories and Variations

1. Bank of England, *Finance for Small Firms*, report dated January 1997, p. 2.
2. D. Carson and S. Cromie, 'Marketing Planning in Small Enterprises: A Model and Some Empirical Evidence', *Journal of Marketing Management*, vol. 5 (1989) pp. 33–50

3. N. C. Churchill and V. L. Lewis, 'Growing Concerns: The Five Stages of Small Firm Growth', *Harvard Business Review*, May–June 1983, pp. 31, 32, 34, 40.
4. R. Peterson and R. Rondstadt, 'A Silent Strength: Entrepreneurial Know-Who', *The 16th ESBS, efmd IMD Report* (86/4) p. 11.
5. S. Birley, 'The Start-up', in P. Burns and J. Dewhurst (eds), *Small Business and Entrepreneurship* (Basingstoke: Macmillan, 1989) p. 15.
6. S. Birley and S. Cromie, 'Social Networks and Entrepreneurship in Northern Ireland', Enterprise in Action Conference (1988).
7. Forum of Private Business, 'The Internal and External Problems that Face Small Businesses', paper presented at the *Sixteenth ISBC* (October 1989) p. 6.
8. Ibid., p. 49.
9. Ibid., p. 6.
10. S. Birley, 'The Way Ahead for Local Enterprise Centres', presentation (1988).
11. Forum of Private Business, op. cit., p. 7.
12. *The 3rd Annual Report of the European Observatory for SMEs* (Zoetermeer: Netherlands: EIM Small Business Research and Consultancy, 1995) pp. 50–51.
13. See S. Cromie, B. Stephenson and D. Monteith, 'The Management of Family Firms: An Empirical Investigation', *International Small Business Journal*, vol. 13 (1995) pp. 11–34 for some definitions.
14. P. Leach, *The Stoy Hayward Guide to Family Business* (London: Kogan Page, 1994).
15. H. Levinson, 'Conflicts that Plague the Family Business', *Harvard Business Review*, March–April 1971, p. 94.
16. H. Levinson, 'Don't Choose Your Own Successor', *Harvard Business Review*, November–December 1974, pp. 53–62.
17. *Managing the Family Business*, A Stoy Hayward Survey in Conjunction with the London Business School (1990) p. 3.
18. Ibid.

7 Distinctive Features of Small Businesses

1. E. T. Penrose, *The Theory of the Growth of the Firm* (London: Basil Blackwell, 1959).
2. A. A. Gibb, 'Towards the Building of Entrepreneurial Models of Support for Small Business', *The 11th National Small Firms Policy and Research Conference* (1988) p. 14.
3. For a discussion on the various sources of influence on organisations, see H. Mintzberg, *Power In and Around Organisations* (Englewood Cliffs, New Jersey: Prentice-Hall, 1983) pp. 32–46.
4. For a discussion on the overlap between personal goals and business goals in SMEs, see R. Goffee and R. Scase, *Corporate Realities* (London: Routledge, 1995) pp. 1–21.
5. See C. Handy, *The Age of Unreason* (London: Arrow Books, 1990).
6. See A. Minkes, *The Entrepreneurial Manager* (Harmondsworth: Penguin, 1987) for a discussion of entrepreneurial decision making.
7. H. Mintzberg, *The Structuring of Organisations* (Englewood Cliffs: Prentice Hall, 1979) pp. 305–13.
8. R. Goffee and R. Scase, 'Proprietorial Control in Family Firms', *Journal of Management Studies*, vol. 22 (1985) pp. 53–68.
9. J. Hayes and P. Nutman, *Understanding the Unemployed* (London: Tavistock, 1981).
10. R. Lessem, 'Getting into Self Employment', *Management Education and Development*, Spring 1984, p. 44.

11. B. Kirchhoff, 'Twenty years of Job Creation Research: What Have We Learned', *The 40th Conference of the International Council for Small Business* (1995) pp. 201–2.
12. Ibid., p. 202.
13. S. J. Davis, J. C. Haltiwanger and S. Schuh, *Job Creation and Destruction* (Cambridge, Massachusetts: MIT Press, 1996) p. 170.
14. D. J. Storey, *Understanding the Small Business Sector* (London: Routledge, 1994) p. 165.
15. Ibid., p. 168.
16. Ibid., p. 113.
17. Ibid., p. 114.
18. Ibid., p. 168.

■ 8   Business Growth

1. J. Levy, *Small and Medium Sized Enterprises: A Recipe for Success* (London: Institution of Electrical Engineers) as cited in D. J. Storey, *Understanding the Small Business Sector* (London: Routledge, 1994) p. 24.
2. DTI, *Competitiveness: Helping the Smaller Firm* (May 1995) p. 2.
3. Extract from an interview, in ICSB, 'The Job Generation Process Revisited', *ICSB Bulletin*, Spring 1995.
4. Storey, op. cit., p. 115.
5. NIERC, *Job Generation and Manufacturing Industry 1973–86* (Belfast : Northern Ireland Economic Research Centre).
6. E. Garnsey, 'A New Theory of the Growth of the Firm', *Proceedings of the 41st ICSB World Conference*, Stockholm (1996) p. 126.
7. A. Gibb and L. Davies, 'In Pursuit of Frameworks for the Development of Growth Models of the Small Business', *International Small Business Journal*, vol. 9.1 (October–December 1990) p. 26.
8. Storey, op. cit., p. 121.
9. Gibb and Davies, op. cit., pp. 16–17.
10. B Kirchhoff, personal communication.
11. Ibid.
12. Ibid.
13. Ibid.
14. C. Hakim, 'Identifying Fast Growth Small Firms', *Employment Gazette*, January 1989.
15. B. Kirchhoff, 'Twenty Years of Job Creation Research: What Have We Learned', *Proceedings of the 40th ICSB World Conference* (1995).
16. Storey, op. cit., pp. 126–37.
17. Gibb and Davies, op. cit., p. 18.
18. Ibid., p. 20.
19. Storey, op. cit., pp. 137–43.
20. European Network for SME Research, *The European Observatory for SMEs – 1st Annual Report* (Zoetermeer: EIM Small Business Reaearch and Consultancy, 1993) p. 24.
21. Storey, op. cit., pp. 144–54.
22. OECD, *Small & Medium Sized Enterprises: Technology & Competitiveness* (Paris: OECD, 1993) p. 21.
23. CBI, *Managing to Grow* (London: CBI, December 1995) p. 11.
24. Storey, op. cit., pp. 138–40.
25. P. Westhead and D. Storey, *An Assessment of Firms Located on and off Science Parks in the UK* (London: HMSO, 1994).

26. Kirchhoff, op. cit.
27. D. Smallbone, R. Leigh and D. North, 'Characteristics and Strategies of a group of High Growth SMEs in the UK, 1979–1990', paper presented at the First Venezuelan SME Management Seminar, Caracas, Venezuela, 7–11 March, 1993.
28. P. Vaessen and D. Keeble, 'Growth Oriented SME's in Unfavourable Regional Environments', Working Paper to ESRC Centre for Business Research, University of Cambridge, February 1995.
29. Institute of Directors, *Your Business Matters: Report from the Regional Conference* (London: Institute of Directors, 1996) pp. 6–7.
30. Local Enterprise Development Unit, *Annual Report* (Belfast: LEDU, 1995) p. 8.
31. M. E. Porter, 'The Competitive Advantage of Nations', *Harvard Business Review*, March–April 1990, no. 2.
32. Ibid., p. 82.
33. OECD, op. cit., p. 23.
34. Cambridge Small Business Research Centre, *The State of British Enterprise* (Dept of Applied Economics, University of Cambridge, 1992).
35. ICSB, op. cit., p. 9.
36. Storey, op. cit., p. 159.
37. Ibid., p. 115.

■ 9   Intrapreneurship

1. P. Drucker, 'Our Entrepreneurial Economy', *Harvard Business Review*, January–February 1984, pp. 59–64.
2. P. Drucker, *Innovation and Entrepreneurship* (London: Heinemann, 1985) p. 132.
3. G. Pinchot III, *Intrapreneuring: Why You Don't Have to Leave the Organisation to Become an Entrepreneur* (New York: Harper & Row, 1985).
4. D. F. Kuratko and R. M. Hodgetts, in *Entrepreneurship* (Fort Worth: Dryden Press, 1995) use this term.
5. J. A. Timmons, *The Entrepreneurial Mind* (Andover: Brick House, 1989) p. 1.
6. A. Gibb, 'The Enterprise Culture and Education', *International Small Business Journal*, vol. 11 (1993) p. 16.
7. J. Curran and R. Burroughs, 'The Sociology of Petit Capitalism: A Trend Report', *Sociology*, vol. 20 (1986) p. 269.
8. Pinchot, op. cit., p. 46.
9. D. F. Kuratko and R. M. Hodgetts, op. cit., p. 95.
10. S. Caird, 'How Important is the Innovator for the Commercial Success of Innovative Products in SMEs?', *Technovation*, vol. 14 (1994) p. 81.
11. Green Paper on Innovation, *Bulletin of the European Union*, Supplement 5/95 (Brussels: ECSC-EC-EAEC, 1996).
12. C. Handy, *The Age of Unreason* (London: Arrow, 1990).
13. E. A. Johns, *The Sociology of Organisational Change* (Oxford: Pergamon, 1973).
14. G. Zaltman and R. Duncan, *Strategies for Planned Change* (New York: Wiley, 1977).
15. Handy, op. cit.
16. H. H. Stevenson and D. E. Gumpert, 'The Heart of Entrepreneurship', in W. A. Sahlman and H. H, Stevenson (eds), *The Entrepreneurial Venture* (Boston: Harvard Business School, 1993).
17. H. Mintzberg, *The Structuring of Organisations* (Englewood Cliffs, New Jersey: Prentice-Hall, 1979).
18. Ibid., p. 233.
19. P. Selznick, *Leadership in Administration* (New York: Harper & Row, 1957).

20. W. Starbuck, *Organisational Growth and Development* (Harmondsworth: Penguin, 1971).
21. Drucker (1985) op. cit., pp. 136–7.
22. R. Lessem, *Intrapreneurship* (Aldershot: Gower, 1987).
23. Ibid., p. 7.
24. J. Sherwood, 'An Introduction to Organisational Development', in R. T. Golembiewski and A. Blumberg (eds), *Sensitivity Training and the Laboratory Approach* (New York: Peacock, 1973) p. 431.
25. Drucker (1985) op. cit., p. 142.
26. Ibid., p. 156.
27. H. Mintzberg, op. cit., pp. 431–67.
28. D. F. Muzyka and N. C. Churchill, 'Fostering the Entrepreneurial Spirit', in 'Mastering Enterprise', *Financial Times*, 17 February 1997, pp. 10–11.
29. C. Hales, *Managing Through Organisation* (London: Routledge, 1993) p. 44.
30. G. Haskins, 'Entrepreneurship Inside Corporations', *efmd Forum*, 94/2, p. 15. The ForeSight Group 1990, diagram and the quotation are found on p. 200.
31. See W. G. Biemans, *Managing Innovation Within Networks* (London: Routledge, 1993) for a discussion on networks and innovation.
32. C. Alter and J. Hage, *Organisations Working Together* (Newbury Park, California: Sage, 1993).
33. A. H. Van de Ven and D. Ferry, *Measuring and Assessing Organisations'* (New York: Wiley, 1980) p. 312.
34. B. G. James, 'Alliance: The New Strategic Focus', *Long Range Planning*, vol. 18, (1985) p. 76.
34. Green Paper on Innovation, *Bulletin of the European Union*, op. cit., p. 19.

■ 10   Why Intervene?

1. D. Birch, cited in D. J. Storey, *Understanding the Small Business Sector* (London: Routledge, 1994) p. 161.
2. C. Gallagher, cited in Storey, op. cit., p. 165.
3. D. J. Storey, *Understanding the Small Business Sector* (London: Routledge, 1994) p. 253.
4. Z. J. Acs and S. Gifford, 'Innovation of Entrepreneurial Firms', *Small Business Economics*, vol. 8 (1996) pp. 203–18.
5. See H. Mintzberg, *Power In and Around Organisations* (Englewood Cliffs, New Jersey: Prentice-Hall, 1983) p. 636, for a discussion on the fallacy of economic markets.
6. See W. R. Scott, *Organizations*, (Englewood Cliffs, New Jersey: Prentice-Hall, 1992) ch. 10, for a discussion on the impact of size on organisations.
7. C. Mason, R. Harrison and J. Chaloner, *Informal Risk Capital in the UK* (Southampton: Venture Finance Research Project, 1991).
8. M. B. Slovin and J. E. Young, 'The Entrepreneurial Search for Capital: An Investment in Finance', *Entrepreneurship, Innovation and Change*, vol. 1 (1992) pp. 177–94.
9. G. Bannock and A. Peacock, *Governments and Small Business* (London: Paul Chapman, 1989).
10. See R. J. Bennett, 'SMEs and Public Policy: Present Day Dilemmas, Future Priorities and The Case of Business Links', paper presented to the *19th ISBA National Small Firms and Research Conference* (Birmingham, 1996) for arguments in favour of leaving matters to the market.
11. Bannock and Peacock, op. cit.

12. Mintzberg, op. cit.
13. A. A. Gibb, 'Enterprise Culture and Education: Understanding Enterprise Education and its Links with Small Business, Entrepreneurship and Wider Educational Goals', *International Small Business Journal*, vol. 11 (1993) pp. 11–34.
14. M. Cross, *New Firm Formations and Regional Development* (Aldershot: Gower, 1981).
15. Bennett, op. cit., p. 6.
16. Business Week Editors, *The Reindustrialisation of America* (New York: McGraw-Hill, 1982). Cited in K. Vesper, *Entrepreneurship and National Policy* (Chicago: Heller Institute for Small Business Policy Papers, 1983) p. 74.
17. A. C. P. de Koning, J. A. H. Snijders and J. G. Vianen 'SME Policy in the European Community', paper presented at *Gateways to Growth – Opportunities for Smaller Firms in the EC* (1992); cited in Storey, op. cit., p. 258.
18. See Mintzberg, op. cit., pp. 171–83, for a discussion of the conditions that favour political behaviour.

■ 11   Theories and Assumptions

1. J. Curran and R. Blackburn, *Young People and Enterprise: A National Survey* (Kingston Business School Occasional Paper no. 11, 1989).
2. A. A. Gibb, 'Enterprise Culture and Education: Understanding Enterprise Education and its Links with Small Business, Entrepreneurship and Wider Educational Goals', *International Small Business Journal*, vol. 11 (1993) pp. 11–34.
3. N. F. Krueger, Jr, *Prescriptions for Opportunity: How Communities Can Create Potential for Entrepreneurs* (Washington, DC: The Small Business Foundation of America, Working Paper 90-03, 1995).
4. See N. F. Krueger, Jr, op. cit., and K. Vesper, *Entrepreneurship and National Policy* (Chicago: Heller Institute for Small Business Policy Papers, 1983) for a thorough discussions on the creation of a supportive community for enterprise.
5. Krueger, op. cit.
6. R. Peterson and R. Rondstadt, 'A Silent Strength: Entrepreneurial Know-Who', *The 16th ESBS, efmd IMD Report* (86/4) p. 11.
7. See R. T. Harrison and C. M. Mason, 'Finance for the Growing Business: The Role of Informal Investment', *National Westminster Bank Review*, May 1993, pp. 17–29 for a discussion on business angels.
8. See D. Deakins, *Entrepreneurship and Small Firms* (London: McGraw-Hill, 1996) for an up-to-date discussion on support for innovative firms.
9. P. M. Blau, J. W. Gustad, R. Jessor, H. S. Parnes and R. C. Wilcox, 'Occupational Choice – a Conceptual Framework', *Industrial and Labour Review*, vol. 19 (1956) pp. 531–43.
10. K. Roberts, 'The Social Conditions, Consequences and Limitations of Careers Guidance', *British Journal of Guidance and Counselling*, vol. 5 (1977) p. 3.
11. V. H. Vroom, *Work and Motivation* (New York: Wiley, 1964).

■ 12   Intervention Methods

1. R. J. Bennett, 'SMEs and Public Policy: Present Dilemmas, Future Priorities and the Case of Business Links', presented to *Nineteenth ISBA National Small Firms Policy and Research Conference*, November 1996, p. 3.

2. L. Stevenson, 'Lessons Learned from the Implementation for Entrepreneurship Development Strategy in Canada: The Case of the Atlantic Region' (Canada, Atlantic Canada Entrepreneurship Agency, April 1996, unpublished) p. 2.

3. D. Storey, *Understanding the Small Business Sector* (London: Routledge, 1994) p. 258.

4. A. C. P. de Koning, J. A. H. Snijders and J. G. Vianen, 'Policies in Small and Medium Enterprises in Countries of the European Community', *International Small Business Journal*, vol. 10, 3 (1992) pp. 25–39.

5. CBI SME Council, Internal Working Paper (unpublished).

6. J. Stanworth and C. Gray, *Bolton 20 Years On – The Small Firm in the 1990s* (London: PCP 1991) p. 20.

7. CBI SME Council, op. cit.

8. Storey, op. cit., p. 269.

9. European Network for SME Research, *The European Observatory for SMEs 2nd Annual Report* (European Network for Zoetermeer: EIM Small Business Research and Consultancy, 1994).

10. K. de Lind Van Wijngaarden and R. Van Der Horst, 'A Comparison of SME Policy in the EU Member States', *Business Growth and Profitability*, vol. 2, no. 1 (March 1996) p. 40.

11. H. Rees and A. Shah, 'The Characteristics of the Self Employed: The Supply of Labour', in J. Atkinson and D. J. Storey (eds) *Employment, The Small Firm and the Labour Market* (Routledge: London, 1993).

12. J. Stanworth and C. Gray, op. cit., p. 20.

13. DTI booklet *Competitiveness – Helping Small Firms* (London: DTI, 1995) p. 13.

■ 13   Evaluation and Results

1. R. Scott, personal correspondence based on work for Northern Ireland's Department of Economic Development.

2. D. Yankelovich, *Corporate Priorities: A Continuing Study of the New Demands on Business* (Stanford) CN: Daurer Yankelovich Inc., 1972).

3. H. M. Treasury, *Economic Appraisal in central Government – A Technical Guide for Government Departments* (London: HMSO, 1991).

4. R. J. Bennett, 'SMEs and Public Policy: Present Dilemmas, Future Priorities and the Case of Business Links', presented to *Nineteenth ISBA National Small Firms Policy and Research Conference*, Birmingham, November 1996, p. 20.

5. D. Storey, quoted in D. Smallbone, 'Policies to Support SME Development: the UK Experience', paper presented at a conference in Novara, Italy, June 1995, p. 3.

6. L. Stevenson, *Lessons Learned from the Implementation of an Entrepreneurship Development Strategy in Canada: The Case of the Atlantic Region*, April 1996 (unpublished) p. 2.

7. OECD: '*Jobs Study Follow Up: Thematic Review of Entrepreneurship and Job Creation Policies*' (Paris: OECD, 1996).

8. D. Storey, *Understanding the Small Business Sector* (London: Routledge, 1994).

9. G. Owen, *Aid Regimes and Small Business in the UK France and Belgium. efmd report to ESRC* (Brussels: efmd, 1992).

10. D. M. W. N. Hitchens, K. Wagner and J. E. Birnie, *Northern Ireland Manufacturing Productivity compared with West Germany* (Belfast: Northern Ireland Economic Research Centre, 1989).

11. R. Scott, 'Does a Regime of Intensive Grant Assistance to Small firms Create Jobs?', paper presented to the *23rd European Small Business Seminar*, N. Ireland (September 1993).

12. Storey, op. cit., p. 227.
13. Ibid., p. 229.
14. Ibid., p. 229.
15. R. J. Bennett, 'SMEs and Public Policy: Present Dilemmas, Future Priorities and the Case of Business Links', presented to *Nineteenth ISBA National Small Firms Policy and Research Conference*, Birmingham, November 1996, pp. 3/4.
16. Storey, op. cit., p. 291.
17. Department of Trade and Industry, *Evaluation of DTI Funded TEC Services in Support of Small and Medium Sized Enterprises*, a report prepared by PA Economic Consultants on behalf of DTI (London: HMSO, 1995).
18. D. Smallbone, op. cit.
19. Bennett, op. cit., p. 3/4.
20. Bennett, op. cit., p. 20.

■ 14 Science, Art or Magic?

1. Industrial Policy Review Group, *A Time For Change: Industrial Policy for the 1990s* (Dublin: Stationery Office, 1992) p. 7.
2. M. Penrose, 'Is America in Decline?', *Harvard Business Review* (July–August 1992) p. 44.
3. S. Zadek and E. Mayo, 'Ten Reasons Why Society Does Count', *New Economics Magazine*, 41 (spring 1997) p. 5.
4. S. Hoggart, *America: A User's Guide* (London: Fontana, 1991) p. 6.
5. A. Pettigrew in the Forword to C. B. Handy, *Understanding Organisations* (Harmondsworth: Penguin, 1976) p. 7.

Index